Tax Policy and Economic Development

The Johns Hopkins Studies in Development
Vernon W. Ruttan and T. Paul Schultz, Consulting Editors

RICHARD M. BIRD

Tax Policy and Economic Development

The Johns Hopkins University Press
Baltimore and London

Research for this book was sponsored by the Lincoln Institute for Land Policy.

The Johns Hopkins University Press
701 West 40th Street, Baltimore, Maryland 21211-2190
The Johns Hopkins Press Ltd., London

The paper used in this book meets the minimum requirements of American
National Standard for Information Sciences—Permanence of Paper for Printed
Library Materials, ANSI Z39.48-1984.

Library of Congress Cataloging-in-Publication Data
Bird, Richard Miller, 1938–
    Tax policy and economic development / Richard M. Bird
        p.   cm.— (The Johns Hopkins studies in development)
    Includes bibliographical references and index.
    ISBN 0-8018-4223-9.—ISBN 0-8018-4265-4 (pbk.)
    1. Taxation—Developing countries.   2. Tax administration and
procedure—Developing countries.   3. Fiscal policy—Developing countries.
    I. Title   II. Series.
    HJ2351.7.B57   1992
    336.2'009172'6—dc20   91-16243

For Carl S. Shoup
scholar, teacher, and friend

Contents

Preface and Acknowledgments   ix

PART I   **Approaches to Development Taxation**

1. A Primer on Taxation and Development   3
2. Analyzing Tax Policy   18
3. Assessing Tax Performance   28

PART II   **Taxation, Growth, and Distribution**

4. Redistribution, Growth, and Tax Policy   41
5. Taxation and the Poor   49
6. Taxation and Employment   61

PART III   **Taxing Income, Consumption, and Wealth**

7. The Income Tax in Developing Countries   85
8. Income Tax Reform and Administration   98
9. A New Look at Indirect Taxation   119
10. The Case for Wealth Taxes   130

PART IV **Local Government Finance**

11. Intergovernmental Finance and Local
    Taxation 145

12. Financing Urban Development 159

13. Earmarking Tax Revenues 171

PART V **Tax Reform and Tax Design**

14. Tax Reform and Tax Design 183

15. The Administrative Dimension of Tax Reform 189

16. Tax Reform in Developing Countries 202

Notes 215

References 239

Index 263

Preface and Acknowledgments

The tax system constitutes one of the most important instruments of development policy in any country. Development economists frequently make pronouncements on taxation but seldom know enough about how the tax system really works to make their arguments persuasive. Similarly, fiscal specialists often fail to realize what aspects of the tax system in a developing country are critical. Perhaps at the cost of acquiring full expertise in either speciality, my principal concern for some years has been to integrate fiscal practice with development policy.

Two subsidiary themes derive from this central concern. The first is the importance of administration. Although the poor state of tax administration in most developing countries is often noted and deplored, few seem to have drawn the right conclusions from such observations. If taxes are certain to be administered poorly, this fact must be taken into account in proposing tax reforms in such countries. As Oliver Sacks (1982, p. 234) has said in a quite different field: "A good part of the tribulations of patients (and their physicians) comes from unreal attempts to transcend the possible, to deny its limits, and to seek the impossible: accommodation is more laborious and less exalted, and consists, in effect, of a painstaking exploration of the full range of the real and the possible." This book tries to convey much the same message to those interested in the role of taxation in developing countries.

The second theme—the importance of grounding theory in actuality—is equally pervasive, if not always so obvious. I have not attempted to be comprehensive in covering the myriad fiscal problems of developing countries. There is, for instance, little discussion of such important matters as tax incentives or agricultural taxation (although an extensive treatment of the latter may be found in Bird, 1974). Instead the scope of the book has been largely determined by the range and limits of my own experience in advising on tax policy in a variety of developing countries including Colombia, Bolivia, Venezuela, Panama, Jamaica, Egypt, Senegal, Indonesia, the Philippines, and Papua New Guinea. The book is not a collection of case studies, but it draws heavily on material first worked out with respect to a particular country.

Much fiscal analysis of developing countries is on the following pattern: the academic literature is drawn on to construct a model fiscal system; the existing situation in a particular country is examined to determine how it diverges from the model; and a fiscal reform is then proposed to transform what *is* into what *ought to be*. This approach is deficient because it does not require sufficiently detailed examination of existing reality to ensure that the assumptions postulated in the model are congruent with reality, that the recommended changes can in fact be implemented, or that, if implemented, they will in fact produce the desired results.

In contrast, my approach is first to study in detail exactly *how* the existing system works, and *why* it works that way, in order to have a firm basis for understanding what changes may be both desirable and feasible. My emphasis has thus always been more on what *can* be done than on what *should* be done—if only it could be! This approach is both time-consuming and tends to induce caution with respect to drastic change. Nonetheless, experience shows that many administrative (and political) constraints must be accepted as immutable in the near term if one is to design a useful tax proposal for any country.

Ambitious proposals may be invaluable in introducing new ideas and in widening our cognitive horizons. In the long run, such basic ideas as the comprehensive income tax and the personal expenditure tax are undoubtedly much more important than even the most meticulously designed reform for country X in year Y. Most real tax policy problems, however, are concerned precisely with X in Y, so the more institutional approach advocated, and to some extent illustrated, in this book is both valuable in its own right and widely applicable. Such in any case is the argument underlying this book.

Finally, many of the chapters draw freely on material published previously, although in every case the version included here has been revised substantially to eliminate redundancies, update references, and incorporate new material. The status of the different chapters in this respect is as follows:

Chapter 1 has not been published before, although much of the material appears in Bird (1990c).

Chapter 2 draws on a paper on Colombia originally presented at the U.S. Agency for International Development in 1968 and subsequently published as Bird (1970).

Chapter 3 draws on a paper originally presented at the University of Puerto Rico in 1974 and subsequently published as Bird (1976).

Chapter 4 is based in part on a paper presented at the 1968 conference of the National Tax Association and subsequently published as Bird (1969) and in part on unpublished remarks made at a 1985 Washington conference on supply-side taxation held under the auspices of the U.S. Agency for International Development.

Chapter 5 is based on a paper with Barbara Miller growing out of our joint work for the Jamaican tax project led by Roy Bahl. The paper was originally presented to a conference on government policy and the poor held at the University of Toronto in 1985 and later published as Bird and Miller (1989).

Chapter 6 draws heavily on a paper presented to a conference organized by the Committee on Taxation, Resources, and Economic Development in 1975. It was subsequently published as Bird (1982).

Chapter 7 incorporates material both from a paper prepared in 1975 for the Government of Mexico with Oliver Oldman and subsequently published as Oldman and Bird (1977) and from an unpublished paper prepared for a fiscal study mission to Bolivia led by Richard Musgrave in 1976 (see Musgrave, 1981).

Chapter 8 is a revised version of a paper first written in 1981 for the Indonesian tax project led by Malcolm Gillis. The paper was presented at a conference organized by the French Ministry of Finance in 1982 and subsequently published as Bird (1983).

Chapter 9 draws heavily on a paper originally presented at a conference at the University of Illinois in honor of John Due in 1985 and later published as Bird (1987) by Pergamon Press Ltd., Oxford, United Kingdom.

Chapter 10 is based on a paper originally presented in Spanish at a conference at Javeriana University in Bogotá, Colombia, in 1978 (see Arango et al., 1979). A version was published in English as Bird (1978).

Chapter 11, which incorporates some material from a report prepared for the Institute on National Affairs of Papua New Guinea and published as Bird (1983a), was first prepared as background material for the 1988 World Development Report of the World Bank. A slightly different version was published as Bird (1990). Reprinted by permission of John Wiley & Sons, Ltd.

Chapter 12 is based in part on a paper originally prepared for the Lincoln Institute of Land Policy in 1976 and later published as Bird (1977) and in part on a paper on Colombia presented with William Rhoads to the Committee on Taxation, Resources, and Economic Development in 1966 and subsequently published as Rhoads and Bird (1967) and, in an expanded version, as Rhoads and Bird (1969).

Chapter 13 has not been published separately although much of this material is incorporated in the report of the Colombian Commission on Intergovernmental Finance (Finanzas, 1981), an English version of which was published as Bird (1984).

Chapter 14 is based on a paper originally presented at a special session of the American Economic Association in honor of Carl Shoup in 1976 and subsequently published as Bird (1977a).

Chapter 15 is based on a paper presented to a conference on tax reform in developing countries held in Washington in 1988 and later published as Bird (1989).

Chapter 16, based on a talk originally delivered at the India International Centre in New Delhi in 1987, was published in a slightly different form as Bird (1990a).

The major debt incurred in the preparation of this book is of course to the many officials and scholars concerned with the developing countries from whom I have learned so much. In particular, my prolonged association with key policy-makers in Colombia at intervals over the last twenty-five years has undoubtedly shaped my attitudes to some of the issues discussed in this book: Eduardo Wiesner, Guillermo Perry, Roberto Junguito, Lauchlin Currie, Jorge Ospina, and Enrique Low, along with many other Colombians—and of course the many officials with whom I have worked in other countries—have, over the years, taught me much about the reality of taxation in developing countries. In addition, I have been fortunate to be associated at various times with such leading scholars of public finance in developing countries as Carl Shoup, Oliver Oldman, Richard Goode, Richard Musgrave, Charles McLure, Malcolm Gillis, Roy Bahl, John Due, and Sijbren Cnossen, among many others. From each of these people, as well as from those with whom I have collaborated on earlier versions of some of the material included here—William Rhoads, Oliver Oldman, and Barbara Miller—I have learned a great deal.

Finally, I am of course most grateful to the Lincoln Institute for Land Policy for making the present volume possible, as well as to the two institutions that housed me during most of its preparation—the National Centre for Development Studies at the Australian National University and the Faculty of Economics at Erasmus University Rotterdam.

About the Lincoln Institute

The Lincoln Institute of Land Policy, which supported the research for *Tax Policy and Economic Development* by Richard Bird, is a nonprofit educational institution where leaders explore the complex linkages between public policies, including taxation, and land policy, and the impact of these linkages on major issues of our society. The Institute is a tax-exempt school providing advanced education in land economics, including property taxation, and offering challenging opportunities for learning, research, and publication.

The Institute seeks to understand land as a resource, the choices for its use and improvement, the regulatory and tax policies that will result in better uses of land, and effective techniques by which land policies can be implemented. The major goal of the Institute is to integrate the theory, understanding, and practice of land policy and its influence on the lives and livelihood of all people.

PART I Approaches to Development Taxation

1   A Primer on Taxation and Development

The potential role of the tax system in helping to achieve desired social and economic objectives has been much discussed in the context of the developing countries. So have criteria that might serve as guides to the design of an appropriate tax system. This chapter, which reviews the usual criteria for tax design in the context of a discussion of the developmental role of the tax system, assumes that the reader has relatively little knowledge of the conventional public finance discussion of the design of tax systems.

Taxation as a Lesser Evil

Why does any country subject itself to the unpleasant experience of levying taxes in the first place?[1] The obvious answer is that taxation is required to provide government with the money needed to purchase the goods and services it requires to carry out its functions. This answer must be wrong. Governments do not need to levy taxes for this purpose.

They may instead, for example, commandeer resources directly. Most governments do this in wartime, both with respect to people (conscription) and with respect to such scarce materials as steel. Indeed, in centrally planned economies, this technique of obtaining command over resources was so dominant until recently that such countries were called "command economies."

Such direct methods have generally been rejected in peacetime market economies, however, as being both capricious and inefficient. Direct methods are also as a rule difficult to administer effectively, which makes them especially unsuitable for use in developing countries. Even totalitarian states have found such methods to be costly and inefficient. Centrally planned developing economies such as China are therefore increasingly moving to less direct methods of attaining developmental goals, such as taxation.

Another alternative to taxation is simply to print money. In the circumstances of most developing countries, however, more than modest recourse to such practices will usually result in inflation (even at high levels of open and concealed unemployment), owing to such bottlenecks as scarce foreign exchange and to fragmented markets that reduce the responsiveness of supplies to price signals. In any case, inflation is not a particularly desirable way of financing government activity. It acts as a capricious and often regressive tax, affecting most adversely some of the poorer groups in society. Inflationary distortion of financial markets also exerts undesirable allocative effects on investment and savings decisions (McKinnon, 1973; Shaw, 1973; Fry, 1987). In an important sense the principal role of taxation in macroeconomic terms is to reduce the inflationary pressure that would result if both government and the private sector tried to buy the same goods and services. Taxes are needed not to provide governments with money but to take money away from the public.

Governments may also borrow money from the public rather than tax it away. In practice, however, the limited domestic capital markets in most developing countries make recourse to domestic borrowing difficult, except in the form of selling bonds to the central bank, a practice that is economically equivalent to printing money. As for borrowing abroad, not only is the credit of most developing countries in international financial markets far from unlimited, but such borrowing also carries its own dangers, as a number of countries have found out all too painfully in recent years.

A final possible alternative to taxation as a means by which governments can obtain command over resources, while at the same time reducing the danger of inflation by removing purchasing power from the private sector, is to sell the goods and services they produce. Such sales may be made directly, through the operations of a state enterprise, or indirectly, by charging fees in accordance with the actual or presumed benefit that people obtain from government activity. There is thus a spectrum of possible ways to finance government activities ranging from a voluntary payment made by an individual for a commodity or service sold by government (a "price") to a compulsory contribution (a "tax") levied on an individual without reference to any special benefits conferred on him or her by government expenditures. The wide variety of fees, charges, and benefit taxes which lie between these extremes fall within the domain of the "benefit principle" of taxation.

The Case for Benefit Taxation

The benefit approach to taxation may be advocated on both equity and efficiency grounds.[2] In equity terms, the benefit principle is essentially identical to the commercial principle that it is fair to pay for what you get. When a consumer buys a loaf of bread in the store, she gets the loaf of bread and the storekeeper gets the money. Similarly, when a citizen receives a direct and measurable benefit from a government activity, it seems only fair that she pays for what she receives.

The case for the benefit approach is even stronger on efficiency grounds. If each taxpayer pays for each public service an amount just equal to his or her evaluation of the marginal benefits received for the service, then the total taxes collected from all individuals will provide a measure of the worth of the public services. Given this information, the provision of any service can then be extended to the point at which the marginal evaluation of the service by all individuals, as measured by what they are willing to pay for it, just equals the marginal cost of providing the service. In such an ideally efficient fiscal system each individual will pay a marginal tax for collective goods and services that is just equal to the marginal benefits he or she receives, and just enough of each good or service will be provided to make the total incremental benefits (and taxes) equal to the marginal cost of supplying the service. This ideal benefit tax system thus determines both the level and structure of public expenditure and the level and distribution of taxation. Little more can be asked of any tax than this.

The application of the benefit principle in practice is much more limited. Benefit taxation is quite unsuitable as a means of financing that part of government activity which takes the form of providing "public goods," that is, services which by their very nature cannot be sold to individuals. Once such services are made available to one, they are automatically available to all.[3] A surprisingly large share of government activity in developing countries, however, consists of providing what are essentially "private" goods (such as education) to readily identifiable persons.[4]

Similarly, it would clearly be ridiculous to tax away the very benefits it is the main purpose of the redistributive activities of government to provide. Nonetheless, in most developing countries explicitly redistributive policies are limited, and even those are seldom very effective (De Wulf, 1975; World Bank, 1988).

However, the principal barrier to more effective use of the benefit principle in most developing countries is not these inherent limitations, but public attitudes. Once a set of ideas—for example, that most public services should be provided free and that charging for such services is regressive—is embodied in the public psyche, it is singularly difficult to dislodge it.[5] Once the rules of the game have been set, people consider it grossly unfair to change them. Attempts at charging for public services, even where perfectly feasible administratively, commercially desirable, and distributively beneficial, almost always incur strong opposition from some groups and support from no one. Few political points are to be won by moving toward a revenue system restructured on the benefit principle.

Nevertheless, with thorough preparation and effective implementation, the gains from introducing more rationality into public pricing through this means may be great, particularly in countries that can ill afford to waste scarce public resources. A larger "benefit" element in development finance is especially needed with respect to urban finance. Too often developing countries direct a substantial fraction of scarce public sector savings to the construction of urban infrastructure and the provision of urban public services that can, and should, be better paid directly by the direct beneficiaries—the inhabitants of the urban areas.[6]

The Case for Redistributive Taxation

No matter how far benefit taxation is pushed, substantial nonbenefit taxes are always necessary. In one view, "fairness" with respect to such taxes— sharing the cost of giving up the resources needed by government in a fashion considered to be "fair," or at least politically acceptable, such as in proportion to "ability to pay"—should be the most important criterion in the design of the tax system.[7]

The principal redistributive role that can be played by the tax system is not to make the poor richer, but the rich poorer. Taxation cannot level up, but it can level down. For this reason, the direct taxation of wealth, although not very important in quantitative terms in any country, is of particular interest from an egalitarian or "ability" perspective, as argued in Chapter 10 below.

If the principal aim of redistributive policy is to "level up," to make the poor better off, the main role the tax system has to play is the limited and essentially negative one of not making them poorer. If the main distributional concern is with alleviating poverty as such, remedies must be sought primarily on the expenditure side of the budget, either by direct public provision of such services as housing, medical care, and education, by simple transfers of income—not very important in developing countries—or through employment-creating policies.[8]

Nevertheless, it is important not to downplay the role of taxation in affecting the poor. The "supply-side" (incentive) effects of taxes affect the primary generation of incomes through the market by affecting the level and use of available capital and labor (see Chapter 6 below). Moreover, indirect taxes in particular may substantially affect the scanty cash resources available to the poor in developing countries (see Chapter 9).

In short, if income redistribution is considered a desirable social goal, then taxation is clearly an important means to this end—and moreover one that every country in fact utilizes, whether explicitly or otherwise. Seldom, of course, is there complete consensus in any country on the desired degree of redistribution. Everyone may perhaps agree, at least in principle, that the poor should become less poor. But when it comes to making the rich poorer, not only are the rich and the poor unlikely to agree, but the less rich, the just plain rich, and the more rich are also likely to be at odds. In the end, the desired distributive pattern of taxation in most countries reflects as a rule a more or less stable resolution of this fundamental conflict of interests and values.[9] The extent to which the desired pattern is actually attained depends upon both the administrative capacity and the economic structure of the country in question.

At best, then, the two traditional tax principles of "benefit taxation" and "ability to pay" provide rough and general guides to what a tax system should (or can) be. The benefit principle has greater economic merit than is usually thought; but it is difficult to apply appropriately, and as a rule the public has been conditioned to think poorly of it. The ability-to-pay principle has, at least until recently, had a better press in both academic and popular circles; but in the end it amounts to little more than a vague injunction to be "fair," where "fairness" is an inherently relativistic concept, subjective or socially determined in nature.[10] In practice, both principles seem often to be employed as justifications of policies adopted for other reasons.

The Objectives of Tax Policy

Many of the goals or objectives commonly attributed to tax policy in developing countries are really those of public policy as a whole. Economic growth, internal and external stability, and the attainment of an appropriate distribution of income and wealth fall into this category. Taxation is only one, and by no means the most important, means of achieving such national objectives. Indeed, the potential efficacy of taxes in achieving many of these purposes has often been exaggerated. Nevertheless, since taxes are one of the most pervasive instruments of government policy in any economy, it is both inevitable and proper that the effects of taxation on such general public policy objectives as growth, distribution, and stability should be taken explicitly into account in designing the tax system (Levin, 1971).

GROWTH

An important policy concern in most developing countries, for example, is the rate of economic growth. The most obvious "growth" objective for tax policy is to provide the resources needed for public sector capital formation and other necessary development-related expenditures. Many developing countries have also considered it desirable to encourage private investment in new physical capital (at least in certain lines of activity) through tax "incentives."[11] The desire to increase and direct private investment may also shape the design of business income taxes in general. Higher taxes may be imposed on retained profits than on distributed profits in order to encourage distribution, the development of capital markets, and the flow of savings to the highest-return investment opportunities. Alternatively, higher taxes may be imposed on distributed profits than on retained profits in order to encourage the retention and reinvestment of profits where they are earned.

There appears to be almost no limit to the tax gadgetry that has been used in one country or another in order to stimulate economic growth and, in particular, investment (Lent, 1967; Shah and Toye, 1978). Nonetheless, such policies are of uncertain effectiveness in achieving their alleged goal, in part because we know so little about the relationship between the financial factors that are influenced by tax policy and the real factors underlying growth performance. This uncertainty, combined with the inequitable and administratively complicated character of most tax incentives, suggests that many countries may have greatly overestimated the net benefits that can be achieved through incentive policy.[12]

The supply of labor and social risk-taking may also be affected by tax policy. Taxes do affect these factors, so such effects should not work against the (presumed) basic policy goal of growth in a developing country. But this does not mean either that taxes should be designed specifically to make people work as hard and take as many risks as possible or that taxes are necessarily the best (or even good) instruments for this purpose.

The best approach in the circumstances of most developing countries is probably to emulate the ancient physicians' motto "above all, do no harm" rather than trying to stimulate and direct growth through ingenious fiscal devices. The cost of attempting to direct market forces through tax measures may be not only an unsustainable growth pattern but also a severely distorted and ineffective tax system. Creating a tax-free sector of economic activity within a country, for instance, in effect establishes an on-shore "tax haven" with accompanying pressures and strains on the limited administrative capacity available. The potential rewards seem too little in most cases to run such risks. Developing countries would seem well advised to avoid fine-tuned tax incentive policy.

DISTRIBUTION

Similar remarks may be made with respect to the role of taxation in achieving other public policy goals, which may often conflict with growth. Tax concessions to investment may raise the rate of growth in certain situations but only at the cost of increasing the inequality with which wealth and income is distributed. On the other hand, sometimes measures aimed at one objective may simultaneously move a society toward another. Heavy taxes on land, for example, may induce more efficient utilization of existing assets and raise the level of output, while at the same time reducing inequality.[13] The importance of such arguments can be determined only by a close examination of the situation in each particular country.

The connection between the distribution of income and the rate of economic growth has sometimes been considered to be a simple, straightforward matter. Economic growth may be viewed as primarily a function of the rate of investment, which must be matched by savings. Since it is supposedly well known that the rich save more than the poor, the characteristically unequal distribution of income in poor countries should at least have the virtue of permitting a higher rate of economic growth than would otherwise be possible.[14]

The implications of this view for tax policy seem clear—and have been much heralded by recent advocates of the so-called supply-side approach to taxation.[15] High taxes on the rich should be avoided, since private saving is the wellspring of economic growth. In particular, light taxation of industrial profits and capital gains would appear to be an essential part of a growth-oriented tax system (Shoup, 1966).

In this view, redistributive taxation is a luxury poor countries can ill afford. Since the interests of the well-to-do in maintaining their position are thus buttressed by the economic argument that it is really better in the long run for the poor that the rich are rich, it is not surprising that in fact few developing countries have very progressive tax systems.[16] Hard economic common sense thus seems to have overcome soft socio-political rhetoric. Or has it?

Even in this "classical" case, where growth is limited by inadequate savings and where the rich are savers, the saving "instinct" may need considerable stimulation in the form of low taxes on the rich, and such policies may build up problems for the future.[17] Other countries, in which growth may also be characterized as "savings-limited," but where the rich spend rather than save, may find redistributive tax policy a more efficient way of producing growth than tax concessions. Moreover, if the key constraint holding back growth is inadequate foreign exchange, as has been true for some countries at some times, increasing savings as such is not a very useful growth policy anyway.[18] In these circumstances, if the rich are spenders, the needed changes in the pattern of final demand may again point toward redistributive tax policy (Bird, 1970a).[19]

The connection between income distribution and economic growth in any country is a factual matter. Surprisingly little is known about the relevant facts, but on the whole there seems to be little case in most countries for maintaining inegalitarian tax policies in the name of economic growth. The distributional impact of the tax system is in any case uncertain owing to such factors as the unknown extent to which such important taxes as company income taxes and property taxes are "shifted" (that is, the person who pays over the money to the government adjusts his behavior in some way and thus passes on the tax to someone else). Indeed, it is arguable whether the impact of the tax system as a whole on income distribution can be estimated in a meaningful way (Prest, 1955; Shoup, 1969; Bird, 1980a).

In any case, the distributional role of taxes in developing countries is less important than one might think. The main explicitly "redistributive" tax (that is, with rates graduated in accordance with personal income) is of course the personal income tax. In practice, however, personal income taxes in developing countries are far from the global progressive levy envisaged in textbook discussion (see Chapter 7 below).

It has long been accepted that income, broadly defined to include all accretions to economic power (potential spending power), provides a particularly suitable measure of ability to pay and hence perhaps the best basis for personal taxation.[20] From an equity point of view, the tax implications of an additional dollar of income should be the same, regardless of the source of that income.

Exactly the same rule of uniformity may be advisable to avoid distorting unduly the pattern of economic activity by diverting resources into relatively lightly taxed activities. Neutrality need not, however, always be an appropriate characteristic of the tax system in developing countries, in which one aim of policy is often precisely to change the prevalent pattern of resource allocation.[21] Administrative realities have forced considerable modification of the ideal of a truly global income tax even in the most highly developed countries. The easiest income to tax effectively is wage and salary income: everything else gives rise to problems of varying difficulty (see Chapter 8 below). In the past, many countries concluded that the resulting lower probability of catching a dollar of capital (or self-employment) income in the tax net should be recognized by imposing a higher tax rate on such income than on wage income. The belief that such differential rates take care of the problem is almost certainly wrong, however, because evasion tends to escalate to offset the differential.

This argument against "schedular" taxes is by now widely accepted (Shoup et al., 1959). What seems to be less widely understood, however, is that simply abolishing schedular taxes in name resolves no problems. Indeed, unless a move toward globalization is accompanied by significant administrative tightening with respect to nonwage income, the immediate effect of such a change may even be to increase taxes on wage earners relative to those receiving other forms of income (Musgrave, 1981).

In the end, the administrative constraint is usually decisive with respect to what can actually be done in any country. Administrative limitations suggest, for example, that it might be wise to avoid large, sudden changes in tax structure. "Nature," said Alfred Marshall (1890; 1948), the well-known nineteenth-century economist, "does not proceed by jumps"—and neither, it may be argued, should tax changes. Small, regular changes (e.g., gradual increases in withholding rates) may perhaps be absorbed more easily than large, abrupt shifts, thus providing less occasion for extreme adverse reactions and more time for the necessary accompanying administrative improvement.[22]

Similarly, there are two main constraints on wealth taxes in most countries: their possible effects on capital flows and the difficulty of satisfactorily assessing wealth (or even real property). The first of these constraints counsels caution in pushing wealth taxes to the high levels that might otherwise seem indicated by such goals as reducing the concentration of wealth—though perhaps not as much caution as most countries have shown (see Chapter 10 below). The second constraint suggests that restraint in designing elaborate tax structures for distributive (as for allocative) ends is likely to prove the better part of wisdom.[23]

In the end, of course, the appropriate design of wealth taxes, like that of all other taxes, reduces to the political question of whether it is likely to be any easier to reduce the concentration of wealth indirectly through taxation than directly. Within limits, the problem, as is so often the case in tax reform, is not so much administrative or economic—though the former has some effect on the structure of what is possible and the latter on the level—but political.

STABILIZATION

The characteristic of the tax system most relevant to the objective of price level and balance of payments stability is its "elasticity" with respect to changes in the level of income, that is, the extent to which tax yields rise when national income rises.[24] The more elastic the tax system, the less the need to rely on (often inflationary) deficit financing to maintain and expand the level of public-sector activity in a growing economy.

Whether an elastic tax system is desirable or not depends upon one's objectives and position. Properly structured taxes (and expenditures) can help loosen both the immediate and the long-term import constraint on growth, and more taxes will in any case be needed to transfer increasing real resources to the public sector (or through the public sector to private investment) (Bird, 1970b). Such analysis implicitly assumes, however, both that government expenditure is "useful" and that the structure of government expenditure is determined independently of tax structure. Those who question these assumptions may be less enamored of the results of a highly elastic tax system (see also Chapter 16 below).

Governments are obviously constrained in what they can do when revenues do not accrue automatically as a result of economic growth and inflation but must instead be obtained painfully and openly. Making the cost of expanded government activity more visible may constitute an important means of making governments more responsive to the real needs and desires of citizens, as the "public choice" literature suggests (Mueller, 1989). But the result may also be to restrain unduly the growth of the public sector, particularly when taxes are less elastic than current expenditure, as is frequently true in developing countries suffering from inflation (Tanzi, 1977). Again, one's view of the suitability of tax elasticity depends not only on economic considerations but also on basic questions of political philosophy and practice.

Other Criteria for Tax Design

Taxes constitute a set of rules determining the extent to which different people have to yield command over resources to the government. To establish the legitimacy of rules in any society, it is customary to appeal to criteria both external and internal to the tax system. The most important *external* criteria are the policy objectives of growth, stability, and distribution discussed above. In contrast, *internal* criteria are attributes, primarily with respect to equity and administration, which, it is thought, people would like to see in their tax systems. One such rule, called the principle of "horizontal equity," is that people in equal circumstances should be treated equally by the tax system. The circumstances determining whether individuals should be equally treated are unlikely to be universally agreed, however. Some may wish, for example, to vary taxes in accordance with economic class, ethnic group, geographic location, type of income, or some other criterion. Examples of such discrimination (legal or administrative) are not hard to find in developing countries.[25]

Other tax criteria are common in the literature: revenue adequacy, revenue stability, simplicity, multiplicity of revenue sources, economy of collection, neutrality, tax consciousness, and so on. In the end, the appropriate design of a tax system for a particular country at a particular time is not a matter of satisfying such a list but rather of accommodating such specific factors as (1) the initial economic, political, and administrative conditions of the country, (2) the precise objectives of national policy, and (3) the availability of policy instruments other than taxation.

The Administrative Constraint

A safe general statement about most developing countries is that the administrative aspect of taxation is overwhelmingly important (see Chapter 15 below). It is thus important to concentrate on the essential task of producing adequate revenue in a politically acceptable fashion and not to overload the tax system with too many refinements.

Tax reform in a developing country should not, for example, depend upon such inevitably tenuous matters as assumed tax incidence or an assumed relationship between such unknown magnitudes as the elasticity of factor substitution and the elasticity of labor supply. When the success of a tax policy is sensitive to variations in such largely unknown facts, the policy is not a good bet. A strategy of not putting all one's water in one probably leaky bucket seems advisable in most countries (see Chapter 14 below).

Policies that depend for their success on administrative "fine-tuning" are doomed to failure in the circumstances of most developing countries, or at least to such perversion in the process of implementation as to produce results quite different from those intended. The best tax policies are those that offer little latitude for officials further down the line to mess them up. There are clearly many distortions and much fragmentation in the economies of most developing countries. The tax system, like all other policy instruments, can and should be used to the extent possible to rectify these problems. In view of the administrative constraint, however, any necessary interventionist component of tax policy should be as general in nature as possible and should not depend on the discretionary decisions of officials.

Moreover, since the problems requiring correction may well have arisen in the first place as a result of other government policies (over-valued exchange rate, inappropriate credit policy, etc.), the indicated direction for tax policy may not always be intuitively obvious. Examples are the common (and usually correct) advice to levy compensating domestic excise taxes on goods taxed by high luxury import taxes (Gillis and McLure, 1971) or, more controversially, to tax capital goods in order to increase utilization and reduce the rate of unnecessary investment in excess capacity (Bird, 1968; Due, 1970). Such corrective policies may indeed be useful in particular cases. On the whole, however, it would seem best for developing countries to be cautious and careful in such fiscal intervention, in order to avoid creating still more unforeseen distortions in the economy, leading to still more interventionism and still greater strain on administrative capacity.

The Personal Income Tax

A brief consideration of the role of the personal income tax in developing countries illustrates the point (see also Chapter 7 below). As noted earlier, the personal income tax is the only significant component of the tax system which has the potential of being "fair" in the sense that the taxes paid by different individuals may be explicitly related to their socially determined ability to contribute to the financing of government activity. For this and other reasons, most tax reforms proposed by Western-trained economists for developing countries have, until recently, suggested an increase in the degree of reliance on the personal income tax.

Yet in most developing countries the personal income tax amounts in reality to little more than a tax on wages and salaries in the organized sector of the economy. Although the tax applies in principle to all forms of income, in practice it is enforced effectively only in the organized sector. Increasing such an "income" tax will therefore discourage entry into the modern (taxed) labor force—the traditional method by which development proceeds and its benefits are spread throughout the population (Kuznets, 1966).

Moreover, pretax wages in the modern sector may tend to rise relative to those in other sectors, thus accentuating the characteristic capital bias of the modern sector in most countries. Fewer people will be employed in this sector, but at higher wages. This tendency will be reinforced by the resulting rise in the relative prices of the goods produced by the modern sector and the fall in its output. It is an empirical question, to which no one as yet has the answer in any country, as to whether the reduction in employment resulting from such "excise" effects of the personal income tax will be offset by the effects of the tax on the after-tax distribution of income and consequent alterations in the composition of demand (see Chapter 6 below).

Given the importance of providing employment in developing countries, some analysts have concluded that an employment-oriented tax system should not contain any payroll taxes (Prest, 1971). Payroll taxes in industrial countries have usually been condemned for their regressive distributional effects, just as personal income taxes have been praised for their progressivity. In the context of many developing countries, however, the distributional effects of both taxes may be much the same. In developing countries, the payroll tax, like the personal income tax, is invariably a selective tax, affecting only some workers in some industries. In these circumstances, so far as the effects of the payroll (and income) tax on employment are concerned, it makes little difference who ultimately pays the tax—workers, consumers, or capitalists. The result will unambiguously be to discourage the taxed modern sector relative to the untaxed traditional, labor-intensive part of the economy (Bird, 1982).

Tax Reform and Tax Design

The preceding discussion implicitly assumes that the taxes discussed will be implemented in some sort of "clean slate" new world: it is concerned with *tax design*. In practice, of course, most national tax systems have not been designed or planned; rather, they have, like Topsy, just grown over time through the cumulation of historical happenstance and passing political expediency. Any *tax reform* in a particular country must start from what already exists. It is therefore constrained by countless political and social conditions peculiar to that country and time.[26]

Too often tax reformers appear to have taken as their objective the remodeling of the tax system to fit some preconceived idea of what a "good" system should look like, with little attention to the specific policy objectives and initial conditions of the country in question. Whether the "model" pursued is based on the system in some other country or on some ideal system derived from economic reasoning ("optimal" taxation) or ethical precepts (various "equity" notions), such exercises are likely to be neither accepted nor, should they happen to be accepted, successfully implemented (see Chapters 2 and 3 below).

Theoretically oriented reformers, for example, often unwarrantedly generalize from skeletal models to always complex local realities. Their empirically oriented brethren at times make similar mistakes by deriving prescriptions for particular countries from the statistically "average" situation in other countries—a route that lacks even the virtue of internal logical consistency, as noted in Chapter 3 below.

It is all too easy for analysts to assume that when reality does not conform to the dictates of a model, the fault lies in reality, which should be cleaned up—so that, for instance, the market will work as theory says it should.[27] Piecemealing reform-mongers, who take the world as it is and try to improve it, are often considered to be mealymouthed compromisers rather than the pragmatic realists they may well be. The "all-or-nothing" approach favored by out-and-out reformers may occasionally pay off tactically, but on the evidence to date it seems to be a clear failure as a general strategy of tax reform. The slate is *not* clean in any country, and there is much to be lost by pretending it is.[28]

This brief defense of the virtue, indeed the necessity, of piecemeal reform is in no sense to be read as a defense of the blind groping in the dark that too often characterizes the views of the "practical man" on tax reform. On the contrary, the prerequisites for a successful major tax reform are exceptionally difficult to satisfy: (1) an explicit statement of policy objectives, (2) a theoretical model explicitly relating the instruments (tax changes) to the objectives, (3) an empirically grounded assessment of all relevant initial and final conditions, and (4) a clear understanding of the political and social, as well as economic, context.

Unfortunately, the social sciences are, for the most part, simply not yet up to satisfying such stern prerequisites as these. Even the best theoretical model will not yield results immediately applicable in a real-world context. Good models produce questions, not answers. In the context of tax reform their virtue is to make clear the key empirical magnitudes upon which the hoped-for results turn. Indeed, it is probably in the estimation of such key parameters that our knowledge in most countries is weakest, even on such ancient questions as the effects of tax changes on saving (Ebrill, 1987). To improve the results of tax reform efforts, much more careful empirical work on such relationships is a prime requisite.

Generalizations about the *substance* of tax reform in developing countries are thus of little use. To be relevant, policy recommendations need to be geared specifically to the prevailing circumstances and objectives of that country. The task of the would-be tax reformer in a developing economy is inherently complicated. When the complexity of the task is combined with the inevitably underdeveloped administrative system of developing countries, it should occasion no surprise that actual performance in most countries falls far short of what might be considered ideal in an unconstrained world. The more that analysts of ability are willing to turn their minds to understanding and improving tax policy in the real conditions of developing countries, the more relevant fiscal economics may become in improving the lives of their billions of inhabitants. Such at least is the belief motivating the present book.

2   Analyzing Tax Policy

Many writers seem to have assumed that there is one particular tax structure that is optimal for all developing countries. Nicholas Kaldor (1965), for example, argued that heavy taxation of the agricultural sector was essential in a developing country.[1] Ursula Hicks (1965) said that an effectively administered global income tax was an essential component of a development tax structure. On the other hand, Walter Heller (1954) had earlier suggested a much more limited role for the income tax, as had Richard Goode (1952). John Due (1967) stressed the importance of heavy taxes on consumption and lighter taxes on business profits in developing countries. More recently, prevailing professional opinion has tended to favor lower income tax rates and a broad-based value-added tax in almost all circumstances.

The conception of the optimal tax structure for a developing country held by many appears to rest on a general notion of the appropriate role of government finance in the development process, a concept of the appropriate nature of the tax system for *any* country, or both. A different approach to designing an optimal tax structure is the comparative approach reviewed in the next chapter. The study of average tax structures and levels in other countries, however, is no more helpful in the design of an optimal tax system for any particular country than are the more explicitly normative propositions cited above. Taxes must be designed for the economic, political, and administrative conditions prevailing in a particular country, not for some average abstract hybrid of all countries. Useful as comparisons may sometimes be for limited purposes, in no way do they indicate the extent or even the direction of change either needed or feasible in any particular country.

The search for an optimal tax system suitable for all developing countries is misguided.[2] If there were no significant differences between developing countries, if the process of economic development were fully understood, if there were no conflicts in achieving the objectives of social and economic policy, and if these objectives and the connections between tax policies and their achievement were fully understood and articulated, then perhaps—and only then—the pursuit of the elusive ideal of an "optimal" package of tax policies would have meaning. Those interested in these problems are better advised to turn their attention to the more limited question of whether there is in any sense an optimal tax structure for a particular developing country at a particular point in time.

Tax policy in a developing country constitutes an essential part of development policy. Within the limits set by a country's institutional and economic structure, meaningful tax reform requires the specification of the appropriate policy framework and the implementation of the best feasible tax system within that framework. The required approach to tax policy thus involves the blending of considerable fiscal expertise with a coherent analysis of the development process and a good stiff dose of knowledge of local conditions.[3] Without the presence of all three ingredients both the palatability and the nutritional benefit of the tax concoctions prepared by visiting experts are in doubt. Given the difficulty of satisfying fully the demands of this recipe, it is not surprising that surveys have found the development tax literature has had relatively little operational impact.[4]

The Welfare Methodology of Tax Policy Reform

The appropriate welfare framework within which to approach the problem of providing advice on tax reform has seldom been considered by practical men. "Practical" tax experts in developing (as in developed) countries, however, are often the servants of a set of intellectual and institutional concepts so deeply imbedded in their way of thinking that they are not consciously aware of their existence.

Two concepts in particular appear to underlie many tax policy proposals in developing countries: first, that there are "desirable" characteristics of any tax in any country at any time, and, second, that the process of economic development is everywhere inherently similar in some important respects, so that there are universally desirable characteristics of the tax system as a development instrument.

The first idea has a long and honorable tradition dating from the time the first canons of taxation were laid down by Adam Smith (1776; 1937). Many have since sung the virtues of such administrative characteristics of taxes as certainty, convenience of payment, and economy of collection. Other commonly cited tax criteria such as horizontal equity (equal treatment of equals) and neutrality (minimal interference with market processes) are more explicitly ethical and normative in nature. However much positive analysis is employed to illustrate the effects of recommendations based on these criteria, to depict the divergencies between the present tax system and the "desirable" one, or to quantify trade-offs between objectives, such norms as horizontal equity and neutrality in the end derive from views of both the nature of society (and of the market) and the initial conditions in the country which may not be shared by all relevant actors in the policy process.[5]

Tax policy recommendations based on such criteria illustrate what may be called the "ethical approach" to normative theory, in which the underlying ethical postulates are simply *assumed* to be of such power and cogency that the desirability, even the necessity, of the recommended policy change cannot be questioned by men of good will.[6] The fact that such ethically derived recommendations are often presented as scientific truths in no way strengthens their uneasy political foundations.

Another example of the ethical approach to tax reform in developing countries is afforded by those who argue that heavier taxation in general, or heavy land taxation, or light taxation of corporations, or the non-taxation of capital gains, or whatever, is essential to achieve some development goal. The judgment involved here relates both to the desirability of the goal and to the connection between the tax instrument and the achievement of the goal. Again, the problem is not so much that such targets are postulated: it is rather that policy recommendations are often presented as though they have some independent validity, some element of inherent "rightness" or necessity about them.

The ethical approach need not be rejected completely, however. Indeed, perhaps the best way to analyze taxation in developing countries is a combination of this version of the "ethical approach" and what may be called the "positivistic" and "acceptability" approaches. The "positivistic" approach analyzes some phenomenon without implying that the analysis says anything about the *desirability* of any particular policy. The aim is simply to provide potentially useful information for policy discussions

The "acceptability" approach, on the other hand, stresses the importance of generating acceptable policy proposals. Essentially, this approach requires that, at least for purposes of the analysis, the technical advisor accept the values of his client. The relevance of this approach to tax policy analysis is obvious. Only if an advisor attempts to relate his advice to the real interests of those in control rather than, as in the strict "ethical" approach, attempting to impose his own conception of social welfare as the goal at which all policy changes should be aimed, is he or she likely to be effective. Governments in democratic states, for example, like to be reelected and are unlikely to embrace policies not conducive to this end. Governments in nondemocratic states are not keen on fomenting unrest and their potential overthrow. Tax policies thought likely to produce such results, no matter how great their technical merits, are unlikely to receive much of a hearing from the powers that be, and those who propose such policies are unlikely to be taken seriously.

This argument implies that effective technical assistance in the tax field must be attuned to the real objectives of government policy. Nonetheless, strong strands of the ethical approach remain even in completely client-centered advice. No client's interests are ever fully articulated, so that advisors in order to advise have to make assumptions about the client's values and aims. If an advisor feels unable to do this (or if there is some divergence of objectives), he or she can adopt a more "positivistic" approach and offer analysis of points—such as the effect of higher income taxes on personal saving—which should in principle be relevant no matter what the precise policy objectives may be.[7]

The best approach to designing a useful tax reform is thus "ethical" in the sense that the desirability of certain objectives is inevitably simply assumed—notably, in most developing countries, the aim of increasing the level of per capita income. It should also be "acceptable" in that there is considerable congruence between the objectives specified and the real aims of those currently in power. And, finally, it may also be "positivistic" in that on points where there may be disagreement in values—often, notably with respect to the effects of progressivity or the efficacy of tax incentives—objective analysis is provided which should be relevant no matter what one believes (though of course no analyst would be human if he or she did not believe the evidence supports his or her position!).

The distinction between this approach to designing a tax reform and that (usually implicitly) adopted by most other writers on this subject is primarily one of degree rather than of kind. Too much tax analysis, however, has been based far too heavily (though almost never explicitly) on the ethical approach alone. An advisor might, of course, be justified in presenting as objectively necessary a set of recommendations that he or she suspects to be completely unacceptable when a radical change in the values of government is expected in the near future. Positing some all-or-nothing alternative such as a drastic reform in present fiscal institutions might be justified in such circumstances in order to have the new tax order ready to hand when the revolution arrives. In general, however, this tactic seems unlikely to pay off in any relevant terms.[8]

The Politics of Tax Reform

In theory, the tax system in most developing countries can be made a more responsive and responsible instrument for development. But is it possible, politically and administratively, for such changes to be made in practice? The existing tax structure in any country reflects the past equilibration of conflicting political forces, as constrained by economic structure and scarce administrative resources. The optimal strategy of tax reform may be defined as that which involves the minimum political cost (Hettich and Winer, 1988). One of the scarcest resources in developing countries is the capacity to make and implement effective policy decisions. The best approach to tax reform in such countries is thus to obtain the desired change for the minimum expenditure of scarce political and administrative capital.

Economic policy is invariably subordinated to the needs of political stability. Decisions on painful and potentially dangerous matters like major tax reform can thus generally be made only in times of crisis, particularly external crisis, when the changes can be blamed on external forces and when it is obvious to all that disaster will ensue if they are not made.[9]

If this assessment of the probability of adopting a major tax reform is correct, one implication is that such changes cannot be expected to be put into force as a package but must instead be viewed as a set of goals toward which, over time, the crisis-induced changes inevitable in any tax system might tend. In this view, a long-run strategy of tax reform can be implemented in most countries at minimum (political) cost—or perhaps at all—only by a series of tactical seizures of the opportunities for change created by crises, with the strategic policy decisions setting the ground rules that constrain and mold the tactical decisions. This approach, however, assumes a fundamental political continuity and hence constancy of objectives over time—conditions that are unlikely to be satisfied in many developing countries.

An alternative approach might be to try to adopt a major set of proposals as a "package." All too often in developing countries, tax reform means tax increase, with the result that no one is likely to be made too happy by the process. The package approach to some extent attempts to neutralize the political damage both by spreading the unhappiness around and by compensating for the "bads" (e.g., higher tax revenues) by "goods" (e.g., lower tax rates). For this approach to be successful, however, would-be reformers again need a solid enough political base to carry out substantial preliminary education of policymakers and, where relevant, the public.

Despite these difficulties, even urgent short-run revenue problems should not be resolved without considering the long-run implications of tax structure for development. To the extent basic tax changes can be made only in times of acute fiscal crisis, there is considerable danger that tax reform —regarded simply as something to be gotten out of the way before going on to the real task of long-range planning (and spending)—may inadvertently establish undesirable economic incentives.[10] Once such incentives are created, experience suggests all too strongly that it will be more difficult to change the policy in question than it would have been to set it up properly in the first place.[11]

Tax policy should be constructed with an eye not merely to the revenue it will produce but also to its probable effects on the structure of incentives in the economy and on the key variables affecting development possibilities and patterns—the balance of payments, the composition of final demand, the size of the public sector, income distribution, and production techniques. Since the initial cost of good tax structure design is generally little higher than that of bad design and the potential long-run benefits are so much greater, more attention to the design of new taxes and the reform of old ones would appear to be a worthwhile investment for most developing countries.

Finally, there is the delicate question of how to present tax reforms. The need to sell reform lies in part behind the later emphasis in this book on earmarking and benefit taxation (see Chapters 12 and 13 below). Similarly, as part of a tax reform package, such archaic and complex taxes as stamp taxes might be abolished to make the increase a little more politically palatable (Bird, 1967).

The political aspect of tax reform has two dimensions. The first dimension relates to the *will* of the government to make such decisions and the second to its *ability* to carry them out. Some efforts at tax reform in various countries in the past have amounted to little or nothing—even if they resulted in the appearance of a new law on the statute books—simply because the reforms were not the real policy of those in power but a game performed for the international lending agencies or other interested spectators. The political autonomy of a government may be defined as its capacity to make decisions independent of the wishes of other groups and interests in society. Is tax policy the reflection of the pressure of vested interests or of the decisions of relatively autonomous policy-makers?

In Colombia, for example, evidence pointing both ways may be found. Somewhat optimistically, both the 1953 income tax reform (Fluharty, 1957) and the 1965 sales tax (Bird, 1968) might be taken to indicate the relative independence of government decision-makers, once they make up their own minds.[12] The role of interest groups—regional and sectional, as well as economic and social—in these decisions was hardly negligible, but there is considerable evidence that a strong, determined Colombian government can overcome such obstacles to reform if it really wants to do so.[13] Past performance is less encouraging with respect to the ability of the government to tax the traditional agricultural sector very heavily. The power of the coffee interests in determining coffee policy in Colombia is well documented.[14] Cattle interests seem to have been similarly successful in blocking moves to tax them more effectively. Indeed, the relative impotence of industrial as compared to agricultural interests in determining economic policy has been noted as a general characteristic of Latin American politics by many observers (Hirschman, 1968), and Colombia is no exception to this rule.[15]

Obviously, no definitive conclusion on such complex, delicate, and country-specific matters can be reached here. The point, however, is simply that the prospects of substantial tax reform in any country are no more than a reflection of those for real change in the political and social balance. It may be frustrating to an expert when advice formulated after careful and objective study goes unheeded by policy-makers, but such neglect is not necessarily wrong. The task of politics is to reconcile conflicting interests in order to bring about acceptable and workable solutions. In some instances, technical advice on taxation may be too narrowly formulated to be acceptable as it stands. In other instances, private interests, whether those of the decision-makers themselves (elite, oligarchy) or of nongovernmental groups (pressure groups) may conflict with the technician's view of the "public interest." Who is to say which is "right" in such cases? Elements of all these conflicts seem present in most countries, and to make the chances of substantial tax reform murky at best.

The Importance of Administration

Tax reform would seem to have no natural allies and many enemies. Some private-sector support for fiscal changes to reduce "tax evasion" almost always exists, however: "Why should government penalize honest taxpayers by raising tax rates when so much revenue is foregone by evasion?" (Taylor, 1967).

By definition, it is difficult to get a good idea of the extent of illegal evasion, but the scanty evidence cited in Chapter 15 below suggests that tax evasion is common. This result is not surprising in countries in which government is considered by most taxpayers to waste what it gets, and where the penalties for evasion are both low and poorly enforced, so taxpayers know that the possible cost of evading taxes is low or zero. Better tax design and more equitable and tougher administration are the only answers to tax evasion, but such changes, if possible at all, will take time even with the best will in the world, and thus cannot be counted on to provide much of the revenue needed for development.

The second dimension of the politics of tax reform referred to above relates to the ability of the government to make its policy decisions effective. Success in this regard depends both on its ability to hold its political base in the face of change and on its administrative capacity. J. K. Galbraith (1964) once noted of economic administration that "there is no problem for which intimacy breeds such respect." This dictum certainly holds true for tax administration. In the hands of an incompetent administration, good tax policy and bad tax policy may end up looking remarkably alike. Tax reform proposals that assume good tax administration exists are unlikely to be relevant in most poor countries. Similarly, comparisons between an existing badly designed, badly administered system and a better-designed alternative that assume the new system will be well administered are more misleading than helpful. A safer assumption is that the present poor administrative machine, perhaps with some marginal improvements, will continue to function at the same low level, no matter what changes are made in tax policy or in tax structure. Indeed, it often seems to be easier to make drastic changes in tax policy than to overcome the inertia of the system and improve the administration of existing taxes. Once a policy change has been made, however, there is usually little reason to expect the new tax to be administered better than the old, for the same people must administer both. (See Chapter 15 below for further discussion.)

There is little economic advisors on taxation can do about the important administrative constraint on tax reform except to take it into account as explicitly as possible in formulating tax reforms for developing countries. Hard as this truth seems to be for some to accept, it is, as a rule, *much* more difficult to administer a tax policy effectively than it is to devise it in the first place.[16]

Tax administrations necessarily reflect the society in which they operate. If the common view of government is disaffected, as is often the case in developing countries, tax administration is bound to be a difficult and unpopular task. Institutional difficulties such as the greater relative importance in developing countries of the always hard-to-control farm and small-business sectors also make tax administration difficult and inequitable. The social and economic structure of a country thus conditions the feasibility of effectively administering different taxes, just as it determines their desirability from a policy point of view. To the extent the problems affecting tax administration reflect political forces, their resolution must be political, not technical. Improving tax administration, like improving tax structure, is inherently a political process.

Since the quality of tax administration is such an important constraint on the possibility of tax reform, it appears logical to suggest only those reforms that can be administered by a relatively low-quality administration. Sound tax policy must be premised on a realistic understanding and appraisal of the capabilities of the tax administration. As argued in Chapter 8 below, one path to improvement in many countries might be to recognize explicitly the need for crude, arbitrary solutions in many instances and to attempt to be consistent in applying them rather than to assume that some "perfect" law can be perfectly administered—which in practice means that the inevitable imperfections spring up unexpected and unprepared for. A less than ideal tax designed for a poor administration may work better—its effects may be more in line with those desired—than a "good" tax badly administered. Unfortunately, in tax policy, as with so many other aspects of development policy in poor countries, it seems both more necessary and less possible to do things well than in more developed countries.

Conclusion

Tax reform, whether in policy or administration, will in most instances be a piecemeal process, given the intractable and ongoing nature of the problem and the limited political and human resources available to deal with it. Tax reform is also a continuous, if episodic, process.[17] Not only can no grand once-for-all reform scheme be realistically expected to be adopted in most countries, but even if such a scheme were adopted it would seldom be sufficient for long. Circumstances change, and policies must change with them. Crisis implementation of tax reforms will likely continue to be the rule in the future in most countries, as it has in the past. The key to an improved tax system is to be ready with soundly worked out proposals when the crisis comes. The first requirement of a full-fledged tax reform effort is of course a real desire on the part of a strong government to carry it out. But inspired leadership alone is not enough. The second essential requirement is that concern with tax policy and tax administration be sufficiently institutionalized so that good intentions may be converted, when the time comes, into workable reality.

3   Assessing Tax Performance

How can one assess the performance of a developing country? Officials responsible for allocating international aid, for example, are not content with such qualitative appraisals as "country X is doing all right" or "country Y seems to be slacking." They need comparable performance indicators, preferably simple and quantifiable, to provide a basis for assessing which "clients" are doing well and which are not—or, in somewhat stronger terms, which countries are not putting forth as great an effort to help themselves as they can or should. If a standard of the performance to be expected from countries at various stages of development can be established, the actual performance of a country, its "effort," can be defined in terms of how closely the indicator approaches the standard.

Such a standard with regard to tax performance may conceivably be established in two quite different ways. One approach is to postulate an ideal (minimum) tax level and structure which any developing country that is "serious" about development ought to achieve.[1] As noted in Chapter 2, such an ideal may be derived from textbooks, or from currently fashionable reasoning such as the distributive bias characteristic of the 1960s or the supply-side bias of the 1980s. Such "ethical" reasoning, however, possesses little inherent merit when applied to any particular country even if buttressed by the observation that some other countries have in fact attained the specified goal. An alternative approach to establishing a norm for evaluating tax performance is to take the average performance of countries defined to be similar in certain respects: in effect to say, as the head of the Philippine planning office once did, that "judging from the tax efforts of more progressively developing countries, the low tax effort in our country can only suggest that there is a wider room for further taxation" (Sicat, 1972, p. 3).[2] Conversely, Marsden (1983) has argued that "low tax" countries grow more rapidly than do "high tax" countries, with the implication that the latter should emulate the former.[3] In both instances, the average performance of other countries is taken not only to show what a particular country could do if it wanted to, but also what it *should* do. It is this interpretation of international tax comparisons, still all too common both in the academic literature and among policy-makers, with which this chapter is concerned.[4]

Why Assess Tax Performance?

The need to assess tax performance and the usefulness of international tax comparisons in doing so have been urged for many reasons. One reason is simply because most economic formulations of the development problem imply that the adequate mobilization of domestic resources is the key to self-sustained growth. In the classic words of Sir Arthur Lewis (1955, pp. 255–56): "The central problem in the theory of economic growth is to understand the process by which a community is converted from being a 5 percent to a 12 percent saver." The arithmetic underlying the usual development plan may be crudely summarized as follows: a certain rate of growth is required (or desired, or considered feasible); to attain this amount of growth, a certain amount of new capital formation is needed; but this level of investment can be achieved without unwanted inflationary pressure only if it is equaled by *ex ante* savings; and since private and foreign savings can be expected to amount to only x percent of GNP (x being less than the required amount), public savings must be increased through taxation to make up the difference. More succinctly, "the simple arithmetic of growth involves mainly an increase in tax revenues" (Sicat, 1972, p. 4).

One rationale for comparative studies is thus to see if a country can achieve the level of taxation required to attain plan targets: to determine "whether a given country could not, if it wanted to, raise more taxes without seriously 'burdening' the economy" (Chelliah, 1971, p. 259). In the extreme, the levels achieved in other countries may even be taken to set some sort of absolute standard, as when Lewis (1966, p. 129) asserted that "most underdeveloped countries need to raise at least 17 percent of gross domestic product in taxes and other government revenues, taking central and local authorities together."

This approach assumes, of course, that increased taxes do not reduce saving to any significant extent. Others have suggested that increased taxes may result in increased current government expenditure and hence make no net contribution to total saving.[5] Indeed, if one assumes, as many do today (albeit on difficult to interpret evidence of variable quality: see Ebrill, 1987), that increased taxes also reduce private saving, more tax "effort" might even mean worse savings "performance"! Moreover, higher taxes may be associated with higher levels of output distortions and hence with lower rates of growth (Skinner, 1988). All in all, information on the level of taxation in one country relative to that in others is a poor guide to the contribution of the tax system to growth.

A second rationale that has been put forward in support of systematic international comparisons is that policy-makers in developing countries, as elsewhere, are in the habit of comparing themselves with others, so that such comparisons may sometimes play an important role in the domestic appraisal of domestic policy.[6] That this proposition is true is obvious to anyone who has worked in a finance ministry in any country, whether developing or developed. The comparisons that are made are all too often oversimple, misleading, and irrelevant.[7] The fact that policy-makers are drawn to, and impressed by, "bad" international comparisons may be sufficient reason to make "good" ones.

Thirdly, in contrast to the additive model postulated in the simple capital formation view mentioned above, it has sometimes been argued that foreign capital, particularly aid, has tended to replace, or substitute for, domestic saving in recipient countries.[8] The receipt of foreign aid leads to taxes being lower than they otherwise would be, with any possible offsetting increases in private savings as a result of lower taxes considered to be negligible. The obvious policy importance attached to this question by aid donors gave a major impetus in the 1970s to studies of saving (and tax) effort and performance.

In a sense, the extent to which foreign saving is substituted for domestic saving is a variant of an older question related to the problem of "project aid" versus "program aid." A major criticism made of project aid in the 1960s, for example, was that because money is fungible, aid cannot really be tied to specific projects. Aid donors, it was argued, would be better advised to focus their attention on the entire development program rather than solely on the particular part of it they wrongly thought they were financing.[9] Similarly, program aid was criticized in the 1970s for financing something—namely, tax reduction—that the donors did not want to finance.

The growth of structural adjustment lending in the 1980s brings up another important reason for the considerable attention that has been paid in the literature to measures of fiscal performance. Such loans are generally conditioned on the attainment by the recipient country of satisfactory standards with respect to certain performance criteria. Given the centrality of saving in the usual development model, the close link between deficit financing and inflation in most developing countries, and the ready availability of fiscal data, it is not surprising that measures of fiscal performance are often dear to the hearts of those concerned with using the "leverage" of aid in this fashion to affect key domestic policies.[10]

In principle, though not yet in practice, international comparisons in relation to aid might also serve as a basis for allocating aid, a possibility at one time canvassed in a number of studies (Rosenstein-Rodan, 1961; Dosser, 1963; Strout and Clark, 1969). The cruder versions of this approach suggest some sort of simple per capita income basis for allocating aid. Experience with intergovernmental aid in federations suggests strongly that it would not be long before some sort of measure of "fiscal effort," probably based on some comparatively derived standard, would come back into the discussion.[11] Should the world ever become more unified, as those concerned with development must hope, this use of international comparisons of tax performance may in the long run turn out to be the most important of all. At present, however, it is clearly utopian.

Even in the imperfect world in which we live, international comparisons are sometimes used as one component of the assessment of credit-worthiness, that is, of the ability of the recipient to pay back a loan without undue internal or external financial strain. Tax capacity and the willingness to make use of it—which may sometimes be judged in part by some internationally determined average standard—are clearly as relevant to this question as the resources and character of a prospective borrower are to a bank manager.[12]

Last, but by no means least as a reason for examining a country's tax performance in quantitative terms, is the simple fact that it is an interesting exercise. Even if one does not accept the simple capital formation model of development put forward above, no poor country can get very far without mobilizing more resources, at least to some degree through taxation. The extent to which any country is judged able to do so is therefore an important intellectual and practical concern for those interested in the well-being of humanity. Moreover, the availability of a large body of at least superficially comparable financial data which lends itself to the techniques of quantitative manipulation with which students of economics are imbued these days makes it likely that the data will indeed be so manipulated, almost regardless of the point of doing so.[13]

The Assessment of Tax Performance

Most early international tax comparisons were carried out without any reference to their rationale. As Shoup (1972, p. 40) said in a somewhat different context: "Too often the information is hardly more useful, directly, than data on the proportion of taxation imposed on inhabitants over six feet in height."[14] This characterization applies to studies of the determinants of national tax ratios (the share of government revenues in the national income) or tax structures which have little or no theoretical basis underlying the choice of variables or techniques.

Despite their theoretical limitations, such studies may provide interesting information on the statistical association between various measurable characteristics of a country and the size of its tax ratio, such as the apparently significant influence exerted on this ratio by the size of the foreign trade sector (Hinrichs and Bird, 1963). Some authors have used such essentially cross-sectional analysis as the basis for a theory of the evolution of tax structure over time, focusing on the declining role of foreign trade taxes and the rise of various income-related taxes (Hinrichs, 1966; Musgrave, 1969).

Undoubtedly, the most thorough studies of the determinants of national tax ratios and structures have been those conducted by the Fiscal Affairs Department of the International Monetary Fund (IMF). In one such study, for example, the average tax ratio of a group of forty-seven developing countries was shown to have increased from 13.6 percent in 1966–68 to 15.1 percent in 1969–71, with the ratio increasing in almost four-fifths of the countries covered and not falling significantly in any. The composition of taxes did not change much over this period, with "income" taxes (which include mineral royalties) accounting for 27 percent, property taxes 5 percent, foreign trade taxes 32 percent, and internal transaction taxes also 32 percent of the total in 1969–71. That is, so-called "direct taxes" yielded only about one-third of total revenues in this group of developing countries. Marked regional variations in both the level and pattern of taxation also emerged from this study (Chelliah, Baas, and Kelly, 1975). A similar picture emerges from more recent studies of tax levels and structures in developing countries (Tait, Gratz, and Eichengreen, 1979; Tanzi, 1987; World Bank, 1988).

The presentation of such descriptive data has obvious informative value. Most such studies, however, attempt to explain statistically the observed difference in tax ratios. The study cited above, for example, found that the tax ratio could be best explained in terms of the sectoral composition of the gross domestic product (GDP), with mining (including petroleum) making a positive and agriculture a negative contribution. What this analysis thus appears to tell us is that some (by no means most!) of the variation in national tax ratios is statistically associated with the shares of agriculture and mining in national output. This result is perhaps interesting, but it can hardly be considered to be very exciting or to have much policy significance in terms of evaluating fiscal performance: a country wishing to raise revenues cannot go out and discover oil at will!

Largely for this reason, the study cited actually rejected the equation with the greatest statistical merit as a "standard" of tax performance in favor of a statistically inferior equation incorporating somewhat different variables. Several reasons were given for this choice. (1) "Per capita income has considerable normative significance in considering taxable capacity and in assessing tax effort"; it should therefore be included.[15] (2) On the other hand, "there are grounds for believing that the share of the agricultural sector affects not only taxable capacity but also, perhaps more importantly, the willingness to tax"; it should therefore be excluded. (3) As for mining, "because of the heavy fixed investment associated with extractive industries, operations tend to be confined to a few large firms and as long as world demand conditions ensure high profitability, there exists a combination of taxable 'surplus' and administrative ease"; the mining share ought therefore to be included. (4) Finally, the nonmining export ratio is needed to "make allowance directly for the export factor in countries where mining is not so important." As these quotations make clear, the main purpose of the statistical exercise in this study was not to explain variations in the ratio among different countries but rather to measure "taxable capacity": the variables selected are those thought to explain capacity best.

The proper measurement of taxable capacity, however, depends critically on the a priori justification of the explanatory variables as affecting *only* taxable capacity and not at all either demands for higher public expenditures or willingness to tax.[16] The inherent problem with this approach is therefore obvious, given the debatable nature of the variables chosen. Per capita income, for example, is presumably included because it is a proxy for a potentially higher tax base (or a larger "taxable surplus"). But in fact income is as much a "demand" as it is a "supply" factor: the identification problem is insuperable.

Similarly, Chelliah (1971, p. 297) argued that the agricultural share should *not* be included because "many developing countries have found it difficult to tax agriculture adequately, for historical and political reasons"—an incontestably true statement (Bird, 1974). The size of the agricultural sector thus reflects not just capacity to tax but also willingness to tax. But then why include the mining share? One might just as well say, equally truly, that many developing countries have, for historical and political reasons, found it easy to tax the mining sector (which is controlled by foreigners in many countries and employs relatively few people). If one sectoral share can be said to affect "willingness" as well as "capacity," then so can the other, on equally firm (or infirm) grounds. The distinction between "capacity" and "willingness" is at best fuzzy. Indeed, one might say that "capacity" without "willingness" is not really "capacity"—or "effective capacity"—at all.

In short, it is inherently difficult to specify correctly any model of (usable) taxable capacity. Any particular specification may be criticized and academic purists will never find such analysis very satisfactory. Practical men will doubtless continue to say, when faced with such quibbles, "What's that to me? I want a number I can understand," and economists will doubtless continue to provide such numbers, even if they shouldn't.[17]

Let us therefore pretend that something called "taxable capacity" can be adequately measured. The obvious next step is to calculate *tax effort*, defined as the ratio of the actual tax ratio in a particular country to that which would be predicted on the basis of the taxable capacity equation. Since, by assumption, all capacity factors are allowed for in the equation, the observed difference—the residual—presumably measures the "effort" that a country makes to exploit this capacity. In the usual form of such analysis, regression equations are used to calculate the predicted tax ratio directly, a procedure which is equivalent to saying that "taxable capacity" is the tax ratio that would result if a country utilized its tax bases to the average extent they are utilized by the sample with respect to which the regression has been calculated. A tax ratio of less than 1.0 implies that the country exploits its estimated tax potential less than average. In other words, it has a "preference" for a level of taxation below the average, or a low tax effort.[18]

Such calculations serve at least a limited function in the sense that the ranking derived is generally quite different from that obtained by ranking countries simply in terms of their tax-to-income ratios. In the 1975 IMF study cited above, for example, only three of the first ten countries ranked by the tax ratio made it, for better or worse, into the first ten in the tax effort league. If for some reason one insists on ranking countries by some simple tax index, the picture suggested by this "effort" index is less misleading than that suggested by the simple tax ratio.[19]

A more usual interpretation of these tax effort figures is that if a country has a low index, "the main impediment to a higher tax ratio is the unwillingness of the Government to raise taxes" (Bahl, 1971, p. 572). The calculated index is thus used as a guide to the feasibility of raising additional revenues in individual countries, and the "international league table" aspect of the exercise is downplayed.

The correct emphasis is precisely the opposite. So long as pressure from "practical" men requires the compilation of such international comparative exercises, the use of adjusted ratios is more likely to give rise to policy-relevant questions (not answers!) than unadjusted ratios. Even if one is a dedicated believer in the tax-savings-growth model, however, the difference between predicted and actual values does not measure in any meaningful way either the scope for change in any particular country or the gap that can (or should) be closed through additional "effort." Reality is too complex and particularistic to be captured by such a mechanistic approach.

Consider, for example, the case of Nicaragua: in the first five years of the Sandinista regime the tax ratio rose from 18 to 32 percent of GDP (Bird, 1985). Only politics can explain this rapid increase. On the other hand, the explicitly political analysis of Best (1976) is also inadequate to explain what happened in Nicaragua since, quite contrary to his model, the "progressive" Sandinista government relied entirely upon (regressive) indirect taxes to accomplish this increase—as, indeed, it had to do given the administrative impossibility of relying on direct taxes in the circumstances of Central America. Assessing the potential fiscal performance of a country with models that leave critical political or administrative realities out of account obviously leaves much to be desired.

Conclusion

Of course, the many good economists who have carried out studies such as those criticized here have generally recognized the validity of many of these points in principle. In particular, the IMF is now much more cautious in its use of such studies.[20] Nonetheless, the lure of quantifiable international comparisons continues to draw even good scholars into misusing such data.[21] Numbers, particularly "scientifically" derived numbers such as these, appear to have undue influence on the attitudes of many people. In conclusion, therefore, it may be useful to summarize the basic problems in using international comparisons to assess tax performance in any particular country.

First, there is almost invariably inadequate a priori justification in international tax comparisons for the use of the selected variables. Furthermore, it is far from clear that taxable capacity can be measured in any meaningful sense. The complex problem of the relation between government revenues and expenditures is only one of the many problems that are obscured in this exercise.[22]

Second, the data are very bad. Everyone who works in the comparative game recognizes this, but too many seem to forget what they know. One cannot take per capita income figures seriously in many developing countries, for example.[23] Even fiscal data in many countries are questionable. These data problems are very serious, and no one can truthfully claim to be aware of all the biases they impart to the result. All cross-sectional studies are thus suspect.[24]

Third, virtually all of the work that has been done on quantitative international comparisons is cross-sectional in nature. Yet the policy inferences that are drawn from such work are invariably concerned with changes in particular areas. Few exercises are more questionable than drawing inferences about *changes* from data on *differences*.[25] The choice of the sample, the possibility of technological innovation in the tax field (the value-added tax), the problem of "tastes" and international demonstration effects—such factors suggest how treacherous such use of cross-section data is. Cross-section data may provide—they often do—the only game in town. But to say this does not imply what it is too often taken to do, that we should therefore play this game.

Fourth, another problem concerns the nature of the norms that are applied in the tax effort analysis. As Tanzi (1973) said: "If we believe, as we all seem to do, that the tax structures of most developing countries are far from what they should be and that they should be changed, why should we use as our reference point the average of all those distortions? A statistical average of 30 or 50 distorted tax structures cannot give us the norm against which a country should evaluate its own tax structure. And if those statistical relations don't do that, what do they do then?" There is no meaningful sense in which the average of distorted reality can be considered a *standard*.[26] Nor is it conceptually useful—though it may sometimes serve as an additional persuasive argument in political debate—to assert that such an average shows what is *feasible* in any particular country.

Finally, despite the growth of econometric sophistication in recent years, all too often authors seem to have forgotten their own initial warnings on the limitations of such exercises and their limited usefulness for policy purposes by the time they reach their conclusions. Tax ratio studies are too often used to imply either that country X should reach some computed ratio or that it could readily do so, if it wished. Both inferences are improper, and studies that lend themselves so readily to misuse ought to be avoided, particularly if undue attention to such international comparisons detracts from the needed analysis of problems and policies in individual developing countries.

In short, the effort that has gone into "effort" studies would have contributed more to both knowledge and policy formation if it had been directed to less glamorous but more rewarding studies of particular problems in particular countries. Economists concerned with taxation and development would be well advised to find out more about the subject they are studying before attempting to generalize on the basis of aggregative and often ill-understood data. Admittedly, it may be tempting to forget the deficiencies of applied economic analysis when the even more flagrant deficiencies of everyone else's approach to public policy are so often made obvious in policy discussion. Too often one feels when listening to a sociologist or political scientist or lawyer discussing taxation that (to paraphrase Sir Winston Churchill), economics is the worst of all the social sciences—except for all the others. Economists clearly have made some progress in understanding the complex aspects of social reality reflected in the fiscal systems of developing countries. Still more progress might be made if we refrain from succumbing to the temptation to become the high priests of a new version of the old mystique of numerology.

PART II

Taxation, Growth, and Distribution

4 Redistribution, Growth, and Tax Policy

As noted in Chapter 1, the connection between the distribution of income and the rate of economic growth is often considered to be simple and straightforward. Growth is a function of investment, and investment must be matched by savings. Since the rich, particularly the rich recipients of industrial profits, save more than the poor, high taxes on the rich will likely reduce private saving and should be avoided. Any deficit in revenues resulting from this prescription should be made up by shifting the tax mix toward heavier reliance on (often regressive) consumption taxes. Redistributive taxation is a luxury that poor countries can ill afford. To retain the mass support necessary for continued political power in any modern (or even semimodern) state, tax policies that appear to be redistributive in character may need to be legislated. For the sake of economic growth, however, such policies ought either to be so full of loopholes (usually called "incentives") as to be ineffective—"dipping deeply with a sieve" in Henry Simons's (1938) immortal phrase—or else they simply ought not be enforced.

Even if a genuinely redistributive policy is thought necessary for some sociopolitical reason—for example, to break the control of the upper classes over income, wealth, and political power so that the poor can receive more of the benefits of economic growth—the economist customarily notes down in the debit column the cost of this policy in terms of economic growth forgone. Since the interest of the present elite in maintaining their position is thus buttressed by the economic argument that it is really better in the long run for the poor that the rich (or at least some of them) *are* rich, it is not surprising that few developing countries have progressive tax systems (Bird and Dewulf, 1973; DeWulf, 1975). The fact is, however, that the relation between income distribution and economic growth is far from a settled issue.

Inequality and Growth

The model of economic growth sketched above, which appears to underlie much tax policy, has growth depending on investment, investment depending on savings, and savings depending in large part on the rate of profits. The classical assumption was that all savings came from profits, the propensity to save out of wage income being zero. Even theories of economic growth which take explicit account of the distribution of income generally have the average propensity to save—the key determinant of the rate of economic growth—varying directly with the share of income accruing to profits, that is, to the rich (Allen, 1968).

A lucid and informed study of Pakistan's development in the 1950s by Gustav Papanek (1967), for example, argued in effect that this classical model works. The great inequalities of income characterizing Pakistan's development, and encouraged by government policy, were *necessary* to provide the savings that permitted the creation of an industrial base and thus some real improvement in the level of consumption of the lower income groups. As Papanek (1967, p. 110) said: "It was the consensus of all industrialists, of most professional observers, and of some civil servants that effective tax enforcement in the 1950's would have aborted Pakistan's industrial development. It was only by widespread evasion of direct taxes that industrialists could earn the large profits which provided the spur and capital for industrial entrepreneurship." Similar views lie below the surface of many supply-side arguments today (e.g., Krauss, 1983; Rabushka and Bartlett, 1985).

In fact, however, the Pakistani case gives little comfort to extreme advocates of laissez-faire. As Papanek (1967, pp. 207–8) went on to note: "The tremendous disparities of income which resulted from the Pakistani pattern of development were not translated into equally wide disparities of consumption. The extraordinarily high incomes of the new industrial entrepreneurs were not as galling when they were invested rather than consumed. The private sector, particularly industry, was a superb machine for squeezing resources out of a poor society, but it took government-imposed restrictions on consumption to assure that returns from industry were saved not consumed." Through tax, tariff, and, especially, quota policy, the Pakistani government prevented inequalities of *consumption* from being accentuated, albeit at the expense of substantial economic distortions. This point seems crucial to the argument for the virtues of income inequality in Pakistan in the 1960s.[1] Nonetheless, Pakistan's policy of forcing the rich to become richer by preventing them from spending their incomes at once may well have accentuated its subsequent political problems once the pent-up spending power of the rich could no longer be restrained. Moreover, the distortions introduced in order to reduce the visible consumption of the wealthy accentuated its economic problems.

Even if problems are not simply postponed to the future, the allegedly beneficial effects of increased inequality may be doubted even on its own terms. Indeed, it can equally be argued that income redistribution is not a "welfare" measure but an essential component of the political stability needed for sustained growth. Recent studies of the relative success of certain growth-oriented policies in East Asia and the relative failure of similar policies in Latin America, for example, suggest that the great difference in the pattern of income inequality in the two regions may be one important differentiating factor (Deyo, 1987). The link between increased saving and increased growth is far from clear either analytically or empirically. Even if there is such a link, it is not at all obvious that income inequality is a very efficient way to get more saving.

As Keynes showed over fifty years ago, increased saving in advanced countries may in certain circumstances lead not to higher, but to lower income levels. Exactly the same result may ensue for different reasons in developing countries. If, for example, increased saving must be matched by increased *imports* if it is to result in increased investment, increased saving alone, with no change in foreign exchange availabilities, may lead not to higher investment and income, but to lower income and more unemployment.[2]

Even if the savings-investment-growth chain of reasoning is accepted, the implications for tax policy are not clear. If more savings are needed for growth, the most efficient way to get them may be not by leaving more money in the hands of the wealthy—who will after all spend at least some of it—but rather by taking it away from them by taxes. Higher taxes, not lower taxes, may be the most efficient way of increasing saving.[3] Increased *public* saving, of course, need not preclude increased *private* investment if desired, for example via reduced government borrowing (Musgrave, 1963).

Increasing income inequality—or, what amounts to the same thing in a dynamic context, refraining from attempts to lessen income inequality—may thus not always be a particularly efficient way of increasing saving, and increased saving may not always imply faster growth.

Redistribution and Growth

The high proportion of nonwage income and the great inequality of income characteristic of many developing countries does not mean that private saving has been an important source of capital formation. In Colombia, for example, the marginal propensity to save out of private disposable income in the early postwar period was extremely low, in part no doubt because of inflation. Since the average propensity to save out of current income of the public sector exceeded that of the private sector, it was suggested that increased taxation of the wealthy might even *increase* saving (Bird, 1970a). In these circumstances, redistributive tax policy, even in terms of the classical growth model sketched above, would encourage rather than retard economic growth. Chile in the 1950s offered a similar example (Kaldor, 1964).

The classical model is inappropriate for countries in which growth is limited not by a shortage of saving but by a shortage of foreign exchange. When inadequate foreign exchange is the binding constraint on economic growth, increasing income inequality to induce more saving is perverse. Indeed, in these circumstances, the only way (other than foreign aid) to escape the foreign exchange bind may be by changing the pattern of final demand to a less import-intensive one, for example, by changing the distribution of income toward greater equality (assuming food production can be expanded).[4] Egalitarian fiscal policy might be of more direct use in fostering economic growth in such countries than tax favoritism to profits or incentives to saving and investment.

As these examples indicate, the classical growth model is merely one of at least four possible models that should be considered by the tax policy designer in a less developed country concerned with economic growth. It is the case where growth is limited by inadequate savings and where the rich are savers. Even in this case, as the Pakistani experience of the 1950s suggests, the saving instinct may need a lot of stimulation, and a laissez-faire policy may be building up problems for the future. Countries characterized by savings-limited growth, in which the rich spend rather than save—a description that to some extent fits Chile and Colombia in the same period—may find redistributive tax policy a more efficient way of producing growth than tax incentives. When the key constraint holding back growth is inadequate foreign exchange, however, increasing savings is not a very useful growth policy anyway. In these circumstances, if the rich are spenders, redistributive tax policy may perhaps be a useful policy instrument to alter the pattern of demand. On the other hand, if the rich are savers, a sort of quasi-Keynesian situation may perhaps prevail in that reducing savings may, paradoxically, increase employment and income, again suggesting that redistributive policy may make economic sense.

The bottom line is simply that the connection between income distribution and economic growth is a factual matter. Although distressingly little is known about the relevant facts, there is no case in most countries for such actively inegalitarian tax policies as are now often pursued in the sacred name of economic growth, even if one shrinks, for administrative or other reasons, from active redistributive policies.[5]

Tax Rates and Growth

Similar strictures may be applied to the recently fashionable emphasis on the connection between the top nominal marginal rate of the personal income tax and the rate of economic growth (Rabushka and Bartlett, 1985). Here too, the argument seems largely unsupported by either evidence or logic.

Does anyone really believe that the developing world would, so to speak, turn upside down if the tax rate on the highest bracket were cut—especially since, in practice, no entrepreneur ever pays anything near these rates? Would a reduction to Hong Kong tax rates produce Hong Kong growth rates? Is there no end to this process? And why has everyone been so obtuse as not to see this magic solution to the growth problem before?

No doubt, there are significant effects of tax rates on growth in developing countries. But it is questionable to draw simplistic conclusions with respect to this relationship. This is not the place for a detailed accounting of the extensive, conflicting, and often obscure evidence on the arcane matters that lie at the heart of this discussion—the effects of taxation on savings, labor supply, and growth.[6] A brief tale of two countries, however, may help to make the point.[7]

The story concerns one country—call it G (for Guatemala)— in which taxes as a percentage of GDP fell by 40 percent in the five years up to 1984. Moreover, the deficit was cut by almost the same proportion in this period. Should not such a country be a veritable fiscal paradise —particularly if one notes that by 1984 only about 5 percent of the GDP was taken in taxes? True, the top statutory marginal tax rate in G was still a relatively high 48 percent on taxable income over $150,000. But this level was three hundred times higher than per capita income. Since there were numerous exemptions and deductions, in fact no one paid anything near this rate even on the small part of their incomes reported to the tax administration. Moreover, not just income taxes but all taxes steadily declined over this period.

Unfortunately for simplicity, at the same time that all these good things were happening, G's growth rate, instead of increasing, declined and indeed became negative. Simultaneously, what little evidence there is on such nebulous matters suggests that the "unofficial" part of G's economy grew rather than shrank during this period of declining effective tax rates.[8]

One should not, of course, conclude from this episode that growth fell *because* taxes fell. But one should also not draw the opposite conclusion had growth risen. Nor is there any reason to expect the outcome to be different had the government been wise enough to cut that top bracket rate down to, say, 15 percent. On the contrary, consideration of G's fiscal and development history in the postwar period suggests that nothing would have been very different.

The point of this story, of course, is simply that the broader economic and political environment is much more important than the top marginal rate of the personal income tax. To illustrate further, consider country J (for Jamaica). In J in 1984, unlike G, taxes and expenditure were very high in aggregate terms; the deficit, while shrinking, was doing so more as a result of tax increases than expenditure reductions; and the highest marginal tax rate really did hit some people (especially the higher levels of the civil service). On all counts, then, J would seem to provide a much worse fiscal environment for economic growth—and, some would argue, political freedom—than G. In fact, however, while both countries were in fairly bad economic shape, in neither case was this condition much connected with the tax system—and moreover G was decidedly a less "free" place than J in any relevant sense.

Again, one should not draw any sweeping conclusion from this brief comparison between these two countries, avoiding the facile connections that tend to be drawn by some from low taxes to high growth to political freedom.[9] The point is rather that one could keep running through the alphabet of countries and not find the simple, obvious connection for which some analysts seem to be searching, because it is not there.

Conclusion

Consider what an ideal growth-facilitating tax system in a developing country might look like. Such a system might include the following characteristics:

1. Little or no taxation of profits, in order to avoid discouraging entrepreneurship and risk taking.
2. Little or no taxation of undistributed profits in particular, in view of the underdeveloped state of capital markets.
3. Taxes aimed at discouraging consumption, especially luxury consumption, relative to saving, in order to encourage the latter.
4. Little or no taxation on the very poorest people, who need an adequate level of consumption to enable them to be productive.
5. Taxes that are stable and certain, to facilitate sound business decisions.
6. Taxes that are well-administered, especially in the nonmonetized sector in order to encourage its incorporation in the monetary economy.

This particular "supply-side" prescription comes from a paper written twenty-five years ago (Shoup, 1966). In many respects the tax systems in many developing countries come surprisingly close to this prescription. Most such countries, for example, levy few effective taxes on profits or on income from capital at all. Most levy few taxes on the very poorest (those in rural areas who are outside the scope of the tax system), tax at least some luxury consumption heavily, and tax consumption more than saving (at least through their explicit tax systems).[10] Many even have fairly low marginal effective rates and a more or less stable—even stagnant!—tax administration.

On the other hand, few developing countries have effective tax administration outside of the larger enterprises in the organized sector of the economy—a critical defect that may vitiate many of the virtuous results that might otherwise be expected to flow from such "growth-oriented" tax systems. Indeed, as Shoup (1966, p. 397) concluded, in most poor countries "it is the other values—equal treatment of equals, avoidance of socially dangerous concentration of wealth, promotion of a rational tax consciousness, and so on—that are being sacrificed by the tax systems of the underdeveloped countries, rather than the goal of growth. The sacrifice is being made, not so much from a desire for growth, as from the self-centered views of those who shape policy in those countries, from administrative limitations, and, no doubt, from indifference to the issues, growth or other."

We know more now about the connections between taxes and growth than we did two decades ago. Nonetheless, Shoup's conclusion seems still to provide a better description of the reality in many developing countries than does the simplistic picture of tax-choked growth painted in some recent studies of taxation and growth (e.g., Marsden, 1983; Wolf, 1988).

5 Taxation and the Poor

Taxation cannot make the poor richer. Even the complete removal of all taxes on the poorest members of society would not make them much better off, simply because of the small absolute amounts of income and tax involved. Furthermore, many poor people, particularly those in rural areas, take only a marginal part in the economic life of developing countries and are thus little affected by taxes. While regressivity of the tax system ought to be reduced as much as possible in order not to make things worse, if our main concern is with poverty as such, with the waste and misuse of human resources and the stunted opportunities in life afforded those with income below some minimum level, any fiscal corrective must be exercised primarily through the expenditure side of the budget (Bird, 1974a).

The potential of tax policies relative to expenditure policies to redistribute income in developing countries has thus been played down in the literature (Harberger, 1977; Goode, 1984). Nevertheless, for several reasons the relationship between taxes and the poor in developing countries deserves reconsideration. Recent developments in incidence analysis have, for instance, cast doubt on the earlier consensus as to the relative regressivity of those taxes that most affect the poor (Aaron, 1975; Browning, 1978; Whalley, 1984). General equilibrium analysis of the effects of taxation has cast new light on the complex relationships between taxation and income distribution touched on in Chapter 4 above.[1] As shown in the next chapter, the potential scope for tax policy to affect factor prices and hence income distribution in developing countries is greater than has usually been thought. New data sources on income and expenditures have begun to be developed and exploited in developing countries (Ahmad and Stern, 1983; Bird and Miller, 1989a). Moreover, skepticism has grown as to the effectiveness of public expenditure policy in reaching the very poor.[2] A new look at taxes and the poor in developing countries seems opportune.

The State of Knowledge

A decade ago, a comprehensive review of fiscal incidence studies in developing countries concluded that the tax system was basically progressive; that is, that the rich, broadly defined, appeared to pay a larger proportion of their incomes in tax than the poor in twenty of the twenty-two countries studied, although in a number of other cases there was evidence of some regressivity toward the bottom of the income scale (DeWulf, 1975). Little attention was paid in any of these incidence studies to the dispersion around the average of the effective tax rate within each income class. The focus of tax incidence studies has been almost invariably on the vertical equity of taxes (do the rich pay a larger share of their income in taxes than the poor?), rather than on the equally interesting horizontal equity question (do two equally poor or rich people pay the same taxes?).

A given degree of dispersion has more important equity implications at lower than at higher income levels. An early study of Guatemala, for example, suggested that low-income heavy smokers and drinkers probably paid 3 percent of their income in taxes on liquor and alcohol compared to only 1 percent for moderate consumers (Adler, Schlesinger, and Olson, 1952). Similar variations are evident in other studies. Differences of this magnitude at low-income levels raise important equity questions, particularly since the low price elasticity of demand for such "sumptuary" products implies that it is mainly the consumption of other goods ("basic needs"?) that is necessarily reduced as a result of taxing them.[3]

McLure (1977) subsequently reexamined the results of seven of these incidence studies with particular attention to the effects of taxes on the poor. He concluded that, while no study really provided the necessary data to analyze the tax burden on the poor in detail, on average taxes in most countries accounted for something like 10 percent of the incomes of the urban poor and a bit less of the incomes of the rural poor, with indirect taxes accounting for a high proportion of the taxes paid by the poorest 60 percent of the population. Moreover, the incidence of indirect taxes was broadly proportional across income classes among the poorer half of the population.[4]

Since taxes on food are generally low, and the income elasticity of nonfood consumption is probably close to unity, a proportional consumption tax would produce more or less these results. This outcome actually results, however, from the complicated interplay of the effects of the quite different tax ratios that are found for different indirect taxes—some rising with income, some falling, and some remaining essentially flat.

Few incidence studies focus explicitly, or in detail, on the poor. Moreover, incidence studies rest on rather questionable logical and statistical bases in the first place.[5] Nonetheless, the available evidence lends little credence to the popular belief that the taxes now levied on the poor in most countries impose a crushingly regressive burden.

A comprehensive recent review of urban finance in developing countries, for example, turned up nineteen studies of the incidence of property taxes in thirteen different countries (Bahl and Linn, 1991). A few studies found the burden of the property tax to be regressive, but most found it to be generally progressive, or even very progressive. Incidence studies employ so many different and sometimes inconsistent assumptions that it is difficult to know what to make of these results. On the whole, however, the conventional view that the property tax is regressive seems unlikely to be correct in developing countries, largely because the income elasticity of housing is likely to be unity or greater.

The scanty evidence on the incidence of the user charges levied to finance various urban services in some developing countries was also reviewed in the same study. In the case of water, perhaps the most important such service, both the precise nature of the rate structure employed and the physical nature of the city in question affected the distributive impact of user charge systems. In Nairobi (Kenya), low-income areas can be supplied at lower cost, so efficient water charges would have a generally progressive incidence. The opposite, however, is true in Cali (Colombia) and other cities, where it is the poor who live in areas where land values are low due to difficult access and unfavorable physical factors. On the whole, property taxes probably constitute a more progressive way to finance the expansion of basic urban services than even progressively structured service prices, essentially because housing consumption is more income-elastic than water consumption.

Studies of the distributive effects of various tax and pricing systems in different developing countries thus suggest that the tax systems existing in developing countries are not very regressive, contrary to the view expressed in some development literature (Chenery, 1974). As emphasized above, however, little is known about the horizontal equity of the tax system within the heterogeneous group called "the poor." Moreover, the precise results estimated for any country often depend on a very detailed understanding of the precise structure and working of the fiscal instruments in question.[6]

The incidence of taxes and charges constitutes only a small aspect of the distributional effects of government policy and may well be swamped by the effects of inflation, trade restrictions, and the like. Nevertheless, the evidence is that taxes, even if not as regressive as sometimes painted, do take a relatively substantial fraction of even very low incomes in most developing countries. To the man who has little, even a 10 percent burden is a lot. Moreover, focusing on the redistribution of income through the fiscal system after it has initially been distributed by the economic system may give a misleadingly small impression of the potential of the tax system to redistribute income. Taxes, like other policies that affect relative prices, may also affect the initial distribution of income in important ways, as illustrated in the next chapter.

The principal way income is redistributed in the long run in most countries, for instance, has been the move out of agriculture (Kuznets, 1966). Aspects of the tax system affecting this move may therefore have more long-run impact on the poor than such minor factors as the current regressivity of tobacco taxes. Similarly, even though properly structured land taxes might seem at first to penalize poor peasants, they may well in the long run improve the well-being of both the rural and the urban poor through encouraging more efficient utilization of land and rural labor (particularly if coupled with appropriate land reform, as argued in Bird, 1974).

Financing Urban Services

A striking phenomenon of recent decades is the increasing urbanization of the developing world. Average incomes are much higher in urban than in rural areas, but so is open unemployment; relatively fewer urban than rural households are poor, but the incidence of slums and squatter settlements as a proportion of urban population is often high. The level of public utility services is much higher in urban areas, but even in the most developed parts of Latin America large numbers of urban dwellers have no access to even rudimentary services. Furthermore, the quality and reliability of such services has deteriorated (Linn, 1983). The level and nature of urban services depends on the manner in which they are financed, particularly at the local level.

The subject of local government finance in developing countries has not received the attention it deserves. One reason may be that many think only central governments matter financially in most developing countries. In many countries, however, local government finance is quite important. State and local governments account for close to one-third of the taxes collected in the non-oil developing countries (International Monetary Fund, 1984).[7] An important local financial role does not necessarily imply any real local independence or autonomy. Nevertheless, those interested in fiscal impacts on the poor should take a close look at the nature of urban government finances, especially in the larger cities (Smith, 1974; Bahl and Linn, 1991). The urban poor *do* pay significant taxes, and many of the taxes they pay (as well as service charges) are levied by local governments. How local governments finance the services they provide may thus have a significant impact on the poor, particularly in urban areas.

A second reason for neglecting the distributional effect of local finances is the belief that distributional aims *should* not be explicitly pursued by local governments. Distribution policy (like stabilization policy) has traditionally been considered by public finance analysts to be the proper concern of central governments alone. Moreover, explicit local distributional policies would in any case generally be ineffective and inefficient in view of the openness of local economies (Oates, 1972).

In developing countries, however, these arguments are not very persuasive (Bird, 1980b). In the first place, as noted above, local revenue systems are important in many developing countries. Their impact on the well-being of the poor is therefore a legitimate matter of concern, especially in countries in which the assumption implicit in much public finance theory that there is (or can be) a smoothly operating central government tax-transfer system is simple fantasy. Secondly, the fact that the local governments in most developing countries have little autonomy—and may therefore be considered to be agents of the national government—means that local fiscal taxes and charges constitute as much a part of redistributive policy as do national taxes. Because what is going on is not locally differentiated redistribution but the local implementation of national policies, openness is also a less serious constraint on policy effectiveness than is usually thought.

Apart from the strong case that can be made for more local use of generally progressive taxes on automobile use and ownership (Smith, 1975; Linn, 1979), the main progressive revenue source available to local governments in most countries is the property tax. As mentioned above, there is increasing evidence that the property tax is, or can be, a fairly progressive way to finance urban services (Bahl, 1979). The precise distributive effect of property taxes depends on such details as the treatment of rental versus owner-occupied properties, of land versus improvements, of low-value versus high-value properties, and so on.

Higher taxes on land than on buildings, for example, might well increase both the progressivity and the efficiency of the property tax (Holland and Follain, 1985). Since the value of landholdings generally rises with income class, a tax levied solely on land—the burden of which falls on landowners—is obviously more progressive than a tax on all real property, which in an open economy will inevitably bear more heavily on labor and on the consumption of locally produced goods than on capital.

There may also be substantial distributional (and administrative) benefits from combining an exemption with a flat rate. In Jamaica, for instance, the property tax in the early 1980s was levied on the basis of the unimproved value of land at rates varying from 1 percent to 4.5 percent. Parcels valued at less than $J2,000, however, paid only a flat tax of $J5. Approximately the same distributional effect could be attained with less administrative and efficiency cost by levying a flat rate of 1.5 percent and exempting the first $J6,000 in value (Holland and Follain, 1985).[8] In some circumstances such features as the exemption of improvements or the imposition of different tax rates in different locations (Holland, 1979) may provide sufficient gains in terms of both equity and efficiency to seem worthwhile.

As stressed in this book, however, advocating complexity in tax design is a dangerous game in countries in which the limits of administrative feasibility are very real. Moreover, conclusions about the relative burden of different versions of property taxes on the poor can be put forward only with limited confidence. It is difficult to talk about "the" incidence of the property tax because of the theoretical and empirical uncertainty about the incidence of the tax, the importance of detailed differences in tax structure in determining distributional impacts, the wide intraclass variations in such impacts depending on the distribution of land ownership and other factors, and the possibly differential effects of such administrative aspects as assessment, collection, and the appeals process. Nevertheless, despite such complexities it seems safe to conclude in most circumstances that moderately well administered property taxes are likely to be progressive.

User Charges and Public Services

Complexity introduced for distributional reasons may at times produce perverse results. Nominally progressive public utility rates proved to be an inefficient technique of income distribution in Malaysia, for example, because poor families often consumed more water than rich families (Katzman, 1978). That portion of the poor population receiving services was in effect penalized by a supposedly "pro-poor" rate structure. Similarly, in Colombia, where the subsidization of urban public services through progressive rate structures is relatively important, the benefits of this subsidy are generally regressively distributed within the poor population (Selowsky, 1979). At the same time, the large group of the poor who receive no such services are often burdened, either through taxes or inflation, in order to make up the deficits of public utility enterprises.

Once again, one must be clear about the details before generalizing. In some instances, for example, "life-line" tariffs (a low tariff for an initial small block of consumption) may provide both an efficient and an equitable way of pricing water, provided that the low rate is not below the amount appropriate to reflect the presumed external benefits from such consumption and that it is not financed by charging larger consumers prices higher than marginal cost. Since the income elasticity of demand for water is relatively low even in poor countries, however, and since to some extent at least household size and income may be negatively correlated, in other instances (e.g., Malaysia) this policy may produce perverse distributional results.

Other water pricing schemes than rising block prices (progressive tariffs) are found in many countries. In Colombia, water charges were until recently related to property values in a progressive fashion. Again, however, the distributional effect of such charges depends on a variety of factors. A study of the incidence of the public service charges levied in Colombian cities for residential water supply and sewerage, electricity, garbage collection, and local telephone service found (using some strong assumptions) that the incidence of these subsidies was generally progressive. But relatively few of these benefits flowed to the lowest 20 to 30 percent of the population, owing to their lack of access to services (Linn, 1981).

Indeed, the most important consideration is often whether the poor receive services at all, not how much they have to pay for them (Meerman, 1979; Selowsky, 1979). In Colombia, for instance, even in the largest cities about 25 percent of the population had no access to services in 1974, with the poorest being those most likely to do without (Linn, 1981).[9] One reason is that the poor are less able to afford the high connection and installation costs charged by the largely self-financing public enterprises responsible for providing urban services in Colombia.

Another reason for lack of access may be simple political bias in favor of the better-off groups who constitute the traditional and expected recipients of such services. Yet another reason may be, in contrast, that the relative insulation of public enterprises from day-to-day political pressures may result in reduced access to services by the poor. The more technocratically determined investment decisions of bureaucrats may result in higher investment levels, with favored (and usually relatively high-income) consumers receiving better services. The poor may thus lose out in several ways: through having to bear through taxes or inflation some of the cost of providing subsidized services to the rich, through being faced with high "benefit" charges for a self-financing system, and through the bureaucratic and political machinations that determine who gets service in either case.

Urban transit provides another instance of the potential importance of public service financing and pricing and the need to consider both the details and the broader context in order to determine the distributional impact of public service finance. Most public mass transit operations in developing countries are heavily subsidized and beset by management and operating problems. Experience suggests that the subsidization of urban mass transit is so inadequate in most financially pressed developing countries that public transit systems are seriously underfinanced and provide correspondingly poor service.[10] The resulting problems are normally exacerbated by the political difficulty of raising fares—even though it seems likely that much of the subsidy thus extended at least nominally to the traveling poor in fact accrues to landowners or employers. Moreover, it is by no means clear that public transit users are those who need subsidization most. A 1978 study of Kingston, Jamaica, found that the poorest people used a higher-cost private system more than they did the public system, partly because the private service to their areas was better (Heraty, 1980).[11] This study also found that many poor people in Kingston spent a high fraction of their income on travel. Similar results are common in other countries (Linn, 1983).

Another aspect of the inefficient pricing of public services such as transit and water is that low-density development and urban sprawl is encouraged (Downing, 1973). The waste of resources through such subsidization may initially seem distributionally worthwhile. Over time, however, as inflation eats away at public resources and at the effective degree of subsidization, and as more and more poor people get locked into costly and inefficient commuting and living patterns, the resulting mixture may well prove to be politically explosive.

The "oil crises" of recent years have set off such explosions in a number of countries. The urban poor may not drive cars, but they do ride buses and minibuses, and fuel costs account for a large proportion of transit fares. With a public bus system, fares can be held down—at the expense, of course, of an increase in operating deficits and the sorts of problems already mentioned. Jamaican experience suggests, however, that matters may be even worse in the absence of a public transit system.

The public bus system in Kingston ceased operation early in 1984 largely as a result of pressure from international lending agencies to reduce the burden on government finance arising from public enterprise deficits. As a result, all public road transportation in Jamaica is now in the hands of private minibus operators, a result that believers in competition and efficiency should presumably applaud. In fact, however, as Smith (1984, p. 53) shows, "for every dollar saved through the elimination of the publicly owned and operated bus company, more than a dollar may be lost in fuel tax revenues because of social and political pressure to keep the taxes low given the anticipated effect on public transport fares."

In view of the general attractiveness of higher fuel taxes in developing countries as an equitable and efficient means of raising revenue, such a constraint on fuel taxes may be very costly. The demonstrations in Kingston and other parts of Jamaica in 1983 and 1985 following fuel tax increases underline both the importance of keeping fuel taxes from impacting too heavily on the poor and the difficulty of doing so when there is no public bus system to provide an administratively feasible vehicle for delivering the subsidy. The "privatization" of public transit in Jamaica may indeed have had the promised benefits of providing transport more efficiently. But it has done so only at the expense of making it increasingly difficult to raise fuel prices sufficiently to reflect the real opportunity cost of oil to Jamaica, let alone to add to scarce public sector resources through more reliance on this most administratively feasible of progressive taxes.

Indirect Taxes and the Poor

Indirect consumption taxes, particularly those on the traditional "excisables"—tobacco and alcohol—account for most of the existing direct impact of taxes on the poor in developing countries. Fuel taxes may also have a substantial indirect impact on the poor through increasing transport costs. A review of the incidence of different excise taxes in developing countries found the tobacco tax to be the most regressive of all indirect taxes in most countries (Cnossen, 1977). In Lebanon and the Philippines, however, studies have found the tobacco tax to be progressive, largely because of the higher tax content of the imported cigarettes consumed by the rich (De Wulf, 1974; Asher and Booth, 1983).

The incidence of taxes on such "traditional" excise products as alcoholic beverages and petroleum products is similarly important to the poor in many countries. As in the case of tobacco, however, the precise incidence of these levies varies sharply from country to country, depending on the specifics of local consumption patterns and tax structures. Generalizations about incidence based on predetermined value judgments about the "inherent" progressivity or regressivity of particular levies can be very misleading.

In Jamaica, for example, many consumption goods are subjected to three separate consumption taxes with highly differentiated rate structures. As part of a general tax reform it was proposed a few years ago to consolidate these three levies into a uniform general consumption tax or GCT (Bird, 1985a). On average, 36 percent of the expenditure of low-income households was estimated to be taxed by the existing levies. The variation in this proportion from household to household was very large, however. The taxes paid by the different groups were calculated on the basis of a set of (more or less conventional) assumptions which seemed reasonable in the Jamaican context. Under these assumptions, the regressivity of the existing system, despite its varied rates, was apparent even in relation to expenditure, let alone income, although it was also notable that the variation in effective tax rates *within* expenditure groups exceeded the variation *between* groups.

The differential impact of applying a uniform GCT rate of 20 percent to all presently taxed items was then calculated and compared to the existing taxes using the same assumptions (Bird and Miller,1989a). This tax change appeared both to increase taxes on low-income households as a group and also slightly to increase the regressivity of Jamaica's already regressive consumption tax system. These results emerged both because many consumption items of low-income groups were previously taxed at rates lower than 20 percent and because such lower-taxed goods as certain processed foods constituted, on average, a slightly larger proportion of the consumption of the poorer households than of the relatively less poor households. Exempting food reversed these results, however, and lowered all taxes on low-income families dramatically and in a progressive fashion.

In contrast, taxing some items at a higher "luxury" tax rate of 35 percent actually made the tax a bit more regressive than a uniform tax because the very poorest people in the sample spent relatively more on "luxury" cosmetics than the others. This observation suggests the danger of imposing predetermined judgments about what is and is not a "luxury" so far as low-income people are concerned.[12] Attempting to make sales taxes more progressive by imposing "luxury" rates on arbitrarily selected items is at best a very crude redistributive tool and at worst may have perverse results.

The exercise described above suggested strongly that at least a few additional exemptions beyond the unprocessed foods (and services) required for administrative reasons were warranted on distributional grounds. Close examination of the detailed expenditure data collected for the Jamaican study indicated that exempting just a few basic food items (such as cooking oil) would eliminate almost all the regressivity from taxing processed food under the GCT and would make the incidence of the GCT roughly proportional to expenditure, compared to the strong regressivity exhibited by the taxes to be replaced by the GCT.[13]

While much can obviously be done to refine such analysis, results such as these provide strong evidence of the potential impact on the poor of relatively small changes in the design of indirect taxes. In the face of the apparent strong direct impact on the poor of taxes on basic foodstuffs, for example, it would take a very low inequality aversion coefficient indeed not to recommend their exemption.[14] Similarly, the perverse distributive effect of some avowedly "progressive" rates (e.g., on cosmetics) should also carry some weight in designing consumption tax structures in countries like Jamaica, particularly given the high administrative costs associated with such rate differentiation.

Conclusion

The tax system in most developing countries impinges on the lives of many poor people in potentially important ways. The poor, especially the urban poor, often pay relatively substantial taxes. Moreover, the extent, nature, and perhaps duration of their poverty are affected in many ways by the characteristics and operation of the tax system. Both governments and researchers concerned with poverty in developing countries should be aware of these effects. The interaction of taxation and poverty is an important subject for research.

Unfortunately, such interaction is very difficult to study. Not only are the underlying theoretical issues inherently complex and the needed facts hard to find, but it is essential to understand the detailed reality of the fiscal instruments under examination and to ground that understanding firmly in the relevant broad policy context. New data and techniques may make it possible in the future to refine answers to meaningful old questions ("will the substitution of a general sales tax for a set of excise taxes be progressive or regressive?") and to answer important new questions ("will an increase in tobacco taxes impact differently on children in female-headed households?"), but there is still a long way to go in the analysis of the distributional effects of taxes.[15] Nonetheless, it is gradually becoming possible to carry out serious studies in a field that has for too long been dominated by misleading overly simplistic quantifications of untested, and too often ad hoc, hypotheses.

As yet, we know little about either the short-run or the long-run impact of taxes on the poor in developing countries. But we are perhaps approaching a point where the economist's increasing understanding of the models underlying incidence analysis and the increasing availability of relevant data are, despite a continued lag on the data side, better matched than ever before.

6 Taxation and Employment

Economists have largely ignored the influence of the institutional structure of the economy on such macroeconomic aggregates as employment, the price level, and national income. The inapplicability of simple-minded macroeconomic solutions to aggregate economic problems has long been apparent, however, in the Third World.

The main aim of economic policy in developing countries is to increase the rate at which per capita income grows. Conventional economic reasoning suggests that the best way to achieve this aim is through the accumulation and utilization of ever-increasing amounts of capital per worker. Even in countries that have managed to fulfill this prescription, however, it has become apparent that investment alone is not enough.

The deficiency of the simple capital-accumulation approach to growth was first brought out in the 1960s by the well-known "two-gap" analysis of development strategy (Chenery and Strout, 1966). This approach stressed the importance for achieving sustained growth of closing not only the "savings-investment gap" but also the "foreign exchange gap," so that the imports of capital and intermediate goods needed to maintain the target rate of growth could be obtained. Since in many countries the shortage of foreign exchange resources is more of a barrier to growth than the shortage of investment resources, this analysis marked a clear step forward. Nevertheless, the approach to economic development remained very aggregative: the only policy target considered was still the growth rate.

What really laid the simple macroeconomic approach to rest in the 1970s was the increasing concern of policy-makers and analysts with such goals as the distribution of income and wealth and the level of employment.[1] *What* is done may matter less than precisely *how* it is done. The "program effects" of tax and expenditure changes may be more important in achieving government's economic (and noneconomic) goals than the effects on the level of aggregate demand (or saving) stressed in conventional macroeconomic analysis. Whether taxes are increased by x or y percent may be less important than the precise manner in which this increased tax bill is attached to the private sector. The recent reemphasis on "growth-first" policies in many countries has by no means eliminated this multidimensional nature of development policy.

The disaggregated (and sometimes conflicting) nature of developmental goals makes the design of appropriate policy measures in a developing country a complex and difficult exercise. Fiscal instruments have a special importance in this task for two reasons. First, by its very nature fiscal action is not global or general in its effects: it is inherently specific, selective, and direct (Levin, 1971). For this reason, fiscal policy is both politically more difficult to implement and analytically a more versatile tool than grosser instruments such as monetary or exchange-rate policy. In principle, the tax and expenditure system affords an extremely powerful means of pursuing the disaggregated approach to development.

Secondly, fiscal measures are often the only ones open to governments in developing countries to influence private sector decisions. The scope of the monetary system is too narrow, and the administrative capacity for managing direct control systems too slight. Almost every part of the economy, however, is touched by the tax collector in one way or another. Indeed, the tax system is in many developing countries the most pervasive and far-reaching policy instrument available to the government. It is therefore especially important that this instrument (or set of instruments) be employed as effectively as possible.

This chapter reviews the use of tax policy to increase employment. A prior question, however, concerns the extent to which tax measures *can* affect employment. Two features of the growth process are of principal concern. The first is the extent to which additional capital is created and then combined with labor to create additional employment. Tax measures to increase capital formation have a long and rich history, and the employment-creating dimension of investment remains important, but this matter is not further treated here, except in passing.[2] The second feature is the amount of labor with which each additional unit of capital is combined to produce output. It is this question, the capital-labor ratio, which is the principal concern of this chapter.

The observed capital-labor ratio in any economy depends primarily upon the sectoral composition of output and the choice of technology within each sector (Morawetz, 1974; Sen, 1980). The composition of output is important because the capital-labor ratio varies substantially from sector to sector, and, indeed, from product to product. Insofar as tax policy affects the composition of demand, it may therefore affect employment. The three principal ways tax policy may operate in this sphere are (1) by altering the distribution of income, (2) by altering product prices, and (3) by altering the relative prices of imports and exports and of agricultural and industrial products. The extent to which tax policy operations on these variables affect employment depends both on the income and price elasticity of demand for output and on supply conditions, which in turn largely depend on the mobility and elasticity of the supply of factors.

In contrast to the *product* orientation of these measures, tax policies affecting the choice of technology focus on the *process* by which output of a given level and composition is produced. The extent to which taxation can affect the process of production depends upon (1) the extent to which different amounts of labor and capital can be combined to produce a given product; (2) the extent to which altering the relative prices of the factors induces such factor substitution in the production process; and (3) the extent to which taxes alter relative factor prices. The first is primarily a technological or engineering question: are there alternative technologies of production? There is also an important economic dimension to this question, however, since technologies do not spring out of the air but reflect both the resources devoted to science and technology and the perceived relative prices of factors. The other two questions are primarily economic: will changes in the wage-rental ratio induce factor substitution? and can taxation alter this ratio?

Finally, the principal points at issue with regard to the direct operation of taxation on factor markets are (1) the extent to which unified factor markets exist in which price differentials can operate, (2) the responsiveness of factor supplies to changes in relative prices, (3) the technical substitutability of factors in production (both statically and in terms of induced innovation), and (4) the extent to which profit-maximizing entrepreneurs dominate in the relevant markets (and may therefore be expected to react to altered relative factor prices by changing their techniques of production).

Even this condensed recital should serve to make two points clear. First, the *potential* scope for tax policy to influence employment is enormous. Apart from the effects of taxation on capital formation itself, the proportion in which capital is combined with labor may be influenced (1) by operating on the "big" relative prices through altering the intersectoral terms of trade, the effective exchange rate, or the wage-rental ratio itself; (2) by altering the distribution of income, and hence the composition of demand; (3) by altering relative product prices; (4) by influencing the rate and nature of technological innovation; and (5) by bringing about a more unified (and price-sensitive) factor market.

The second point, however, is that the *actual* effects of tax measures on these various fronts depend upon the relative magnitudes of several important economic parameters, notably the elasticity of substitution between capital and labor. Although there have been a number of empirical studies of these parameters, little is really known about the size of the relevant elasticities in most countries (Morawetz, 1974).

Much the same is true with respect to the scope for so-called "indirect substitution" through altering the output mix by changing relative product or factor prices.[3] The relatively few empirical studies that have been carried out on the employment implications of alternative income distributions, for example, do not offer very clear guidance to policy, though they do suggest that the effects of different output mixes may not be too large.[4]

Pessimists see little scope for factor and product markets to effect such substitution. They tend to stress the rigidity of much modern technology and the unavailability of alternative technology suitable for the factor proportions found in developing countries (Streeten, 1972). Their recommended solutions tend more to radical reformulations of the world and national economies than to tinkering with factor prices: it is not surprising that most neo-Marxist development economists are elasticity pessimists.

Optimists, on the other hand, stress the possibility of factor substitution in ancillary processes and the ease with which more appropriate technology is invented and adopted, if it is profitable to do so. They are also relatively optimistic about the potential to bring about increased employment and the lower capital-labor ratio required to fit the labor-intensive nature of the factor endowment in most developing countries. Given the tools, the market will do the job of bringing about the right factor proportions. The more justified such optimism in any particular situation, the more important tax influences on employment are likely to be.

Even economists who do not believe it is sufficient simply "to get the prices right" and who advocate a more interventionist policy—including, for example, such prior major structural changes as land reform and factor market unification in order to make a market intervention strategy work—generally agree that once these changes are made, the price system can and should do much of the job of fitting factor use to factor endowment. The dominant attitude of the economics profession (and this chapter) may perhaps be fairly characterized as one of modified "elasticity optimism."

It is sometimes argued that investment takes unduly capital-intensive forms in developing economies for more complex reasons than the lack of suitable technologies or incorrect factor prices.[5] The reasons cited for this view range from the training of engineers to the machinations of multinational corporations. These reasons are, it is argued, deeply rooted both in the political and social structure of the international and national environment and in the individual psyches which reflect (and direct) that reality. Without denying the existence and possible importance of such factors as the drive to emulate others or to build monuments, however, the underlying assumption here is that firms invest in capital-intensive rather than labor-intensive techniques primarily because it pays them to do so.

Granted this assumption, the next step in the argument is to assert that the private cost of capital relative to labor is lower than its social cost in most countries primarily because of the "capital bias" of numerous government policies, including tax policies. This capital bias may itself, of course, reflect such basic political and social factors as who controls the government or how government officials are selected and trained, but the limited task undertaken here is simply to review how to remove the capital bias from tax policies.

The object of this exercise is to develop a more *neutral* tax system, one that does not favor the use of capital relative to labor, rather than to introduce a new "labor bias" into the system. The range and depth of the measures discussed simply indicate the surprising pervasiveness of capital-favoring elements in the tax systems presently found in most developing countries.[6] Capital bias has in the past been viewed with relative equanimity or even approval by those concerned with designing tax systems to facilitate growth. When such policy objectives as distribution and employment are given significant weight, however, one's assessment of many issues in tax structure design changes.

Taxation and the Composition of Output

The extent to which different factors of production are employed in any country depends on what products are produced, and by what processes. A potentially important approach to increasing the employment of (largely unskilled) labor in developing countries is therefore by altering the product mix. The composition of output may be changed in three ways: (1) by altering the distribution of income, on the assumption that different income groups have different propensities to consume labor-intensive goods and services; (2) by altering the mix of exports and imports, or of agricultural and industrial products, on the assumption that these groups of products reflect different degrees of labor-intensity; and (3) by altering the relative prices of different products within any one sector to make labor-intensive products cheaper, on the assumption that the price elasticity of demand for these products is greater than unity.[7]

INCOME DISTRIBUTION AND THE COMPOSITION OF DEMAND

The influence of income distribution on the savings rate has long been a prime concern of development economists, as noted in Chapter 4 above. More recently, it has been argued that the highly unequal distribution of income characteristic of developing countries has resulted in an output mix that is both more import-intensive and more capital-intensive than warranted by the real economic circumstances of these countries. Studies of the effects of income distribution on factor requirements suggest that the capital (and import) intensity of the expenditures of the poor is not very different from that of the rich, partly because the greater labor intensity of the food consumed by the poor is offset by the greater labor intensity of the services consumed by the rich (Cline, 1975). Income redistribution may have many intrinsic merits and even (as suggested in Chapters 4 and 5 above) some instrumental merits, but it is not a particularly powerful instrument for increasing employment.

OUTWARD-LOOKING INDUSTRIALIZATION

Some authors have emphasized the effects on factor requirements of changing from an inward-looking to an outward-looking pattern of industrialization. The main reason for this optimism appears to be faith in the existence of a highly elastic foreign demand for labor-intensive exports from developing countries, coupled with a clear understanding of the strong capital bias of the trade-exchange rate and tax-subsidy policies characteristic of the import-substituting industrialization strategy long pursued in many countries.[8] There is more reason for the understanding than for the faith, however. Indeed, the protectionist bias of developed-country markets against labor-intensive exports from developing countries has become marked in recent years (Bhagwati, 1988). It thus seems to be stretching things to argue that "the most promising attack on that extreme employment problem related to low incomes lies in improved international trade policy—specifically, by placing greater emphasis on exports" (Berry, 1974, pp. 228–29). Nevertheless, revisions of output and factor taxes to reflect a country's factor endowment can alter trade patterns, and hence factor requirements, to some extent.

Implicit taxes levied on export industries through protective tariffs on inputs, for example, ought to be removed as part of the movement toward a more appropriate effective exchange rate.[9] Concessions to protected industries in the form of exemptions for imported materials and capital equipment should also be removed. More boldly, a uniform tariff might be combined with a uniform tax levied on imports and domestic goods destined for final consumption. This system could of course be combined with luxury excises, if desired. If luxury goods are subject to special taxes, such taxes should be imposed by excises applicable to domestic and foreign products alike rather than by tariffs which stimulate the domestic production of luxuries.

The immediate purpose of such tax policy changes would be to allow developing countries to take full advantage of their real comparative advantage in international trade. Since (apart from mineral exports) that advantage is generally in goods that are labor intensive, one result would presumably be to increase the demand for labor. Furthermore, since another consequence of such policies would be to raise the price of capital (much of which is imported) relative to labor, the capital-labor ratio would also presumably be affected in this way, as well as through the change in the output mix.

The efficacy of such policies clearly depends on the elasticity of foreign demand for labor-intensive exports, on the intersectoral mobility of factors, on the responsiveness of producers to incentives, and on the elasticity of substitution between labor and capital. Nevertheless, it is probably a relatively safe bet to say that policies, tax and otherwise, which alter a country's international trading pattern to reflect better its comparative advantage will as a rule tend to increase employment.

THE INTERSECTORAL TERMS OF TRADE

It is hard to express even this degree of qualified optimism about the effects of policies altering the intersectoral terms of trade between industry and agriculture, for two reasons. First, each of these sectors is itself generally dualistic in nature (that is, consists of a labor-intensive and a capital-intensive subsector). Policies altering the intersectoral terms of trade may therefore have very different effects depending on the relative responsiveness of these subsectors. If one makes the plausible assumption that the more modern (capital-intensive) sectors respond more quickly to such changes, the effect on employment of (say) improving the terms of trade for agriculture may be adverse, even though the agricultural sector as a whole is more labor-intensive than the industrial sector.

A second reason for caution is the overwhelming importance (and complexity) of industry-agriculture relations in the development process as a whole.[10] While opinions have shifted on this question over the years, operations on the intersectoral terms of trade do not appear a promising means of employment creation. Although many tax policies inevitably affect the relative price of agricultural and industrial outputs, it is probably more useful to focus on the effect of these policies within each sector rather than on the relationship between them.[11]

COMMODITY TAXES AND EMPLOYMENT

A final means of altering the composition of demand is by changing relative product prices to make labor-intensive products relatively cheaper and capital-intensive products relatively more expensive. If the price elasticity of demand for these products is greater than unity, the result of such policies should be to increase employment. Such labor-favoring commodity tax policies already abound in developing countries, in both explicit and implicit forms.

Perhaps the clearest case of the explicit use of commodity tax policy to foster employment is in India. On the assumption that small

firms use more labor-intensive technology than larger firms, India
grants exemptions, complete or partial, or applies lower tax rates in
its extended excise system to firms in different industries on the basis
of such criteria as the number of workers, whether power is used in
the production process, and the size of output (Mahler, 1970; Purohit,
1988). While this favorable tax treatment may result in some instances
in an increase in the market share of small firms, it is not clear that
any resulting gain in employment is at the expense of lower and less
efficient production levels. It *is* clear from Indian experience, however,
that commodity tax differentiation of this sort is extremely cumbersome to administer.

   An alternative approach focuses not on the size of the firm but
on the technology it employs, by levying lower commodity taxes on
products produced through labor-intensive techniques. In Indonesia,
for example, handmade cigarettes were taxed at a rate of 20 percent,
while machine-made cigarettes (which use a very different tobacco)
were taxed at almost 50 percent. Since the handmade cigarette industry
employed 100,000 people in a very labor-intensive fashion—it takes
one employee, for example, a day to roll the same number of cigarettes
as a machine does in a minute or two—this tax differential presumably
favored employment creation (Cnossen, 1977). A somewhat similar
excise tax differentiation existed for soft drinks in Indonesia and for
cigarettes and distilled spirits in the Philippines. Such measures are,
of course, more palatable when the labor-intensive products are consumed mainly by lower-income groups, as is probably true in these
cases.

   The idea that indirect taxation should attempt not only to tax high-
income consumption but also to alter its composition toward labor-
using commodities is not uncommon in the literature (Chenery, 1974).
This policy may be implemented by tilting the commodity tax balance
toward labor-intensive products, or by favoring labor-intensive processes of producing essentially similar products, as in the cases cited
above.[12] In addition, commodity tax systems in developing countries
implicitly tend to vary sharply in accordance with the production characteristics of different industries.

   For example, food is normally exempted from tax, when unprocessed for administrative reasons and when processed largely on the
distributional grounds discussed in the previous chapter (Due, 1988).
To the extent low-income consumers shift expenditure to relatively
cheaper food products, employment in agriculture will be relatively
larger. There is no presumption, however, that any gains in agricultural

employment on this account will not be more than offset by losses in industrial employment, particularly in view of the dualistic nature of both sectors.

Another common feature of commodity tax systems is that most services are exempted from tax, either in law or in fact. In this instance there is a clear conflict between the distributional and employment objectives of indirect tax policy. As Lord North recognized when a tax on men servants was introduced in England in 1777, those unfortunates with only one servant could not be exempted from the tax for fear that those with two servants would then discharge one of them in order to qualify for the exemption (Dowell, 1965).

Commodity taxes in developing countries inevitably burden most the modern (organized) sector of the economy. Small-scale industry—especially in the "informal" sector (de Soto, 1990)—in effect operates under a tax shelter. It is therefore larger than it would otherwise be, and so is employment in this sector. This implicit differentiation in favor of small-scale and labor-intensive activity is probably about all that should be asked of the sales tax system even in countries that put employment at the top of their list of policy objectives.

A final important characteristic of commodity taxes in developing countries is that export taxes often constitute a substantial part of total tax collections. Export taxes on agricultural exports may fall most heavily on such labor-intensive activities as rubber and copra production.[13] In the Philippines, for example, the agricultural product most affected by export taxes in the 1970s was coconuts. Coconuts were the most important small-holder crop in the Philippines, providing the major source of livelihood for perhaps ten million people. Assuming (as seems likely) that the primary incidence of the export tax on coconuts was on small landowners and laborers, there was a strong case on both distributive and employment grounds for lowering this tax.

The Unification of Factor Markets

The simplest approach to the chaotic factor markets and diverse and often inappropriate factor prices in most developing countries is to tackle these problems directly by establishing prices that correctly reflect relative factor scarcities and by ensuring that these prices operate uniformly throughout the economy. Those who advocate this approach generally stress in particular the need to reform the prevailing foreign exchange system and the related complex of policies which keep interest rates down relative to wage rates (McKinnon, 1973; Shaw, 1973).

In addition to getting factor prices right, however, it is important to ensure that all relevant decision-makers face this set of relative prices. Large, modern industrial complexes do not operate in the same factor markets as small artisans, even though both are "industrial" in nature. Large firms obtain financial capital from internal sources, from government agencies, and from domestic and foreign suppliers. Small firms rely essentially on the personal savings of the owner and his family. This dualism means that the "nonmodern" sector in most developing countries generally faces much higher costs of capital, that is, costs that reflect more adequately the real factor supply conditions.

The institution of correct relative factor prices would therefore have its most direct impact in the modern sector. Such a policy change would have two effects on employment, one positive and one negative. The positive effect is that profit-maximizing entrepreneurs will be stimulated to use less capital in order to minimize costs. In the nature of business, however, changes in production processes take time to effect, especially if new technologies must be developed in response to the inducement provided by the new factor prices. Unfortunately, the negative effect on employment is almost instantaneous. As a result of raising the cost of capital to modern industry (and modern agriculture), the amount of capital flowing to this sector will fall, with a consequent decline in the amount of labor employed.

This shift would give rise to no problems if the amount of capital formation were maintained by other government policies *and* if the capital thus freed were simply combined with more labor in the traditional sector, at least until the modern sector reorganized in the face of the new factor prices. The employment thus created would, by definition, more than offset the employment snuffed out by the fall in investment in the modern sector.[14]

The problem with this scenario is that there is no guarantee that the traditional sector has access to the capital fleeing the modern sector. On the contrary, there is good reason in most developing countries to believe that it will not. An essential part of any strategy hinging on correcting factor prices must therefore be to improve the access to capital of the presently nonprivileged sector of the economy. The only way to do this is by substantial institutional reforms in the financial system, in order to make expansion (and employment) possible in the labor-intensive sectors (Chenery, 1974). In other words, it is not enough to get factor prices right by removing policy-induced (or other) distortions: the correct prices must also be made effective by, in effect, unifying factor markets. Otherwise, the immediate effect on employment of instituting correct factor prices could well be perverse.

This prescription to reduce the fragmentation of the capital market to make capital (at scarcity prices) equally accessible to all entrepreneurs is undoubtedly correct in principle. It is also, equally undoubtedly, impossible to achieve fully in practice: if developing countries could do everything economists say they must do in order to become developed, they would, by definition, already be developed! Nevertheless, simply getting factor prices right will *not* do the whole job. Not only must accompanying institutional reforms be undertaken to improve the availability of capital to the labor-intensive sector, but the new factor prices must be made effective in the capital-intensive sector as well.

An obvious target for tax policy in this respect is the internally generated funds with which corporate enterprises finance most of their expansion. Tax policies that force (or induce) distribution will have their strongest effect on large, often monopolistic, and always capital-intensive firms. The principal rationale for such policies is the desirability of subjecting investment projects to the scrutiny of the market. This argument is reinforced to the extent that the factor prices in this market reflect factor scarcities. The trouble with this proposal is that there is no well-functioning capital market in developing countries.[15] The alternative to reliance on the private capital market is to tax profits away from corporations and channel them via government agencies to labor-intensive sectors—which takes us back full circle to the earlier argument on the need to increase the access of the traditional sector to capital.[16] The likelihood that the hard-pressed public sector can carry out efficiently such a complex redirection of funds is small.

Indeed, the principal offender against market discipline is often the government itself. Government enterprises are big business in many developing countries (Short, 1984). The public sector must not be shielded from its own policies. The "capital bias" of engineers and planners is nowhere more obvious than in the public sector, which is not, in most cases, subjected to even the minimal discipline exerted by the fiscal and financial system on large private firms. If factor prices are to be rationalized for the latter, governments must clean up their own houses and ensure that public-sector activities are subjected to the discipline of correct factor pricing.

The Correction of Factor Prices

The main challenge in adapting the tax policy of developing countries to provide employment is how to rationalize factor prices directly. There are so many tax policies in developing countries which demonstrably go in the wrong direction that there is much to be done.[17]

THE PRICE OF LABOR

Taxation measures affecting the price of labor may be divided into those affecting the real wages received by workers and those affecting the labor cost of employers. The first of these categories may in turn be divided into measures affecting the supply of labor directly—through effects on population, on migration, and on monetization—and those affecting real wages directly. Similarly, the second category may (more tenuously) be divided into measures affecting the quality of labor—through effects on education and training—and those affecting labor costs directly.

Population. An obvious way to increase the proportion of the labor force which is employed is by reducing the rate of growth of the labor force. Fiscal policies have long been thought by some to have an effect on population growth by making it relatively more or less expensive to have children (Prest, 1985). For this reason there have been many suggestions to tax children beyond the third or fourth or at least to disallow dependents' allowances under the income tax for such "excess" children (Myrdal, 1968). In fact, a number of countries (notably in francophone Africa) already limit the number of dependents that may be claimed for income tax purposes, usually to four. The scope of such measures is restricted, however, owing to the small proportion of the population subject to the income tax.

If such measures have any effect in reducing birth rates, they will presumably mildly alleviate the employment problem fifteen or twenty years hence. These effects seem so uncertain and remote, however, as not to be worth further discussion. An additional consideration is that the analysis underlying such proposals views children solely as a consumption good. In the typical developing country, however, children in most families are as much an item of investment for one's old age as they are a consumption good. The development of a public social security system may thus reduce the incentive to have children much more than limiting income tax deductions—a fact that should be remembered in the face of the usual condemnation of social security financing on employment grounds.

Migration. Employment has received more attention in recent years in part because of rapid urbanization. One popular model of migration suggests that the creation of an additional job in the modern urban sector may even result in an *increase* in urban unemployment, because more than one person will migrate to the city as a result (Todaro, 1969). Tax measures that make rural life less attractive than urban life will presumably tend to induce still more migration. Export taxes on agricultural products and rural land taxes have, for example, been condemned on these grounds. The effect of agricultural taxes on migration flows depends on their incidence. If such taxes lower the price of the food eaten by urban consumers, for example, by increasing the marketed surplus, as was at one time reportedly the case with the rice tax in Thailand (Bertrand, 1969), migration will be stimulated. On the other hand, if agricultural taxes raise the price of urban wage goods, migration will presumably be discouraged.

If migration reduction is a policy goal, taxes should be altered to favor farmers rather than industrial workers and residents (Prest, 1971). Since most countries in fact already tax farmers relatively lightly, there may be little scope for further leniency on this score, especially in view of the many other objectives of agricultural tax policy (Bird, 1974). Moreover, "keeping them down on the farm" does not necessarily mean that they will be employed there any more than in the city.

Monetization. Migrants enter the money economy and thus become more subject to market forces and to government interventions in the market. The withering away of the subsistence sector of the economy has long been recognized as an essential part of the development process. In some parts of the world, notably colonial Africa, the tax man has at times stepped in to help this process along by levying taxes on subsistence farmers which had to be paid in money. These taxes forced farmers to enter the monetary economy by selling their produce, their labor, or both. Indeed, it has been suggested that such taxes were major factors in creating an initial urban labor force in much of Africa (Jolly, 1973). There is no place for such levies in modern Africa or in other developing countries concerned with growing unemployment problems, however. Neither a "push" (through head taxes or crop taxes) nor a "pull" (through light taxation of incentive goods or urban wage goods) to migration and monetization seems called for in an employment-oriented tax policy. As with so many other questions in economic policy where there are good arguments for both sides and critical gaps in our knowledge of the relevant empirical parameters, neutrality is probably the appropriate policy goal.

Education and training. The unemployment problem in developing countries is predominantly a problem of unskilled workers—though not entirely so, as the oft-publicized "educated unemployed" of India and a few other countries attest. Generally, however, a more educated and skilled populace (provided the skills are relevant to market conditions) will have a lower level of unemployment. Taxation policy can play a role in influencing the skill level of the labor force. Two fiscal instruments may be discussed briefly in this connection: the personal income tax and tax incentives for training cost.

In practice, the personal income tax usually amounts to little more than a tax on wages and salaries in the organized sector of the economy. It therefore discourages entry into the taxed part of the labor force.[18] Pre-tax wages in the modern sector will therefore tend to rise relative to those in other sectors, thus accentuating the capital bias characteristic of the modern sector in any case. Fewer people will be employed in this sector, but at higher wages. This tendency will be reinforced by the resulting rise in the relative price and fall in the output of the goods produced by the modern sector. A more positive aspect of the limited scope of the personal income tax from the point of view of employment may be that the attractiveness of wage employment, and hence of migration and entry into the monetary economy, is lessened.

Tax deductions for education expenditures may foster education and training. The limited scope of the personal income tax, as well as distributive and motivational considerations, make such measures relatively unattractive in developing countries, though they are hardly unknown there.[19] Special tax concessions or rebates to firms related to the expenses they incur in training their staffs have also been proposed (Jolly, 1973). Left to themselves, firms will provide less than the optimal amount of on-the-job training owing to the "externality" problem—the fact that, in the absence of slavery, workers once trained might move to other firms. A good case can therefore be made for subsidizing such training (Bruton, 1965). Favorable tax treatment of educational and training expenditures should upgrade the skill of the labor force, although any such effect is likely to be minute.

Labor taxes and subsidies. The most important direct way in which taxation affects the price (and hence the employment) of labor is obviously through explicit labor taxes and subsidies. An employment-oriented tax system, for example, would presumably not contain any payroll taxes. Since such taxes are in fact found in a large number of developing countries, this seems an obvious area for reform.[20] Moreover, if the employment problem in part arises because the costs of labor to employers are too high, and if it is not feasible or desirable to lower these costs directly (by lowering real wages or fringe benefits), an obvious second-best approach is to subsidize firms in relation to their number of employees.

The first question to be considered concerns the payroll tax: who pays it? The answer is not entirely clear, but most analysts in the United States assume that labor bears the *entire* burden of the payroll tax (Brittain, 1972; Break, 1974). This conclusion seems questionable in the context of most developing countries, however, where tax-induced changes in labor supply cannot be disregarded and where there is no reason to think that the incidence of the tax in the product market is distributionally neutral. As it applies in developing countries, the payroll tax is in fact invariably a selective tax, affecting the use of some labor in some industries only.[21]

The modern sector (in which the tax is levied) will tend to contract relative to untaxed sectors. So long as the demand for the output of the modern sector is price-elastic, it does not matter whether the payroll tax is borne solely by labor or is passed on to consumers. Indeed, some or all of the tax may ultimately be borne by employers—in developing countries all payroll taxes, whether for social security or other purposes, are invariably paid by employers only—if the elasticity of the supply of labor to the modern sector is as high as is usually postulated and if, as is common, protective trade policies create economic rents in many industries. To the extent a payroll tax is borne by capital, it acts like a partial factor tax on capital (like the corporate income tax) and tends to reduce the amount of capital in the taxed sector. So far as the effects of the payroll tax on employment are concerned, however, whether workers, consumers, or capitalists pay the tax, the result will be to discourage the modern sector relative to the traditional sector. Somewhat paradoxically, then, payroll taxes as they actually operate in developing countries may tend to *encourage* employment through their sectoral effects! *Within* the modern sector, however, the effect of such taxes is almost certainly to discourage employment since they raise the cost of labor to employers.

If payroll taxes discourage employment on balance, reducing such taxes is an obvious way to raise the the labor-capital ratio in the taxed sector and therefore to increase employment. Analytically (and budgetarily) this amounts to paying employers a subsidy related to the extent to which they employ labor. Those concerned with employment have often recommended just such subsidies. The administration of even a simple labor subsidy scheme has sometimes been thought to be beyond the capability of most developing countries, although this is not at all certain (McLure, 1980). Nonetheless, for administrative reasons, labor subsidies cannot easily, if at all, be confined to the margin but would have to apply to all labor; they would therefore tend to be very costly. In any case, such a subsidy should clearly be related to employment, and not to the size of the payroll, in order to stimulate maximum employment.

The effects of such subsidies on employment are unclear. Two formal analyses of this question have reached precisely opposite conclusions. One view is that taxing capital is preferable (in employment terms) to subsidizing labor (Peacock and Shaw, 1971). The other is that a labor subsidy is clearly superior to a capital tax (Ahluwalia, 1973). While the latter, general-equilibrium approach is analytically more satisfactory, its conclusions too are suspect and depend on many strong assumptions. The superiority of the labor subsidy in inducing employment depends entirely upon the assumption that the supply of labor is completely elastic and that the supply of capital is completely inelastic. The supply of labor is indeed probably highly elastic in developing countries, but the effects on employment of selective labor taxes or subsidies cannot be inferred from this fact alone, particularly since the supply of capital to many developing countries is also elastic. More work on the specifics of particular countries is needed before useful generalizations can be made with respect to this question.

Among the specific labor subsidization proposals that have been made are a reduction of social security taxes on unskilled labor only (Balassa, 1975) and subsidization of firms according to their labor input by, for example, varying the corporate income tax inversely with the degree of labor intensity.[22] Another approach is to vary the duration of tax holidays or other tax incentives to investment inversely with the capital-labor ratio (Lent, 1971). Despite the number of such suggestions in the literature, Lent (1971) found no developing country that had introduced any form of explicit labor subsidy policy.[23]

THE PRICE OF CAPITAL

The issues with respect to the taxation and subsidization of capital are the obverse of those sketched above with respect to labor. Two new problems require brief discussion, however: the effects of capital taxes (subsidies) on capital accumulation and the important distinction between the capital stock and its utilization.

Capital accumulation. The principal focus of this chapter has been on the extent to which capital can be combined with more labor. It has been assumed throughout that measures to alter the capital-labor ratio will not affect the amount of capital. This assumption is suspect, however. In particular, when inducing capital inflows from abroad is an essential component of development strategy, as is the case in many developing countries, the conflict between policies to attract capital and policies to reduce the capital-labor ratio is obvious. If the aim of policy is to increase the amount of capital available to the economy, then policies which, in effect, subsidize capital will do so most efficiently. At the same time, however, such policies will also tend, perversely, to increase the capital-labor ratio.

The only apparent answer to the dilemma of how to get more capital, while at the same time using it better (in the sense of combining it with labor in proportions that reflect real factor scarcities), would appear to be by introducing very finely tuned incentives such as those noted above, which in effect confine the subsidy to capital that is appropriately combined with labor. Even in those few countries capable of administering such policies efficiently, this approach obviously involves some risk of diminishing capital inflows. Other measures (tax and otherwise) to keep up saving may therefore be needed. Nothing in this life comes free, and tax structure changes intended to induce employment are no exception.

Capital utilization. Up to this point the word *capital* has been used very loosely. What matters with respect to employment is not the stock of capital as such but rather the services provided by that stock. The extent to which capital is utilized is an important determinant of the capital-labor ratio: a given stock of capital used more intensively will as a rule be combined with more labor, thus lowering the ratio. The same capital-favoring policies that result in too much capital being acquired also result in the low capital utilization rates that many observers have noted in developing countries (Winston, 1974). Policies increasing the price of capital facing private entrepreneurs to a level reflecting its true social scarcity may therefore have a doubly beneficial effect on employment by inducing more intensive use of the existing capital stock, as well as by affecting new investment decisions.

Two specific tax devices have been used to bring about this result. The first is to provide special depreciation deductions or other tax concessions for machinery used on a multishift basis. Such provisions have existed at various times in a number of countries (e.g., Colombia) and have at times been recommended for others (e.g., Indonesia). While increased utilization of existing capital could presumably be achieved by such devices, tax concessions related to capital also reduce the price of capital and hence may have an offsetting effect on employment.[24]

The second approach to increasing capital utilization does not suffer from this defect, however, since it consists of levying taxes on capital rather than subsidizing its more intensive use. One proposal along these lines suggested that a tax be levied on the "potential" output (value-added) of industrial firms at "full" capacity (Tanzi, 1974a). If firms produce more than this amount they are in effect taxed at a marginal rate of zero: the closer their actual production is to their rated capacity, the lower the tax.

Since the idea is to apply to industry the sort of tax on potential output that has so often been recommended for agricultural land, such proposals suffer from many of the same political and administrative shortcomings as the land tax proposal (Bird, 1974). Nonetheless, the idea is interesting because some countries already possess sales and excise taxes which are, in effect, levied on capacity rather than on output, though primarily for administrative rather than incentive reasons. A careful examination of such "capacity taxes" in Pakistan was not able to discern any clear effect on utilization rates (Cnossen, 1974), but did emphasize the importance of examining just *how* taxes are in fact administered before pronouncing on their economic effects—an idea developed further in Chapters 7 and 8 below.

Capital taxes and subsidies. Corporation income taxes fall primarily on large modern firms; regardless of their precise incidence, they probably tend to discourage the more capital-intensive sector of the economy. On the other hand, almost all tax incentives—such as tariff exemptions for capital goods, tax holidays, and investment allowances—also accrue primarily to this sector and, moreover, do so in such a way as to effectively lower the price of capital, thus encouraging capital intensity. The simplest way to reduce this problem would be to abolish such incentives.

If for some reason (e.g., to induce capital inflows from abroad) incentives are thought necessary, it would seem best to tie them to domestic value added rather than to capital inputs in order to attract capital without biasing the capital-labor ratio (McLure, 1971).[25] The objective of incentive policy is not to increase *investment* but *output* (value added): the most efficient subsidy (per dollar of revenue cost) will thus be one tied directly to the thing to be "incented." While such a policy would undoubtedly increase capital formation, it would not do so to the extent an equal-cost subsidy explicitly related to capital formation would do. But it will also not distort factor utilization, the way the latter would. As usual in life, there is a trade-off which must be made.

The above argument is fairly obvious and noncontroversial, if also inconclusive. Another suggestion that has sometimes been made is that capital goods should be explicitly taxed through sales or other indirect taxes. While the taxation of production equipment is of course anathema to traditional sales tax designers, in some circumstances a good case can be made for taxing capital goods to offset the other biases (e.g., overvalued exchange rates) which make capital unduly cheap (Due, 1988). Such taxation is clearly a very crude way of redressing the balance, but it may be better than doing nothing, which may be the only feasible alternative. For much the same reason, the time-honored practice of permitting tax-free imports of capital goods needs careful reexamination and, in all likelihood, elimination in most, if not all, developing countries (Lent, 1974).

THE PRICE OF LAND

Land is a distinct and important factor of production in developing countries. It may be argued (1) that agricultural mechanization has often been unduly fostered by capital-biased policies, (2) that large holdings are less intensively farmed than small ones, and (3) that more intensive farming means more labor-intensive farming (Bird, 1974). A good case can be made sometimes for special taxes on agricultural machinery to offset the biases of other policies; in other cases, the specifics of the country situation may advise against such policies (Gemmill and Eicher, 1973). In *all* cases, however, an excellent argument can be made for heavy land taxes on the grounds that they will encourage more efficient utilization of land. Provided that factor markets are relatively unified—which may well require significant land reform—and that factor prices are not badly distorted by other inappropriate government policies, the result will almost certainly be that more labor will be employed on the farm. Indeed, in the end this rationale may provide the most persuasive case for increased land taxes in many developing countries.

Beyond the Price System

Even if factor prices are corrected, which often means the removal of inappropriate government intervention, significant government intervention is still required in any employment-oriented policy. Three areas where such intervention might be required are with respect to technology, asset redistribution, and factor market unification.

Correct factor prices will presumably foster the development of more appropriate technology over time. In most developing countries, however, the economic problems are urgent and the pressure for quick solutions great, so efforts to stimulate the innovation and adaptation of labor-using technology are likely to form a necessary element of an employment-oriented tax policy.

Similarly, as argued in Chapter 10 below, asset taxes may sometimes induce efficient resource utilization, but they seem unlikely to bring about as much redistribution of assets (e.g., from large to small farmers) as an employment-creating policy would require. Substantial land reforms and other similarly "revolutionary" measures may thus be required both in order to get resources into the hands of those who will use them more intensively and to ensure that all sectors of the economy face the same (correct) factor prices.

What is really at issue in putting employment to the forefront as a policy objective is a fundamental reorientation of attitudes. Such reorientations are seldom painless or rapid, and the probability of a quick reversal of the capital-favoring policies that now prevail in most of the world is obviously severely limited by political and economic realities. Indeed, despite the many technical complexities surrounding the issues discussed here, it is much easier to resolve these issues technically than to prescribe how the required policies might be adopted in any country. As Paul Streeten (1972, p. 1) put essentially the same point in a different context: "Understanding the atom is child's play compared with understanding child's play!"

Nevertheless, three points may be made about the political economy of policy change. The first is that generalizations are generally useless. To be useful for any country, policy recommendations need to be specifically geared to the prevailing circumstances and objectives of that country. At best, some typology of countries may perhaps be constructed to simplify the process a bit, by making the generalizations derived from analytic reasoning more closely applicable to the circumstances of particular countries.[26] Often, however, it is likely to prove more important, and more difficult, to determine the relevant facts in a particular case than to develop an applicable analytical model. In this, as in other fields of development economics, policy-minded economists are continually driven back to first principles, namely, that one must know a country before one can prescribe for it. Historical, institutional, and statistical studies are often more useful for this purpose than exercises in deductive logic.

Secondly, the appropriate tax policy for employment (or any other policy objective) requires the orchestration of many subtle fiscal instruments. At the same time, however, the necessary interventionist component of an employment-creating policy must recognize the severity of the administrative constraint and be as general in nature as possible—unless, perhaps, one is prepared to throw efficiency considerations completely out the window and to create most of the additional employment desired within the ranks of the government itself! Reconciling these two dictates is not easy.

Finally, critics of the present international system have attributed the capital bias and resulting unemployment seen in developing countries to the pernicious influence of capitalist technology, especially as disseminated by that ever-popular villain, the multinational corporation (e.g., Sunkel, 1973). One may equally well suggest, however, that it is in the tax treatment of capital and labor in developing countries that the real instance of inappropriate emulation of techniques developed for other economies and other times occurs. The tax systems in most advanced countries may be argued to be unduly anti-labor. When such systems are transferred to other environments, and their capital bias is reinforced both by political and administrative realities and by the inappropriate application of simple (capital-accumulation) growth models, the problem is accentuated. One area of technology to which those concerned with development need to devote more research and development is thus tax technology. In the end, the greater pressure on the developing countries on this front may result in their developing a technology from which tax experts in other parts of the world may also have something to learn.

PART III Taxing Income, Consumption, and Wealth

7 The Income Tax in Developing Countries

A central purpose of the tax system in any country is to distribute the cost of financing government activities as fairly as possible among the population. As emphasized in Chapter 1, "fairness" is inherently a subjective concept; as a rule, however, a fair distribution of taxes is considered to be one that imposes taxes on people in accordance with their ability to pay, as measured by some socially acceptable index of economic capacity.[1] The personal income tax is the only significant component of the tax system which has at least the potential of being completely "fair," in the sense that the taxes paid by different individuals can be explicitly related to their socially determined ability to contribute to the financing of government activity.[2]

Other taxes—those on luxury consumption, for example—may in practice turn out to be progressive in that those with higher incomes will, on average, pay a larger proportion of their incomes in tax than those with lower incomes. As stressed in Chapter 5, however, such taxes may treat taxpayers with the same incomes but different consumption patterns very differently. Only the personal income tax takes explicitly into account those personal characteristics of the taxpayer which are considered most relevant to his ability to pay. Any tax reform concerned with improving the equity of the revenue system must therefore pay particular attention to the structure and functioning of the personal income tax.

The essential role of the personal income tax in the tax system is thus to treat different people equitably, as equity is defined in the society in question. The ideal is to tax those with the same capacity to pay at the same rate, while levying heavier taxes on those with greater capacity than on those with lesser capacity. In view of the existence in most countries of important taxes that do not have these attributes, it may also be considered desirable to increase the progressivity of the income tax to offset the regressivity of the rest of the tax system. At the same time, of course, the desire to encourage saving and entrepreneurial activity acts as a check on the progressivity of the tax, as may political conditions.

An additional virtue of the personal income tax, particularly one that is effectively progressive in its incidence, is that increased reliance on it for revenues may, at least in principle, add to the elasticity of the revenue structure and hence reduce the need to recur to deficit financing of expenditures.[3] Increased reliance on the personal income tax is in theory an important means of increasing both the elasticity and the progressivity of the tax system.

In practice, the income tax in most developing countries is a collection of taxes rather than a unified levy. At the company level a relatively sophisticated net income tax is needed to deal with foreign corporations and large domestic firms. For small businesses, a quite different "presumptive" approach like that set out in Chapter 8 below is often required. Similarly, at the personal level, the employees of large public and private organizations are usually subjected to wage taxes, while self-employed people are reached to a limited extent through crude estimated assessments. Income from capital is sometimes withheld at source, as is also described in the next chapter. The "income" tax in the circumstances of most developing countries thus consists of a set of different taxes that may in many instances not be levied on "income" at all.

The effect of the income tax on economic incentives is in part determined by its coverage of economic activity. If important sectors (such as agriculture) are, in effect, tax-free, then more resources will tend to flow to these sectors than would otherwise be the case, to the disadvantage of taxed sectors such as manufacturing. Unless such distortions in economic activity are consciously intended (e.g., for political reasons) this result is undesirable. Moreover, the knowledge that some forms of income are taxed more lightly than others may act as a brake on the political acceptability of the income tax, and, indeed, of taxes generally. So long as people feel that others are getting away without paying their "fair share" of taxes, their willingness to meet their own tax obligations is greatly reduced. For both these reasons, an important objective of income tax reform in developing countries is to extend the effective coverage of the tax to a much broader segment of the economy. In many countries what is most needed to achieve this aim is a strengthening and restructuring of income tax administration, as argued in the next chapter.

Conditions for Successful Income Taxation

No appraisal of income taxation in developing countries would be complete without explicit reference to Richard Goode's (1952) famous six conditions "necessary" for the successful implementation of an income tax in a developing country:

1. The existence of a predominantly monetary economy.
2. A high standard of literacy among taxpayers (said to be "not strictly necessary but very helpful").
3. Prevalence of accounting records honestly and reliably maintained.
4. A large degree of "voluntary" compliance on the part of taxpayers (at least in the long run).
5. Absence of "wealth groups" with the political power (and desire) to block tax measures.
6. Honest and efficient administration (the minimal acceptable standards of which were said to be higher for income taxes than for any other taxes).

Subsequent commentators have suggested that the first two of these conditions are in reality irrelevant because the potential income tax base is highly concentrated in the upper-income classes, which are both clearly within the monetary economy and also literate (Tanzi, 1967). This position has substantial merit in many developing countries. Since there is no conceivable way in which the population in the traditional rural sector can possibly be brought within the ambit of the income tax in the near future, the personal income tax in such countries is inevitably more a "class" than a "mass" tax. Nevertheless, the other conditions for successful income taxation listed above appear to retain much of their validity in all but the most advanced developing countries—at least as a counsel of caution, if not despair.

The single most important condition for the successful application of the income tax, whether on a class or mass basis, is the existence of a government that both wishes to enforce the tax and has sufficient political support to do so. In the absence of this essential political prerequisite, no effective progressive personal income tax is possible in any country. Even if one is legislated, those who dislike such taxes will have little reason to fear, because the tax will not be effectively enforced. The importance of the political condition for successful income taxation is as obvious as its absence in many developing countries.

Even if this condition is met, there remains the important problem of tax administration—a problem which, in reality, encompasses the so-called "voluntary compliance" condition listed above. The degree of tax compliance in any country reflects less taxpayer "morality" or "conscience" than it does some combination of taxpayer belief that government is spending its money wisely and administering taxes fairly and taxpayer fear of being caught cheating, which in turn depends on the probability of being caught and the consequences of being caught (the effective penalty structure). For further discussion of these points, see Chapters 15 and 16 below.

The minimal acceptable standards of income tax administration are higher and more difficult to achieve than for any other tax. First, the very raison d'être of the personal income tax is, as noted above, its potential for finely discriminating among individuals: but fine discrimination requires a high level of administration if it is not to result simply in accentuated arbitrariness. Secondly, the incentive (as well as the equity) effects of failure to attain a satisfactory level of administration may be worse in the case of a tax on income than a tax on either consumption or wealth because of the sensitivity of economic agents to factors impinging on marginal earnings. The key to a good income tax is a good income tax administration. In turn, a good income tax administration cannot exist in isolation from favorable political circumstances and a certain degree of economic development.[4]

Schedular versus Global Taxation

Until recently it was customary in considering the design of income taxes to contrast the schedular and the global approaches to taxing income. Today the latter approach has triumphed, at least in principle, throughout the world. The income tax in virtually every high-income developed country is now global in concept. Among developing countries, those influenced by British colonial administrations have long had global-type income taxes, and almost no country in the world now has a "pure" schedular system, with completely separate taxes on income derived from different sources. The prevalent form of income tax in much of Africa is still a "mixed" system (schedular taxes capped by a complementary global tax), but any changes in this situation seem likely to be in the direction of increased globalization (Plasschaert, 1976).

This worldwide move toward a "global" income tax has both an economic and an equity rationale. Although, as noted above, equity rationales are always matters of social judgment (and hence disputable), it remains widely accepted in principle that from an equity point of view the tax implications of an additional dollar of net income (comprehensively defined) should be the same, regardless of the source of that income.[5] Moreover, exactly the same rule is advisable from an economic point of view to avoid distorting unduly the pattern of economic activity by diverting resources into relatively lightly taxed activities.

Nevertheless, there are three reasons why significant schedular elements remain even in the most globalized income taxes: principle, policy, and administration. Perhaps the major question of principle concerns the appropriate tax treatment of "earned" and "unearned" income. A secondary issue that may perhaps also be decided on grounds of principle concerns the treatment of gifts and bequests—a point central to some of the arguments recently heard with respect to the superiority of consumption or "lifetime income" taxes over conventional "annual" income taxes.[6]

In addition to possible "incentive" reasons for differential tax treatment, other "policy" issues arise with respect to the treatment of international income (income going to foreigners and foreign income going to residents) and such matters as personal deductions, the treatment of pension income, and so on.[7]

Finally, and in practice most importantly, administrative realities have forced considerable modification of the ideal of a truly global income tax even in the most highly developed countries. The easiest income to tax effectively is wage and salary income; everything else gives rise to problems of varying difficulty. In the past, many countries concluded that the resulting lower probability of catching a dollar of capital (or self-employment) income in the tax net should be recognized by imposing a higher tax rate on such dollars than on wage income. The trouble with this approach is twofold: (1) it leads to neglect of the need to improve the administration of the tax on nonwage income (precisely because of the belief that the differential rates take care of the problem); and (2) the belief that the differential rate takes care of the problem is in any case almost certainly wrong (precisely because the neglect of administration means that evasion will tend to escalate to offset the differential).

This argument is widely accepted. What seems to be less widely understood, however, is that simply abolishing the various schedular taxes resolves no problem.[8] Indeed, unless the move to a global income tax is accompanied by significant administrative tightening on non-wage income, its immediate effect may perhaps even be to increase taxes on wage earners relative to those receiving other forms of income.[9] Unfortunately, increasing "globalization" in another sense, with respect to world capital markets, has made it increasingly difficult for even developed countries to tax capital income effectively (Bird and McLure, 1990) without chasing capital away and hence lowering real wages.

The Treatment of Earned Income

Despite these problems, there are two principal theoretical rationales for differentiating in favor of earned income. The first is the argument that a dollar of income received from investment carries with it a greater inherent "capacity to pay" than a dollar received from work. He who receives the former dollar (the "man of property") receives two substantial additional benefits: the income flows without taking much, if any, of his time or effort, and his source of income, his wealth, provides a sense of security and power over and above that of the job of the man who works.

This line of thought flatly contradicts the underlying rationale of a global income tax ("a dollar is a dollar is a dollar"). Even if true, it points more to the desirability of an additional tax on wealth as such rather than lighter income taxes on earned income (see Chapter 10 below). Nevertheless, such arguments help explain many income tax differentiations found in practice, such as large exclusions from earned income. Sometimes such arguments for special treatment of one source of income are confused with arguments for favoritism to lower levels of income, for example, when the earnings of those receiving the minimum wage are exempted. These questions are quite distinct in principle, however. The case for exempting low-income earners does not depend on the source of their low earnings.

More consistent with the general framework of a global income tax is the view that income from labor is, so to speak, less "pure" (or net) than income from capital (e.g., because of the lack of explicit tax provision for the costs of acquiring and maintaining "human capital").

This argument reduces to the view that inadequate allowance is made for expenses of earning labor income compared to capital income.

Most countries, even those that do not have special tax treatment for all labor income, have special provisions for employees only. These provisions are of two types: exclusion of various fringe benefits paid by the employer and, more closely related to the basic issue of differentiation by source of income, some allowance for employment expenses.

There is indeed a case for providing some recognition of the "costs" of earning labor income. In principle, optional deduction of itemized employment expenses (excluding such basic costs of living as food, shelter, and commuting expense) is probably the best system. In practice, some countries provide a small "standard" deduction of a certain percentage of employment income (often up to some maximum) for administrative convenience.

Since self-employed taxpayers can usually deduct all costs of earning income anyway, they are not usually extended any special deduction for "employment" expenses. Indeed, in their case the problem is often the opposite, to limit the deduction of what are really "personal" expenses (e.g., for the use of an automobile). Many countries have therefore imposed arbitrary limits on the deductibility of expenses by the self-employed.[10] In addition, the self-employed are often subject to special review and "estimated income" procedures. Small businesses and professionals are subject to such procedures in many countries, as discussed further in the next chapter.[11]

The Treatment of Income from Capital

The rationale for special treatment of income from capital rests not on principle but on considerations of policy and administration. The most important policy rationale for taxing income from capital lightly arises from the desire to increase savings and investment. In addition to exempting (or otherwise favoring) income that is saved or invested, many countries provide favorable tax treatment for some or all income from capital (e.g., interest or capital gains) either in order to raise the rate of return on such activity and hence make it more attractive or on the presumption that such income is more likely to be "used" in a socially useful way (that is, saved). The fact that the efficiency of such incentive measures has been severely questioned in many studies (Shah and Toye, 1978; Usher, 1977; Gillis, 1985) has not, apparently, weakened their attractiveness to policy-makers.

Many varieties of exclusions, exemptions, deductions, and credits for income that is saved or invested (or for income from savings or investment) may be found in different countries (Smith, 1990). It is particularly difficult to generalize about this aspect of income tax design because what is best for any country depends on factors specific to that country, such as its degree of openness (linkages to the international capital market), its preference for financial versus fiscal means of mobilizing and channeling savings, the efficiency of tax-induced changes in the rate of return, and other difficult (and largely unknown) matters.

The administrative problem in taxing income from capital might appear less severe to the extent that such income is received from such organized modern-sector institutions as corporations and banks. Even when bearer securities (those not registered to specific individuals) are important, it would appear easy in principle to avoid income tax collection problems by requiring the paying institution to withhold tax, ideally at the highest rate in the income tax rate scale. The withheld tax could then be fully creditable against income tax otherwise due. In the case of bearer bonds and shares, which provide a means of avoiding capital gains and wealth taxes, a higher, penalty rate may be advisable. Another possible approach might be to levy a higher tax on the retained earnings of corporations whose shares are not registered, in order to obtain at least some compensation for the revenue thus forgone. Despite various problems, interest, dividends, and royalties should all be fairly easy to tax in principle. The fact that they are not very effectively taxed in practice in most countries reflects as much deliberate policy as administrative limitations.[12]

Administrative problems are clearly much more severe with regard to other property incomes (e.g., most rents), interest to moneylenders, etc. There is no easy way to collect tax on such generally unorganized sources of capital income except by arbitrary techniques similar to those discussed in the next chapter. As in the case of the self-employed, there is no short-cut to an alert and well-informed tax administration.

Even if such an administration exists, it will encounter many problems in taxing one particular type of capital income, namely, capital gains. Where a capital gains tax exists, as already mentioned, it cannot be enforced effectively even on shares (usually the easiest case) if bearer shares exist. Nor can it be enforced effectively on real property in the absence of an up-to-date and accurate cadaster (register of property ownership and valuation). Gains on closely held businesses, objets d'art, and similar items tax the taxman in the most advanced countries so severely that it seems hopeless to expect less developed fiscal ad-minstrations to be able to deal with them very effectively. Even in the case of large corporations, it is hard to control the conversion of ordi-nary income of corporations into nontaxable (or partly taxable) capital gains. *Any* differential between the rate of personal income tax levied on, say, dividends and interest and that imposed on capital gains gives rise to avoidance possibilities which must be anticipated and blocked in one way or another if the "global" character of the income tax is not to remain a mere illusion.

The only way to avoid serious administrative problems in this re-spect may be by approximating as closely as possible to a position in which *all* payments from corporations to shareholders are taxed similarly, no matter how they are labeled. This aim may, of course, be achieved by lowering all taxes on income from capital to the rate levied on capital gains, although such a policy would introduce a substantial (and presumably undesirable) degree of discrimination against labor income.

An approach more consistent with the concept of a global income tax would be to treat all such payments (including those arising through liquidation, "thin capitalization," full and partial redemptions, and so on) as ordinary income of shareholders. Obviously, a fairly harsh and arbitrary set of administrative rules would be needed to achieve this aim, but there seems no other feasible way to approach the goal of an equitable global income tax.

Flat-Rate Taxes and Inflation Adjustment

The many problems of effectively administering income taxes in developing countries increase the attractiveness of relatively flat-rate taxes, levied at similar rates on companies and high-income individu-als, with a limited amount of progressivity being achieved by personal exemptions or credits.[13] Even if one is not prepared to go this far, steeply progressive rates have no place in a well-designed income tax in developing countries. A particular advantage of flat-rate taxation in many countries is that it reduces the problems caused by inflation's moving people up the rate structure.

Some countries have introduced automatic indexation schemes for personal exemptions and rates to alleviate this problem (Aaron, 1976; Petrei, 1975). Others have preferred to rely on discretionary adjustments in personal tax structure to offset undesired tax increases as a result of inflation. Still others may even welcome such inflationary increases as a relatively painless way of increasing tax revenues.

More difficult questions arise with regard to adjusting the *base* of the income tax for the effects of inflation. The principal areas of difficulty are depreciation, inventory valuation and—an often neglected but important offset to the other two—financial items on the balance sheet (McLure et al., 1989). Those who owe money in fixed nominal currency amounts, as do many business firms, gain in inflation. While some countries (e.g., Chile: see Casanegra, 1985) have gone further than others in dealing with these problems, there is no consensus in either theory or practice as to how best to take inflation into account in designing tax structure. Partial solutions, such as the indexation of capital gains or depreciation commonly advocated by business, may sometimes be worse from a social point of view than no action, while a comprehensive solution seems beyond the reach of most countries at this time.

In short, whether with respect to inflation adjustment or many other problems encountered in different countries in the process of "globalizing" the base of the personal income tax, the solutions found to these problems in different systems illustrate a changing and varied mixture of rationales derived from principle, policy, and administrative need. There are no simple answers to the question of the appropriate income tax treatment of many items, whether one is operating within the framework of a global system or not.

Perhaps the major contribution of the notion of globalization is to serve as a standard (or principle) requiring all deviations from the treatment applied to the "standard case" of wage income to be specially justified in terms of the social benefits to be achieved from such deviation (policy) or the social costs of not so deviating (administration).[14] The adoption of a global framework alone does little to resolve the hard problems of designing an effective personal income tax in an evolving society.

Income Taxes on Companies

The virtues of the other major component of the income tax structure in most countries—the company income tax—are less overwhelming than those of the personal income tax in terms of equity but may be significant in terms of the potential contribution of this levy to the revenue productivity and elasticity of the tax system. Despite the difficulty of ascertaining the incidence of taxes on companies, on balance they are likely to show a certain degree of "blind progressivity" (that is, in terms of average incidence across income classes, without taking into account the unique characteristics of individual taxpayers, as does the personal income tax). In most countries, the bulk of the company income tax is paid by a small number of private firms. Whether this tax is borne by the consumers of the goods and the services produced by these firms, by their owners (or owners of capital in general), or even by their employees, its incidence will as a rule be progressive because all three of these groups generally have incomes well above the norm.

In principle, it would be possible to treat all taxes levied at the enterprise level as constituting, in effect, "withholding" of personal taxes, thus completely integrating enterprise and personal taxes and explicitly relating the total income tax on enterprise-derived income to the personal characteristics of the taxpayer (presumed in this instance to be the shareholder).[15] Whatever the merits of such integration, however—and some have argued that they are far from clear (Bird, 1987b)—in practice the administrative requirements of this system clearly make it unworkable in developing countries. A more limited alternative is to "integrate" only that part of the enterprise tax assumed to fall on dividends with the personal tax levied on those same dividends. This could be done, for example, by including in personal income for tax purposes the amount of the dividend grossed-up by the presumed corporate tax paid, calculating the personal tax on total income including this grossed-up dividend, and then crediting against this personal tax the corporate tax presumed to have already been paid. Although this system is considerably less administratively complex, it too is dubious on both administrative and incentive grounds. In particular, the debility of the personal tax administration makes it improbable in most countries either that the tax at the personal level is collected very well or that a system of crediting enterprise taxes against personal taxes would work very well either.

In the end, perhaps the most feasible way to integrate company and personal taxes in developing countries may be simply by exempting dividends from personal taxation, as has recently been done in Colombia (McLure et al., 1989). Thus exempting some capital income from personal income tax obviously moves the tax system far away from the initial focus on the income tax as a comprehensive measure of ability to pay at the personal level.

In any case, taxation at the level of the enterprise is a necessary complement to the successful implementation of a personal income tax, particularly when the task facing tax administrators is as enormous as it is in most developing countries. Even when dividends (and other distributions) as well as capital gains on the sale of shares or businesses are successfully taxed at the personal level—which is far from being the general case—an annual enterprise tax on undistributed profits may be justified on equity grounds. Since this justification becomes stronger the weaker the administration of the tax at the personal level, the equity case for enterprise taxation is especially strong in developing countries.

The primary rationale for taxing enterprise profits separately, however, is undoubtedly the relative administrative ease of collecting large sums from a relatively few taxpayers. The role of the profits tax in tapping foreign investment is particularly critical in many developing countries. Indeed, the revenue collected from such operations may in many instances constitute the major national benefit from such investment.[16]

Conclusion

This chapter has sketched a few of the problems countries have encountered in moving toward a more global personal income tax base. Although in principle globalization means the treatment of all income alike, regardless of source, in practice different degrees of "netness," sundry policy rationales, and the various administrative problems alluded to above mean that no tax system anywhere really treats all forms of income alike. Nor does it seem reasonable to posit such uniform treatment as a short-run goal in any developing country.[17] Instead, the attention of would-be income tax reformers should be focused first on strengthening administration in those areas in which it is inherently weakest—the self-employed, rental incomes, etc.—and then considering carefully the extent to which policy objectives (or simply politics?) require more favorable treatment of certain types of income than seems warranted in the name of the principle of globalization.

To the extent that such schedular elements remain, it must also be carefully considered whether it is best to mark them out explicitly (e.g., by special tax rates on interest income) or to allow them to exist in practice but not in law (as with agricultural income in many countries: Lent [1973]). The former is better in principle, but the latter is clearly more common, thus again demonstrating the primacy of political considerations over conceptual neatness in the formulation of tax policy.

Finally, an important function of law in any country is to state social ideals or goals, even if they cannot, for the moment, be fully or adequately implemented. The imposition of a global framework for the income tax may serve an important role in this sense as a statement of goals which may provide administrators and judges alike with some basis for deciding difficult cases of interpretation.

Global income taxes may make sense in principle in both equity and economic terms in the context of many developing countries. They may also (more doubtfully) make sense, at least as an aspiration, even when they cannot be effectively enforced. But there is no getting around two facts: first, the key to moving in the direction of an effectively global income tax in any country lies in improved tax administration—the subject of the next chapter; second, any practical income tax in a developing country will be far removed from the "comprehensive income tax" familiar from public finance textbooks.

8 Income Tax Reform and Administration

Although the present chapter focuses on the income tax, and particularly on the personal income tax, much of the argument is equally applicable to other "modern" taxes based on accounts and records (such as the sales tax) as well as to taxes based on valuations (such as the property tax). The "presumptive" technique described below, for example, is as often used for sales taxes as for income taxes. Similarly, the value-added tax may be characterized as a form of "withholding" intended to implement a retail (or other) sales tax more efficiently (Krauss and Bird, 1971). There is also a strong parallel between the rationale and working of the standard assessment techniques discussed below and the "mass appraisal" methods often proposed for property tax purposes. In both instances, the administrative essence of the system is the development by experts of a detailed manual which can then be applied by nonexperts to individual cases. Only when taxes are based directly on easily identifiable and verifiable characteristics—as are excise taxes—can the problems discussed here be avoided.

The previous chapter concluded that the key to a good personal tax system is good income tax administration. Good income tax administration in turn requires a favorable political environment in the sense of a government that, from the highest level down, has the desire and authority to enforce the tax. In the absence of firm and consistent political support for the revenue authorities over a substantial period of time, no basic improvements can be expected in tax administration. Since without such improvement a good personal tax system cannot be implemented, no matter how well designed that system might be on paper, it is simply assumed here that political conditions are favorable to the sorts of administrative methods discussed. If this assumption is *not* correct, tax reform efforts would be more profitably directed at designing and implementing effective indirect, impersonal means of generating the requisite revenues in an acceptable way (see Chapter 9) than in refining the essentially ineffective and inequitable system of taxing persons in accordance with their income.

The three basic tasks of any tax administration are to *identify* potential taxpayers, to *assess* the appropriate tax on them, and to *collect* that tax. In other words, the "three E's" of administering taxes are to *enumerate, estimate*, and *enforce*. All these tasks are difficult to accomplish in a developing country, where many potential taxpayers are not enmeshed in the set of interlocking recorded transactions characteristic of developed countries. In all countries, it is much harder to tax self-employed businessmen, farmers, and professionals than it is to tax employees of large organizations. One of the misfortunes of developing countries is that so much more of their potential tax base lies in the former group that they need to spend relatively more of their scarce resources on the inherently difficult task of taxing them.

Unfortunately, there are no shortcuts to better tax administration. The best a developing country can do with respect to the "hard-to-tax" is to emulate what is done in developed countries with respect to the same groups: to collect the taxes before they have a chance to hide the income (through a withholding system), to assess taxes on the basis of something more readily verifiable than income (through an estimation system), and, of course, to enforce the tax system as rigorously as possible. This chapter elaborates these three points.

Withholding and Current Payment

Countries that levy relatively successful income taxes collect most of the tax through withholding or "third party" techniques that in effect charge a third party with the tasks of deducting the tax from some payment being made to the taxpayer and then remitting the proceeds to the government. Such withholding may be of two types: provisional or final. Amounts provisionally withheld are credited against a final end-year liability and are in principle subject to adjustment through supplementary payments, or refunds, as the case may be. In contrast, other withholding may be treated as the final payment with respect to certain income, with no provision for subsequent adjustments. Both types of withholding are found in all countries, but the scope and the precise form in which they are applied differ widely, depending upon the structure of the economy and the capability of the tax administration. In addition, in some circumstances tax withholding is supplemented by a "current payment" system for other forms of income.

WAGE WITHHOLDING

Most income tax revenues in every country consist of taxes withheld on the wages and salaries paid to employees by large organizations such as public-sector agencies and private corporations. The income tax is more difficult to apply in developing countries because such modern sector employment income normally constitutes a much smaller part of the potential tax base. Nevertheless, it is invariably with respect to such income that the income tax can and does function most effectively and fairly (at least within the group of employees). Among the most important aspects to be considered in setting up a wage withholding system are its scope and its accuracy.

In principle, the coverage of the wage withholding system should be as broad as possible. The withholding of tax from public-sector employees, for example, is not simply a matter of government putting money into one pocket and taking it out of the other. Instead, it is an essential ingredient of an effective and fair income tax in at least two ways: first, by providing the necessary basis on which to assess and tax the global income of public employees and, second, by removing an obvious rationale for others to rationalize their own (extra-legal) nonpayment of taxes. As in the case of state corporations paying corporate taxes, public employees paying income taxes constitute a valuable "role model" for others less easily reached by the power of the state. Public employees should thus be subject to wage withholding.

Employees of private-sector corporations and other organizations (nonprofit, etc.) should similarly be subject to the wage withholding system, depending on the limit of administrative practicality. All wages with respect to which contributions to social insurance funds (or similar payments) are made, for example, should also be subject to income tax withholding. One exception might be for small firms subject to the "estimated" tax system discussed below, since if their books are so unreliable for other purposes they cannot be trusted for withholding purposes either. In general, however, the scope of the wage withholding system should be as broad as can possibly be managed.

In the absence of careful institutional study, it is not possible to be equally definitive with respect to the precise form of the withholding system that should be adopted in any particular country. An "ideal" system might be one that would leave most employees, who have no significant outside income, with no tax to pay (or refund to receive) at the end of the year. In other words, the tax withheld would precisely equal the tax due. Such a cumulative withholding system has long existed in Britain under the name of P.A.Y.E. (pay-as-you-earn), but the expense of achieving this degree of perfection makes it quite impractical for a developing country.[1]

Nevertheless, the avoidance of the refund problem (see below) makes some features of the British tax system that have facilitated P.A.Y.E. worth noting. In particular, the application of (in effect) a proportional income tax rate to the vast majority of taxpayers and the restriction of applicable deductions basically to exemptions for dependents are desirable features of a workable income tax in a developing country. Striving for undue refinement with respect to either the progressivity of the rate structure or the delineation of the tax base is likely to yield few, if any, benefits in increased equity and substantial administrative cost and complexity.

The noncumulative withholding system used in the United States and a number of other countries shares with the P.A.Y.E. system the characteristic of being in principle provisional rather than definitive in character. Unlike P.A.Y.E., however, the U.S. system is also generally provisional in practice. Many additional payments and refunds are therefore required to reconcile the taxes withheld over the course of the year with the taxes finally determined to be due.

In a developing country, where most taxpayers do not keep reliable or accurate records (or, if they do, cannot be made to reveal them), effective administrative systems depend on official action, or the lack of it. Given the scarcity of administrative resources, however, it is desirable to induce taxpayers (or relevant third parties engaged in transactions with taxpayers) to do as much of the authorities' work as possible. One obvious way to do this (widely used in the United States) is to overwithhold, thus forcing taxpayers to reveal information to the authorities in order to qualify for refunds. Although this policy is surprisingly popular in the United States—most taxpayers appear to regard it as a welcome form of "forced savings"—it would probably not work in most developing countries, owing to the weakness of the tax accounting system and the slowness and unreliability of tax refunds.

Indeed, without a fairly reliable system of tax processing and accounting, *no* system of provisional withholding can work very well. Unless amounts withheld are properly and promptly credited to the correct taxpayer account, the refund process can never be counted on to correct for overwithholding. Even if the withholding rate is kept deliberately low in order to reduce the need for refunds, the amounts withheld have to be credited to the right account if there is to be a final adjustment in tax liability at the end of the year. Moreover, both taxpayer and administration need to be sure that this matching will take place if the withholding system is to constitute, as it should, a principal structural component of the assessment and collection process.

The key to good accounting in this sense is a reliable system of taxpayer identification numbers. Only when each withholding (or other) payment is reliably and promptly credited to the correct account can a refund system be established. Only when both administration and taxpayer are sure that all payments are accurately recorded is it possible to make use of such enforcement devices as requiring proof of tax compliance before issuing passports, business licenses, etc. Indeed, a reliable tax accounting system based on unique taxpayer identifiers is an essential prerequisite to any significant improvement in either tax assessment or tax collection.

An alternative approach to wage withholding is less administratively demanding—but also further away from the presumed ideal of a global income tax. In this approach, a prescribed tax is withheld from wages by employers, transmitted by them to the government, and treated by the latter as the final satisfaction of tax liability on those wages.[2] The tax withheld in this fashion may be a flat-rate levy (in which case it is simply a gross payroll tax) or, more usually, graduated in accordance with the wages received by particular employees. There may, or may not, be some allowance made for the number of dependents or other personal deductions, though the fewer such refinements the better the system will function.

The key point about this approach is that there is no direct contact at all between employees and the government. In effect, each employer acts as a mini-assessing authority, determining who pays what, subject to at most an aggregative review by the revenue authorities. Indeed, where such systems exist, experience suggests that in practice many provisions of the substantive tax law—concerning, for example, fringe benefits and allowances—tend to be ignored. For a system of definitive wage withholding of this sort to function satisfactorily from an administrative point of view, the tax base should be as close to gross money wages as possible, since any variations lead to the need for the sort of detailed official verification that this approach is intended to avoid.

From a policy point of view, such definitive wage withholding is tolerable only when most taxpayers subjected to this regime receive wage income from only one employer and have no other significant income. To avoid substantial abuse, information returns should be required from each withholding agent (employer), showing the amounts withheld and the tax base (gross income less stated deductions) by the name, address, and identification number of the taxpayer. Once this information is obtained, however, it is not clear why anything except administrative capacity prevents the conversion of this system into a provisional withholding system, with final adjustment, as described earlier.

An alternative approach might be to require employees to submit to the employer, to be kept on file for possible audits, a brief form containing identifying information, the basis for any deductions (e.g., number of dependents), and a statement to the effect that they have no other significant source of income. Those who do not comply must file regular individual returns (and pay currently, as noted below). This alternative has the obvious disadvantage of increasing the paper flow, but it has the possible advantage of putting the onus for compliance more clearly on the taxpayer, while still leaving tax collection for the employer to deal with. In many developing countries, however, such potential conceptual benefits should, like many other nice ideas, be forgone to avoid flooding the already overloaded tax administration with still more unprocessable paper.

Wage withholding inevitably constitutes the mainstay of effective personal income taxation in any country. The easiest withholding system to run satisfactorily is one with a relatively simple rate structure (probably not too progressive) and, especially, as simple a base as possible in terms of personal deductions and allowances. For most taxpayers, the taxes withheld could probably be taken as their full tax liability, and they need have no direct contact with the revenue authorities. For such a system to function as part of a decent income tax, however, employees should be required to provide some basic "coding" data to employers, employers need to provide identifying information on all employees to the authorities, and the administration needs to have the sort of reliable tax processing and accounting system that unfortunately does not yet exist in most developing countries.

OTHER WITHHOLDING

Aside from wages and salaries, withholding can be used for income from such "movable capital" as interest, dividends, and royalties. The basic administrative questions are similar to those already discussed with respect to wages, though the answers need not be the same.

It is more common, for example, for withholding to constitute a definitive settlement of tax liability in the case of movable capital. The rationale for this approach is obvious in the case of nonresidents, but it is far from obvious why the same is so often true in the case of residents—or why, indeed, there is so often *no* withholding on such payments domestically. The failure to withhold any tax on payments of interest, dividends, and royalties from corporations (or governments) to individuals greatly weakens the administrative underpinnings of the income tax.

In principle, as noted in the previous chapter, *all* payments from corporations to individuals for the use of movable capital—whether labeled "interest," "dividends," or "royalties"—should be subjected to withholding, preferably at a significant uniform rate.[3] As before, a good system of tax accounting and taxpayer identification numbers is needed if payments withheld in this way are to be credited accurately against final liabilities. In the absence of this infrastructure, such withholding would become in practice the final tax payment. The rates applied are generally lower than the appropriate personal income tax rate since the recipients of most such payments are relatively well off. In principle there is no reason for this concession, since those from whom income is withheld can always file a full return if they are overwithheld. Without at least *some* withholding on income from movable capital, however, such income is all too likely to escape tax entirely in the circumstances of most developing countries, thus reducing the income tax in effect to a discriminatory tax on wages.

Two essential components of an effective income tax collection system are thus withholding on wages and salaries and withholding on interest, dividends, and royalty payments. In both cases, the ideal system would treat the tax withheld as a provisional payment of the final global tax liability, but in practice even a system that treated withholding and the final payment as synonymous would, at least with regard to nonwage income, constitute an improvement in the circumstances of many countries.

Much the same has sometimes been claimed with respect to a third possible form of tax withholding, namely on payments by government or large private corporations—for example, those that are designated as withholding agents for other purposes—to individuals in forms other than wages, interest, dividends, or royalties. Examples are payments for rent, to independent contractors, or for the services of independent professionals. Withholding on such payments would obviously have to be on a gross basis and probably at a fairly low rate. In the absence of a decent taxpayer identification system and reliable tax accounting, a withholding system of this sort would in fact amount to little more than a discriminatory sales (or purchase) tax.[4]

With the right infrastructure in place, however, so that the amount withheld can be attributed to the right taxpayers and credited against their tax liabilities, such an approach may provide a useful stimulus to some members of the "hard-to-tax" groups to comply with their legal obligations. The feasibility and usefulness of this approach as part of an *income* tax depends upon the existence of a workable administrative structure: it cannot be a substitute for the absence of this structure, as sometimes asserted. In fact, attractive as such withholding may appear to hard-pressed revenue authorities, on the whole it seems unlikely to be useful as part of the income tax system in the context of most developing countries.

A final comment to be made about *any* form of withholding is that care must be exercised to ensure that the amounts withheld by third parties on behalf of the government are transmitted to the government as promptly as possible. For this purpose, a special withholding enforcement section is probably needed in the administration, particularly strong financial penalties should be imposed on noncompliers (who, in effect, are misusing public funds), and compliance should be made as easy as possible, for instance, by providing in a timely fashion any needed forms and information, by simplifying the relevant tax law (sometimes drastically), and by making it simple to transfer funds to official accounts. Such things are much easier to say than they are to do in developing countries.

CURRENT PAYMENTS

Even if withholding is used as extensively as possible, self-employed persons will generally escape the system on much or all of their income: they will thus be advantaged relative to wage earners. For this reason, if equity is a concern—as it presumably is in any country implementing an income tax— a system of "current payments" for taxpayers not subject to withholding on most of their income is also desirable. Taxpayers with certain characteristics—for example, with substantial non-wage income—may be required to make payments, often quarterly, of the taxes estimated to be due that year.

One problem with this system is to identify those taxpayers who should be filing on a current basis: like provisional withholding, current payment requires prompt and accurate taxpayer identification and tax accounting if it is to function satisfactorily. Another problem is to determine the basis on which the current payments should be made: as a general rule, the previous year's taxes are accepted, although it has often been proposed that such payments should be adjusted to reflect subsequent price rises.[5] Since one of the principal advantages of not filing currently is the inflation-induced reduction in real tax liabilities, this last point is significant in many countries (Tanzi, 1977).

On the other hand, current payment systems may need a "hardship" provision, in case this year's income falls well below last year's owing to some general or local disorder. This problem may be handled by permitting amendment at the option of the taxpayer (and approval by the administration) subject to a substantial financial penalty if it turns out the revised estimated basis is too far (say 10 percent) below the original base. A similar system might be used to induce taxpayers to *raise* their estimated base above that of the previous year (even if inflation-adjusted), but in this case a greater margin for legitimate error (say, 25 percent) would likely have to be allowed to make such a penalty politically tolerable.

A current payment system could be introduced gradually, over (say) a five-year transition period. Corporations and taxpayers with business income (or substantial nonemployment income) might, for example, be required in the first year (year 1) of the system to pay the tax due for the prior year (year 0) plus 20 percent of the tax estimated for year 1 (e.g., year 0 tax times an inflation adjustment). In year 2, they would pay the balance due on year 1 (final assessment less amount currently paid on year 1) plus 40 percent of the tax estimated for year 2 (inflation-adjusted final assessment for year 1). By year 5, all taxpayers would be on a full current payment system. The transitory revenue gain accruing to the state over this period might perhaps be considered belated recompense for the previous advantages received by these taxpayers. Apart from corporations, however, where this acceleration factor might be significant in (one-time) revenue terms, the primary rationale for a current payment system is clearly equity (fairness of treatment of withheld and non-withheld taxpayers) and politics (improved acceptability of the system by employees), not revenue.

As a final comment, it again deserves emphasis how simplified tax assessment and collection can be if the income tax is linear in form, that is, consists of proportional rate tax, with any desired progressivity introduced by relatively simple personal exemptions or deductions (Head and Bird, 1983). With such a simplified tax structure, *all* payments from governments or corporations to individuals can be withheld at a uniform flat rate without serious injustice being done. Employees can file simple forms with their employers claiming the exemptions to which they were entitled, as described above. Employers can then apply the flat rate to wages net of any permitted deductions, thus yielding a tax with the desired progressivity across employees (at least those who work at only one job). Others would of course still have to file tax returns to claim any refunds to which they were entitled.

There is no way to avoid some rough edges even in a simplified system, but the "rough justice" that could be attained by an effectively collected, albeit relatively proportional and simple, income tax is likely to prove more equitable in practice in many countries than the results of a more refined tax structure that cannot be comprehensively and fairly applied. Whether administration is viewed as a constraint on the design of tax structure or the design of tax structure is viewed as a factor affecting administration, the result is the same. A simple, not too progressive, not too ambitious tax seems the best that can be achieved in most developing countries. Attempts to go beyond this are likely to produce anomalous results: greater nominal progressivity, for example, may induce greater evasion, and consequently less progressive outcomes.

Taxation of Estimated Income

The same sort of pragmatic striving for "rough justice"—the attainable "good" as opposed to the unattainable "perfect"—is the rationale for taxing "estimated" or "presumed" income. *All* countries encounter a great deal of trouble in taxing the self-employed in business, agriculture, and the professions. The techniques used for this purpose—all very much of the "rough justice" variety—are rather similar around the world, although they tend to be used somewhat differently in developed than in developing countries.

The common element everywhere is the estimation of taxable income on a basis that is more readily verifiable by the tax authorities than is the taxpayer's own declaration of income. The factors used for this purpose range from information on sales and wealth to external indicia of earning power (e.g., number of employees) or consumption (e.g., ownership of houses and cars). Developed countries tend to rely more on such accounts-based methods as the "net worth" method of estimating income (as the difference in wealth at the beginning and end of a tax period plus consumption during the period).[6] Developing countries, where taxpayers seldom leave as many financial tracks, necessarily rely more on "objective" external indicia. But both groups of countries use both methods to some extent. The principal difference between developed and developing countries is that the latter more commonly use such estimating methods for the *final* determination of income rather than as a technique for reviewing the income declared by those taxpayers selected for audit, as is commonly done in countries where more reliance can be put on accounting records.

Undoubtedly the best-known and most developed system of taxing estimated income is that developed in Israel (the *takshiv*) (Lapidoth, 1977). For present purposes, however, a variant recently proposed for Bolivia in the Musgrave (1981) report is especially interesting.[7] Under this proposal, taxpayers were to be divided into four groups: (1) very small taxpayers, (2) small taxpayers, (3) other "hard-to-tax" groups, and (4) others. The first group were to be exempted, in line with normal income tax principles on exempting minimum incomes, and the fourth group would be required to keep adequate books and records and be subjected to the regular income tax (including selective audit) procedures. This fourth group, for example, might include foreign enterprises, state enterprises, and corporations benefiting from state grants or fiscal incentives.

The second group distinguished in the Bolivian proposal, the "small taxpayers," were to be subjected to a special tax in lieu of the personal and corporate income taxes *and* the sales tax that would otherwise be applied (at least in principle). "Small taxpayers" were defined as those with not more than two employees and were to be distinguished from the exempt group and the other groups mentioned above on the basis of gross sales. Gross sales figures were to be determined in part by a "short return" to be filed by such taxpayers, supported by a minimal set of books that taxpayers were to be required to keep. Since for obvious reasons no reliance could be put on this information, rough physical indicators (see below) would also be used to estimate gross sales and hence classify taxpayers.[8]

Once taxpayers were classified by type of activity and gross sales, all those in a particular group would be subjected to a flat lump-sum tax, set at approximately the amount that would result if the regular income and sales tax rates were applied to the estimated average income of the group. The exempt level, and the level at which taxpayers are supposed to move to the regular system, varied widely from category to category, depending upon the presumed relation between estimated gross sales and taxable income (and sales).

The system described in the preceding two paragraphs is of course not really an income tax at all (Morag, 1957). Rather, it is a lump-sum minimum tax in lieu of accounts-based taxes on income and sales. It is closer to a set of business license fees than to an income tax since the principal factors determining who pays, and how much they pay, are (a) the nature of the activity and (b) whatever "objective" indicators (e.g., number of employees) are used to estimate gross sales. Crude as it is, however, such a tax may serve the useful purpose of incorporating more taxpayers in the tax net at minimum administrative cost. The tax should, at the very least, be sufficiently high to more than compensate for the cost of establishing and running the system. Its incidence and economic effects are in no sense likely to be those of an income tax, but this is not a very relevant criticism since the option of levying an income tax is by definition not available. Either a simple tax such as this is levied on these small taxpayers, or they are not likely to be effectively taxed at all, at least not directly. This seems sufficient rationale for considering a system along these lines in most developing countries.

The principal problems with such systems are twofold. On the one hand, the taxes charged will likely have to be set on the low side to reduce the level of "tax protesting" as well as the possibility of imposing undue hardship in particular instances. But if the taxes levied are too low, not only will there be no incentive to move to the regular income tax system, but there will also be substantial incentive for larger firms to disguise themselves as "small" (in terms of the indicia used to decide size, such as number of employees) in order to retain the benefits of the fixed-tax system.

On the other hand, if the categorization system is upgraded along the lines discussed below, the costs of administering the system with respect to truly small taxpayers will probably soon exceed the revenues produced. There is no way to avoid such difficulties except by constantly improving tax administration in general to try to confine the use of the presumptive system to the group for which it is intended. Again, however, it must be recalled that reaching small traders and artisans through direct taxes in the context of a developing country is likely either going to be done this way, or not at all. In the circumstances, it seems worth developing a system along these lines in most developing countries. The main feasible alternative is to do nothing, either explicitly (for example, by setting exemption levels high) or, much worse—and more common—implicitly, by simply not enforcing the law that purports to subject these people to income tax, thus increasing the general perception of this potentially fairest of all taxes as "unfair" by those, mostly employees, who cannot escape paying it.

The third group distinguished in the Bolivia report are taxpayers who are not "small." Such taxpayers were to be subjected in principle to the regular income tax, but the regular administrative procedure (of verifying books and records by selective audit) could not readily be applied to them. This important group of taxpayers in most developing countries includes, for instance, the professions and all but the largest businesses. In practice, faced with the difficulty of verifying information supplied by such taxpayers, tax officials generally use either very arbitrary methods of assessment or, perhaps most commonly, bargain with taxpayers as to the amount of tax to be assessed (often within the limits set by the official's need to satisfy the revenue targets that he has been given). Such individual bargaining between officials and taxpayers completely undermines the rationale of the income tax and is obviously highly conducive to fraud and manipulation on all sides. On the other hand, it is usually impossible for overworked and undertrained officials to cope with recalcitrant taxpayers in a hostile environment in any other way. In these circumstances, the method of standard assessment used in Israel, Korea, and other countries, and recommended for Bolivia, seems to be the best possible solution, indeed perhaps the only one.

The essence of this method is the establishment of a set of *standard assessment guidelines* for each major economic activity, on the basis of which the income for any individual taxpayer can be estimated in a relatively objective fashion.[9] Guidelines may be developed for various activities by a relatively small group of experts, and updated from time to time. Such guidelines require little expertise to apply. Basically, all the assessing officer has to do is to obtain information on a series of relatively objective indicators—the number of employees, their skill level, the nature and type of machinery installed, stock on hand (inventory), etc.—, go to the relevant guide, and calculate the tax on the basis of the ratios shown there between the indicators on which he has collected information and gross sales and between gross sales and net income.

The ratios in such guides in principle should be based on careful studies by experts in the particular trade, industry, or profession in question and are intended to represent typical or average rates.[10] Ideally, a different guide is needed for each trade or profession in each major city or region; it would take many years, and much work, to obtain comprehensive coverage in this way. A more realistic aim is not to cover everything but rather to focus on those areas where public perceptions, and the knowledge of officials, suggests there are serious problems.

Several aspects of this approach to implementing income taxes in the "hard-to-tax" sectors should be underlined. In the first place, although a principal reason for moving to the estimation system is to reduce the scope for bargaining or negotiation about individual cases, trade organizations should likely be closely consulted in the initial stages of developing the relevant guides, both in order to obtain relevant information and also to persuade them that it is better that all their members pay a (roughly) fair tax than have taxes arbitrarily imposed upon them. (Imposition of the system must not, however, be conditional on the *agreement* of such organizations!) Among the information used to develop assessment guides may be available tax information (including customs and excise) on firms with fairly good records, other information on sales and purchases, direct studies of firms, general industry studies, and so on.

Second, it is critical that as many "indicators" as possible be used in determining the tax base in order to avoid the obvious distortion and evasion that could otherwise result. The development of these indicators and the related sales, expense, and income ratios is a difficult and complex task if it is done right, as it must be if this procedure is to be of any use. It will probably therefore take several months to develop a useful guide for any particular line of activity. This means the system should be introduced selectively, preferably concentrating initially on areas in which there is thought to be significant revenue potential and for which reasonable *quantitative* (not qualitative) information is available. As the small group of economists and accountants charged with developing these guides becomes more expert, they can begin to tackle more difficult areas, in addition to periodically revising previous guides (for example, to take account of price changes).

Third, the tax established on the basis of the assessment guides should be a *minimum*, unless the taxpayer can show that his actual liability is less—which he can do only by meeting the detailed record-keeping requirements established by the revenue authorities. Taxpayers should, at a minimum, be permitted to claim losses, investment incentives, and similar concessions *only* if they file a detailed return supported by creditable, and verifiable, records maintained in a prescribed fashion (and externally audited). This provision is important to provide some incentive for taxpayers to move off this "minimum estimated tax" system and into the regular income tax system.[11] Ideally, the estimated amounts should be on the high side to encourage better record keeping, but as noted earlier this may not prove politically feasible, so that some inducements (such as access to incentives) must be used to encourage the upgrading of accounts.

A final point to be considered is whether the standard assessment guides for particular activities, once prepared, should be published in some form. Two reasons in favor of publication are, first, to act as a check on possible corruption or misuse by officials and, second, since the income estimate based on the guide will be a presumptive minimum, perhaps to stimulate more accurate and complete taxpayer declarations. Since the ultimate aim is to move everyone onto the regular income tax system, this point is important in principle, though it may not amount to much in practice given the probable low level of the estimated taxes. The only argument against publication is that taxpayers may obtain too much information on how to arrange their affairs to minimize tax. This argument can easily be overdone, however, since it will not be so easy to do this if a number of indicators are used, as should be the rule, and since such information is often readily available in any case.[12]

On balance, the "guide" approach seems the *only* available way to deal with the "hard-to-tax" groups, whether in the professions, agriculture, or business. The key to success appears to lie in being clear and open about what is being done and why, in the careful and complete study of selected industries, and in allowing field officers as little discretion as possible in applying these rules.[13] Those who wish to rebut the presumed minimum income always have the option of keeping good books and filing regular returns and should, as noted above, be encouraged to seize this option by the restriction of such benefits as incentives, loss offsets, etc., to those who do so.

The result of the almost inevitable bias toward presuming income on the low side is that, unless great care is exercised, the estimated system, instead of fostering movement toward the regular system, will discourage such movement. To offset this "locking-in" of taxpayers to the (favorable) estimated system, the system must be reviewed periodically (preferably yearly) in accordance with price and other changes, so at least matters do not get worse in this respect. The parallel to the need to maintain assessed valuations in a property tax system is clear.

Taxes levied on the basis of standard assessment guides are of course not really "income" taxes, unless the estimated income is an exceptionally good measure of the (unknown) actual income. They are, in effect, taxes on the set of factors used to estimate income, with consequently different incidence and economic effects than a proper income tax. Nevertheless, the adoption of a standard assessment system as a basis for securing a minimal tax contribution from the "hard-to-tax" segment of the population would constitute a significant improvement in the fairness and efficiency of the overall tax system in most developing countries. This approach is not a panacea; nor is it particularly easy to implement successfully. But there is really no other way to go if the direct tax system is to be expanded to encompass all taxpayers above some minimal exempt income, as it should be.[14]

Strengthening Administration

The establishment of an effective income tax in a developing country depends largely on the successful implementation of the two devices to which the bulk of this chapter has been devoted—a withholding and current payment system on the one hand and some form of "estimated" taxation of the hard-to-tax groups on the other. In addition, many conventional aspects of tax administration are also extremely important. Without attempting in any way to be comprehensive—nothing is said here, for example, about the obvious need for good staff training and an appropriate organizational structure—this section is intended simply to call attention to a few other general points that are relevant to improving income tax administration in developing countries.[15]

It was noted earlier, for instance, that before one can assess and collect an income tax one must first identify the potential taxpayers. An important aspect of improving the income tax in any country is therefore a program to bring non-filers into the system. It is important, however, not to put too much emphasis on this problem as compared to the problem of assessing and collecting taxes once potential taxpayers are on the rolls. The number of potential taxpayers is often huge. In all likelihood, however, most of them are not individually very important. Indeed, undue emphasis on adding new taxpayers to the rolls has, in some countries, resulted in a sort of "information overload," clogging up the administrative channels with masses of paper that in the end—in part perhaps because of an inappropriately low rate and exemption structure—hardly produces enough revenue to cover the cost of processing it.[16] Too much stress on expanding the tax roll may thus result in the addition of a large number of small taxpayers, at the cost of substantial diversion of administrative efforts from the more difficult and important task of assessing and collecting tax from the much smaller group evading significant amounts of tax, many of whom are probably already nominally in the system. Efforts to enroll new taxpayers should be focused on areas where there is reason to believe there are significant net revenues to be gained—and should be matched by efforts to clear the existing rolls of duplications and errors.

The principal methods usually suggested for expanding the tax roll are field censuses and unique identification systems. There is little to be said for the first of these techniques. The use of revenue officials to carry out door-to-door canvasses in selected districts looking for potential taxpayers is usually a waste of time and scarce resources. This is particularly true when, as has often proved to be the case in countries employing this technique, the basic assessment-collection system—already weak—is weakened further by this diversion of resources and thus rendered even more incapable of making effective use of any information gathered.

On the other hand, as emphasized earlier, the introduction of a system of unique taxpayer numbers is an essential part of an effective income tax, but it too is not without its dangers. In the first place, it must again be remembered that enumerating taxpayers is in no sense a substitute for taxing them. The best identification system in the world will not produce revenue if no one is out there assessing and collecting tax. It is important not to concentrate too many scarce resources on identifying non-filers in the belief that this exercise alone will be productive in revenue terms.

Secondly, if the identification system is to be used in part as an enforcement mechanism—for example, by requiring "tax clearance certificates" before issuing passports, business licenses, and other official documents—this can be done only if taxpayer accounts are well maintained and up-to-date. Indeed, the main usefulness of a computerized system of taxpayer identification numbers may be to establish a reliable system of current taxpayer accounts. Once such accounts are created and kept up-to-date, information on the state of these accounts can be used to exert pressure on taxpayers to comply through such devices as clearance certificates. In the absence of reliable internal records, however, recourse to this device has usually generated still more bureaucratic delays and opportunities for corruption and fraud (e.g., the industry of producing false tax certificates that flourishes in some countries) and produced little, if any, net administrative gain.

A final potential problem with a mass taxpayer identification program is the potential it holds for undue centralization, particularly if heavy emphasis is to be placed on computerization. It is clear that a modern income tax requires unique taxpayer identifiers, that such numbers must be issued centrally, and that maintaining taxpayer accounts centrally by computer is generally desirable. The basic advantage of a centralized administrative system is clearly the greater opportunity for control it gives to the central administration. But this can also be a serious disadvantage.

In the most fundamental terms, the essential problem facing the tax administration in a developing country is its lack of information. Much of the information needed to administer taxes fairly and effectively can *only* be obtained locally.[17] Indeed, it could be argued that there is no functioning income tax system anywhere that does not, in the end, rest on the knowledge and experience of local tax officials. Such officials, invariably underpaid and often unrespected by their superiors, are the weak point of tax administration in most developing countries. It is therefore not surprising that administrative reformers often try to bypass local administrations and to reduce the discretion open to them by centralizing operations in various ways. To some extent, indeed, this path was suggested earlier with respect to the estimated tax system.

Some centralization is obviously needed, as noted above, but in principle the purpose of collecting information centrally should be to *support* the effective decentralized administration of the tax system, not to *supplant* it. There is nothing more important in improving tax administration in most countries than strengthening local tax offices. The efforts of reformers should be aimed at utilizing local knowledge and improving coordination (and trust) between local, regional, and central administrations. As is so often the case with administrative matters, no shortcuts seem available to bypass this time-consuming and difficult task and attempts to do so may make things worse.

The legal structure of the income tax should obviously be designed to permit and support its effective implementation (Yudkin, 1973). As noted earlier, this aim is facilitated if the rate structure is relatively uniform over a fairly wide range of taxpayers. The rates should, however, be high enough at the lower end to ensure that revenue from those included in the tax net at least cover the cost of processing the associated paper. On the other hand, since a truly mass income tax is not a feasible goal, the tax should not encompass the bulk of the population—that is, it should have an exemption level above the average income level. Similarly, the law should provide for an effective withholding and current payment system and for a system of presumptive taxation along the lines discussed earlier.

In addition, the law should provide an adequate penalty structure, appeals system, and general administrative procedures. The appeals structure, for example, should be as simple as possible to provide some escape from injustice without providing an easy means of tax avoidance (through, for example, unpenalized deferral) for the well-to-do. The penalty structure should be primarily (perhaps exclusively) financial in character and probably progressively related to the amount of tax evaded and the seriousness of the offense (Oldman, 1965; Gordon, 1988). As already mentioned, for example, noncomplying withholding agents should be subject to more severe penalties since they are in effect stealing the funds of others. There should also be adequate provisions for real interest payments on delayed taxes (or refunds). All these matters obviously require a careful and systematic examination in the context of each particular country, but the general rules set out above will probably hold in all cases.

Much the same can be said of the obvious need to improve the audit and collection functions in almost every developing country. The relevant general rules in these cases may perhaps be summed up briefly as follows. Audits, to be effective, must probably be selectively based on some rational criteria,[18] and should in any case include intensive field audits conducted by well-trained officials. The usual "office audits," which amount to little more than numerical verification and/or arbitrary adjustments, as a rule do little more than delay the collection process and jam up the appeal mechanism.

More effort should also be devoted to the collection of assessed taxes. All too often collection agencies in developing countries are little more than "tellering" agencies, waiting for taxpayers to come in and pay up.[19] Effective collection is a field task, requiring intensive efforts to reduce arrears in a number of obvious (usually painful) ways that are spelled out in all manuals on tax administration. In the case of both audit and collection, considerable thought should also be given to the development and implementation of quantitative criteria for appraising the degree of success achieved by different district offices.

This is one sort of "targeting" that seems to be inadequately utilized in most countries.

Conclusion

Two themes run through the subjects discussed in this chapter. The first is that improving income tax administration is an essential part of income tax reform in any country: without administrative improvement, it is simply not possible to have a meaningful direct tax system. To say this is no doubt to repeat a cliché. But it is also a fact, and one that must be kept constantly in mind in considering the merits of the varied and ingenious policy ideas that are inevitably suggested in the course of a major tax reform effort.

The second theme, perhaps less obvious to those who have not gone through the exercise in detail, is that the administrative constraint requires that taxes be kept as *simple* as possible if they are to be implemented effectively. Moreover, the highest aim that can realistically be achieved is likely to secure at best a degree of "rough justice" in the allocation of the cost of government among taxpayers. Most fancy schemes to improve tax administration, for example, collapse of their own weight—by creating information overload (elaborate "cross-checking" schemes), by overcentralizing (rigid "master tax roll" schemes), or by postulating miracles (the instantaneous creation of a well-paid, well-trained group of "incorruptible" officials): see also Chapter 15 below.

In the end, the main lesson emerging from this discussion is that reformers, whether concerned with "policy" or "administration" (what is the former without the latter?), should as a rule be very *risk averse.*[20] Recommended changes should be considered carefully to ensure that their full (or, more commonly, partial) introduction will not damage revenue yields severely or produce unexpected (and undesired) inequities. There are too many instances, for example, of "all-or-nothing" computerization schemes messing up a functioning revenue system to be comfortable about proposals that rely solely on the merits of the magic machine. Tax reformers, like peasants whose survival depends upon their ability to wrest a minimal amount of sustenance from an uncertain environment, should introduce change with caution, incrementally, and experimentally, in order to avoid the fate traditionally foretold for those who tackle the unknown with undue hubris.

This counsel of caution does not mean nothing can be done, and even less that nothing should be done. But it does mean that not much can usually be done quickly and that considerable thought and effort have to be devoted to institutionalizing and implementing even the most desirable reforms before serious—and in the worst cases, irreversible—mistakes are made. An essential element of any meaningful tax reform is thus a careful, detailed, and realistic study of the limits and potentials of the administrative system that is expected to implement it, as developed further in Chapter 15 below.

9   A New Look at Indirect Taxation

Recent developments make another look at the old topic of indirect taxation in developing countries worthwhile. Consumption taxes in general, and indirect taxes on consumption in particular, have received a much better press over the last few years than was the case earlier.[1] Even the regressivity of consumption taxes, their major drawback to many, has been increasingly questioned in recent years (Browning, 1978; Whalley, 1984).

The dominance in developing countries of indirect consumption taxes over the more modern taxes on income and profits was long considered to be little more than an unfortunate reflection of underdevelopment. This lapse would, it was thought, be rectified as these countries moved closer to the exalted status of the industrial countries, where such taxes provide a much smaller share of total revenues. Renewed concern for economic growth in recent years, however, has reemphasized the virtues of taxing consumption rather than income. The new-found glamour of consumption taxes in industrial countries, as well as the growing disillusion with income taxes, has definitely influenced recent thinking in some developing countries (Tanzi, 1987a; Gandhi et al., 1987).

A second reason for reconsidering the role of indirect taxes is that a small but significant literature has developed which emphasizes the potential virtues of selective taxes on the consumption of particular goods and services. This literature stresses the potential (first-best) allocative role of excises in correcting externalities, their obvious administrative advantages in developing countries, and the optimal tax (second-best) argument for non-uniform commodity taxation.[2] Each of these arguments casts doubt on the long-accepted view that a uniform commodity tax, such as a general sales tax, is in principle better—more "modern"—than a differentiated set of taxes on goods and services.

Finally, and in some ways most importantly, we know more now than we did fifteen or twenty years ago about how indirect tax systems actually function in developing countries.[3] Increasing familiarity with reality has led to increasing skepticism about the validity of some of the tax reform advice that has traditionally been offered to developing countries. This new cynicism may not, in the end, prove to be any better founded than the old optimism, but it does suggest that it may be worth re-examining traditional views in light of our increased awareness of the severity of the administrative constraint on tax reform in developing countries.

A Quantitative Overview

The most important single fact about indirect taxes in the developing economies is the dominant role they play in the revenue system of almost every country. Indirect taxes provided over half of total central government revenues—and an even higher proportion of tax revenues—in two-thirds of the developing countries in the 1980s. While taxes on international trade (mainly import taxes) were important, particularly in Africa, domestic taxes on goods and services were as prominent in the revenue systems of many developing countries. Selective taxes on goods and services—notably those on the traditional excise products (alcohol, tobacco, and fuel)—retained their role as important revenue producers in most developing countries. By the early 1980s, however, at least seventy developing countries had also introduced general sales taxes, and in forty countries the general sales tax produced more than 10 percent of central government revenue in 1983.

In contrast, in only two of the twenty industrial countries for which comparable information was available did taxes on foreign trade produce more than 10 percent of total central government revenue; in only four such countries did domestic taxes on consumption yield over 30 percent of revenue; and in only five did the yield from all indirect taxes exceed this figure. On the other hand, all but one of the industrial countries had a general sales tax, and in most the sales tax yielded more than 10 percent of central government revenue.[4] Indirect taxation thus remains a much more important source of revenue in developing countries than in industrial countries, although the structure of indirect taxes is very different in the two groups. Developing countries as a rule rely on import duties, excises, and sales taxes, while in industrial countries this order is reversed.

Although this picture is not very different in broad outline from that twenty years earlier, the number of developing countries with general sales taxes and the revenue importance of those taxes has greatly increased. In the late 1960s, twenty-three developing countries had no revenue from general sales taxes (Due, 1970); by 1983, thirteen of these twenty-three countries had such taxes in place. Almost three-quarters of developing countries (seventy out of ninety-five) had general sales taxes in 1983 compared to only 60 percent (thirty-four out of fifty-seven) in the late 1960s. This trend has since continued.

"The value-added tax," according to Goode (1984, p. 157), "is the most important tax innovation of the second half of the twentieth century." In line with this perception, an increasing number of developing countries—such as Indonesia and Turkey—have converted their sales taxes to value-added taxes (VAT). The continuing introduction and evolution of general sales taxes, and especially of value-added taxes, has been the outstanding feature in development taxation in recent years. In 1977, for example, sixteen out of twenty-six countries in the Caribbean and Latin America had sales taxes of some description (Cnossen, 1977). By 1983, twenty-four out of twenty-nine developing countries in the Western Hemisphere had such taxes. Similarly, in the early 1970s five developing countries in Latin America had some form of value-added tax (Due, 1976). A few years later, there were eleven such countries (Goode, 1984). VAT is clearly on the move, in the developing as in the developed world.

Despite this trend, however, it is important not to overemphasize the role of general sales taxes in developing countries. Many such taxes amount to little more than a new label on an old package of indirect taxes, with most revenue continuing to come from imports and a few traditional excise goods. The growing popularity of value-added taxes in developing countries sometimes reflects a change more in form than in substance. The VAT introduced in Guatemala in 1983, for example, can hardly be said to have advanced the course of rational indirect taxation in that country in view of its disastrous effects on revenue collection and the complete failure to match the changed tax structure with an appropriately changed administration (Bird, 1985).[5]

A recent detailed examination of the tax structure of eighty-two developing countries found that not only is there no correlation between the share of indirect taxes in GDP and per capita income—a familiar result (Due, 1970)—but that there is also no correlation between the share of general sales taxes in GDP and per capita income (Tanzi, 1987). Moreover, in many instances, this study found that the so-called "general" sales taxes in most developing countries collected half or more of their revenue from imports and probably did not reach more than 20 percent of *domestic* value added.[6] On average, as noted earlier, traditional excises were more important revenue producers than general sales taxes. Over 90 percent of excise revenue in most countries comes from petroleum products, alcoholic beverages, and tobacco products.

Import duties continue to be the most important single source of revenues in developing countries. Although a relative decline in the importance of these levies is observable in higher-income developing countries, the traditional argument that this decline can be attributed simply to changing income levels and accompanying changes in the structure of production has been recently questioned. Instead, it has been argued that this decline largely reflects deliberate policy choices by individual countries, particularly with respect to import exemptions and the degree to which import taxes and domestic taxes on goods and services are substitutes for each other (Tanzi, 1987). Since, as noted earlier, the base of most sales taxes in developing countries consists largely of imports in any case, the distinction between the two can easily be overdone. The traditional "tax handles" view (Musgrave, 1969) that the degree of fiscal dependence on trade taxes is closely related to the degree of economic development still has considerable explanatory power (Greenaway, 1981, 1984). To put this point another way, collection costs play an important role in determining the "optimal" tax structure for different countries. Even the old question of the changing role of import taxes in the process of development has thus been reopened in recent years.[7]

Issues in Excise Taxation

Another old question that has recently been reexamined is the choice of specific versus ad valorem rates. The conventional view is that there should be almost exclusive reliance on ad valorem taxes, particularly in the inflationary conditions found in many developing countries. But a strong case may be made for maintaining specific rates in some instances, largely on the administrative grounds that should—but often do not—shape tax design in developing countries.[8] Such rates should of course be indexed to avoid the obvious problems of erosion with inflation.[9]

The traditional view is that specific tax rates discriminate against cheaper varieties, and that this is a bad thing because it is inequitable. The "new view" is that ad valorem taxes tend primarily to reduce product variety and quality since the demand for higher priced goods is more elastic. The appropriate tax policy is thus to use specific rates to raise revenue and ad valorem rates only when it is desired for nonfiscal purposes to affect quality and product variety.[10] The appropriate rate structure of indirect taxes on efficiency grounds thus appears to be almost the opposite to that implied by the traditional concern with equity.

Similar conclusions may be reached on rather different grounds. Lower ad valorem taxes on such widely consumed beverages as beer or wine, which may seem indicated on equity grounds, to some extent work against the presumed aim of maintaining the right "tax-intoxication relationship"—a goal that can be achieved only by specific rates related to the strength and intoxicating effects of various alcoholic beverages (Cnossen, 1981). In contrast, the "optimal" tax system for alcohol would appear to be to put the lowest tax on the products with the highest elasticity, which in general means more on beer and less on spirits (Clements, 1983). This conclusion assumes, however, that there are no externalities associated with the consumption of alcohol, since most alcohol-related costs are borne directly by the individual (or his family). This assumption seems untenable unless no associated medical or policing costs are borne by taxpayers in general, although it may not be too unreasonable in many developing countries. On the whole, if excises are imposed to reflect negative externalities, specific rates are required.

Finally, as Shoup (1983, p. 262) has noted, the social costs associated with both alcohol and tobacco imply that "being poor should not entitle one to an unlimited license to create negative externalities." This position may be contrasted with the strong equity argument against sumptuary taxes in developing countries made by others (McLure and Thirsk, 1978).[11] The "pricing" role of selective taxes has been particularly emphasized with respect to the taxation of motor vehicles and fuel (Smith, 1975; Linn, 1979)—although in practice very little has been done along these lines in any country.

On the whole, it is hard to know what to make of this mixed bag of recent contributions on excise taxes.[12] It seems fair to say, however, that sweeping condemnation of the sumptuary taxation of alcohol and tobacco offers little guidance to what should be done in any particular developing country.

Unfortunately, little attention has been paid to these questions in developing countries. The sumptuary rationale for heavy taxes on traditional excise products appears to be important in most Asian indirect tax systems, for example, although Asher and Booth (1983) express skepticism as to the realism of this rationale in view of the low price elasticity of demand for such goods and quote with approval Due (1970, p. 63) to the effect that "the primary argument for excises on alcoholic beverages and tobacco products is their revenue productivity." In a sense, however, all the observed low price elasticity that underlies this revenue productivity demonstrates is that the tax rate is still some distance below the maximum-revenue rate (Shoup, 1983). The observed reluctance in many countries to maintain the real level of sumptuary taxes in the face of inflation—a reluctance frequently castigated by experts urging ad valorem taxes—also casts doubt on the view that all these levies really constitute is a simple way to gouge the poor.

Those who advocate higher taxes on alcohol on social grounds in developing countries (Marshall, 1982) are thus not necessarily talking hypocritical nonsense, especially when higher alcohol taxes may not be regressive anyway.[13] As always, detailed, quantitative study, not sweeping generalization, is needed to advance knowledge and to formulate good tax policy in this important and unduly neglected area of indirect taxation in the developing economies.

Indirect Taxes and the Poor

This point may be further illustrated with reference to the incidence of indirect taxes. As noted in Chapter 5 above, on average, taxes—mainly indirect taxes—took around 10 percent of the incomes of the urban poor, and a bit less of the incomes of rural poor. Interestingly, Jamaica was found to be an exception in both respects, with taxes on the poor being close to 20 percent of income throughout the island, with indirect taxes accounting for almost all the taxes paid by the poorer half of the population (McLure, 1977).

A more recent study found the incidence of Jamaica's indirect taxes to be proportional, or even mildly progressive, within the poorer half of the Jamaican populace, except perhaps for the very lowest decile, where transitory circumstances reduced the significance of the results

(Wasylenko, 1987). As usual, this outcome is the result of the complicated interplay of the effects of the quite different tax ratios found for different indirect taxes—some (e.g., gasoline taxes) rising with income, some (e.g., tobacco taxes) falling, and some remaining essentially flat. Because traditional excises are often the largest revenue producers in the indirect tax system of developing countries, the precise incidence attributed to these taxes is an important determinant of the overall impact of the fiscal system on the poor. As noted in Chapter 5, however, their incidence varies sharply from country to country, depending on the specifics of local consumption patterns and tax structures. Generalizations about incidence based on judgments about the progressivity or regressivity of particular levies are misleading, even if one ignores the many problems with conventional incidence studies.[14]

In the end, as with so many questions of development policy, the distributional impact of indirect taxes in any developing country comes down to a question of the relative *quantitative* importance of different tax and income characteristics. Such matters cannot be decided on a priori grounds. Textbook advice to discriminate between income groups through higher taxes on goods with higher income elasticities and low price elasticities is as uselessly simplistic as the judgment in Chenery (1984, p. 84) that "in most cases the [existing] structure of indirect taxation is markedly regressive."

A related issue on which there is substantial divergence in the literature is whether commodity tax rates should be uniform or differentiated. Rate differentiation (of different types) has been urged on efficiency grounds, on distributional grounds, and even on stabilization grounds (Asher and Booth, 1983). Many developing countries have, it appears, listened to this advice, at least to the extent of introducing progressive sales and excise tax rates.

A strong case may be made against using rate differentials in a general sales tax in order to achieve distributive ends, essentially because any equity gains from differentiation are likely to be more than outweighed by the additional administrative costs entailed (Cnossen, 1982).[15] On the other hand, in most developing countries there are very substantial differences in consumption patterns between income groups that can be differentially taxed through sales taxes. Moreover, in developing countries one cannot say, as did Cnossen (1982, p. 213) in an article concerned with developed countries, that "whatever meagre progressivity may be achieved by a differentiated sales tax rate structure can be attained far better through a small change in the income tax." With respect to the poor, who are outside the income tax, this statement is not true. With respect to the rich, it assumes that the income tax is in fact an effective instrument of redistribution—a proposition on which Chapter 7 casts substantial doubt.

The sort of research needed to answer the key questions of indirect tax policy in any country—what is to be taxed? at what rates?—may be illustrated by a recent series of studies of India and Pakistan. The approach in these studies derives from the optimal commodity tax literature, in which the aim is to raise a given revenue in such a way as to minimize the welfare loss, subject to socially determined distributional weights.[16] As a rule, this literature yields such general guidelines to taxation that their application to any real-world case tends to be either obscure or else dependent on so many specific assumptions as to be a most unpromising guide to reform in the context of a developing country. Nonetheless, this method may produce some interesting, if tentative, policy conclusions.

The first step in the analysis is to calculate the effective tax rates—in itself not an easy task, particularly since the impacts of taxes on intermediate goods must be traced through an input-output system in order to calculate the final tax components of different products. The taxation of inputs under pre-retail stage sales taxes often produces a quite different pattern of indirect tax incidence than the nominal rate structure would suggest. Food grains, for example, are not taxed at all by India's central excises; nevertheless, these products were found to bear taxes ranging from 1.5 percent to 3.6 percent (Ahmad and Stern, 1983). On the whole, India's indirect tax system, when the effects of all subsidies and input taxes were taken into account, was found to be progressive, although less so than had been indicated in the major previous study, which followed more traditional methods (Chelliah and Lall, 1978). Similar results were found in a more limited study along similar lines in Jamaica (Bird and Miller, 1989a).

The second stage of the analysis involves the examination and evaluation of possible alternative indirect tax structures. Unsurprisingly, the major conclusion emerging from this exercise is simply that "the marginal social cost of taxing different goods is quite sensitive to distributional value judgments. Cereal subsidies, for example, would be unattractive if one has little concern for inequality but more attractive otherwise" (Stern, 1984). While it is not always immediately clear what such results tell us, in the case of India Ahmad and Stern (1983) felt comfortable in recommending reductions in taxes on fuel and increases in taxes on milk products. In Pakistan, a similar analysis concluded that any degree of concern for inequality at all made wheat and sugar poor candidates for increased taxation compared to, say, meat and eggs (Ahmad, Leung and Stern, 1984).

While such specific results are—as is common with optimal tax work—very sensitive to the functional forms used in estimation, a particularly interesting outcome of the analysis of India was that a shift to a uniform value-added tax (VAT) would increase the price of many essentials and hence reduce the expenditures of the poorest rural households by almost 7 percent and those of the poorest urban groups by about 5 percent. Ahmad and Stern (1983) concluded: "The only value judgment for which it [such a shift] would be considered optimum would be that involving no concern whatsoever for income redistribution in favor of the poor." These results ignore the administrative complications of differentiated rates, but nonetheless suggest strongly that there is a distributive case for exempting certain basic food products.

Although less sophisticated, the analysis of the effects on a sample of low-income households of introducing different variants of a proposed new general consumption tax (GCT) on value-added lines in Jamaica outlined in Chapter 5 above yielded similar results. This study too found that replacing the present differentiated taxes by a uniform GCT not only increased taxes on all low-income households as a group but also slightly increased the regressivity of Jamaica's already regressive consumption tax system. Assuming that all food was exempt completely reversed these results and lowered taxes on low-income families. This exercise thus suggested that at least some additional exemptions from the Jamaican GCT beyond unprocessed foods (and services) were warranted on distributional grounds.

The Jamaican results, like those for India and Pakistan, suggest strongly the potential impact on the poor of particular changes in the design of indirect taxes. Even though the greater part of basic foodstuffs are usually *not* consumed by the poor, in the face of the strong direct impact on the poor of taxes on such foodstuffs, concern for their well-being often suggests the need for their exemption.[17]

The main conclusion to be drawn from such exercises, however, is simply that detailed expenditure data, and close attention to the details of tax structure, are needed to reach such conclusions. Generalizations on the expected distributive impact of this or that indirect tax in developing countries are of little use in the absence of such detailed studies. There is good reason for those concerned with distributive issues to pay close attention to the details of indirect tax design in developing countries.

Conclusion

The argument of this chapter may be summed up briefly. First, indirect taxes in most developing countries, while in all likelihood not as regressive as most people seem to think, impinge on the lives of many poor people in limited, but potentially important, ways. Given that the objective of development is presumably to make the poor less poor, their proper design is thus an important question in development taxation.

Second, some of these effects are complex and subtle, and hinge on the detailed structure and administration of the tax in question.[18] Such generalizations as "income taxes are better than sales taxes" or "beer taxes are always regressive" are no help in designing or reforming tax policy in any particular country.

To make further progress on these matters, more attention needs to be paid to collecting and analyzing relevant data, with particular emphasis on trying to obtain a better understanding of the extent and nature of the variations among those classed as "the poor." All too often, the great differences *within* the poor have been neglected. There are important differences between the urban and the rural poor; between the employed and the unemployed; between those in male-headed and female-headed families; between those with and without children; between smokers and drinkers and the abstemious; and so on. If we know anything about the effects of indirect taxes on the poor in developing countries, it is that these effects often vary more with such characteristics than they do with any measure of total income or expenditure.

More detailed data on such variations is not enough, however. We also need better models of incidence patterns as well as a clearer idea than we now have of the normative relevance of the observed deviations among different groups of poor people. Do the nonsmoking poor care that their addicted colleagues pay heavy taxes? Should they? Do those who indulge care? Should anyone care? Questions such as these need more careful consideration than they have received to date in the ongoing discussion of indirect taxes in developing countries. What can be said with certainty, however, is that, contrary to what may have been thought only a few years ago, indirect taxes are important and will continue to be important in terms of their allocative and distributive effects in almost all countries.[19]

The design and reform of indirect taxes will undoubtedly continue to give rise to important economic, political, and fiscal questions in most developing countries for the foreseeable future. What is generally needed is the reform, not the replacement, of the existing structure. More use of microdata sets for incidence studies, more explicit modeling of the effects of tax substitutions in a general equilibrium setting, more thought as to the importance of the considerable horizontal inequities characterizing most indirect tax systems, and much closer attention to administrative realities—all these offer better guides to what is needed to improve policy recommendations in this area than does the search for some unique, all-encompassing solution (such as a value-added tax) to the problems with existing indirect tax systems.[20]

10   The Case for Wealth Taxes

The many words written about taxation over the centuries have not, it appears, dimmed the attraction of the subject. Ordinary citizens dislike taxes, especially those of which they are most aware, and at best view them as a painful necessity. Nevertheless, they seem fascinated by advice on how to avoid taxes and by tales of high "tax-free" living. Tax practitioners such as lawyers and accountants who earn their bread through the intricacies of the tax system of course have self-interest urging them on to further knowledge of at least some aspects of taxation. Economists turn to taxes not only for classroom examples of basic economic principles but also as instruments to achieve this policy goal, or that, or perhaps both. Tax economists as a rule have all three motivations—curiosity (morbid or otherwise) as to the varied ways the human animal reacts under "tax stress," self-interest, and a concern with economic policy—urging them to study the apparently endless ingenuity displayed by man in his unceasing efforts to tax his fellow man. No field of taxation rewards such study more than the taxation of wealth and property, nor does any area better demonstrate the huge gap between tax theory and tax practice in every country.

Both characteristics of wealth taxation—its incredible complexity and variation and the gap between theory and practice—are accurate reflections of the history and the nature of taxes on wealth and property. Taxes on wealth, especially on land, are among the oldest fiscal instruments in most countries. The varied collection of wealth taxes presently found throughout the world represents the result of centuries of accretionary adaptation to the evolving social and political milieu.

Despite its antiquity, wealth taxation has been relatively neglected in recent years. The main efforts of fiscal reformers have been directed to the goal of making the income tax the keystone of the fiscal system—in the first instance by "globalizing" it, with the ultimate aim being a truly comprehensive income tax.[1] More recently, doubt has been cast on both the attainability and the desirability of such a comprehensive income tax, even in developed countries, and a direct personal tax on expenditures has been put forth by some as an alternative ideal.[2]

The emphasis of fiscal writers on expenditure and income taxes, and their relative neglect of wealth taxes, is a fair reflection of the small and declining weight of wealth taxation in the fiscal system of most countries, high-income and low-income alike. Indeed, the only discernible worldwide trend in the wealth tax field appears to be the decline in the relative importance of wealth taxes: there is no trace of any such convergence on details of structural design as one sees to some extent in the income and sales tax fields.

To discuss all conceivable forms of wealth taxation would be a task for several books. This chapter therefore focuses on death taxes, with only passing reference to other forms of wealth taxation.[3]

The Goals-Instruments Approach

As noted in Chapter 2, the tendency of experts charged with designing fiscal instruments is usually to assume some objective—for example, the attainment of "horizontal equity" or of some given degree of income redistribution—and then to appraise different designs in terms of how well they satisfy the assumed objective or goal. This instrumental approach to questions of tax design is a substantial improvement over the alternative approach of copying what was done in some other country or what appears in some textbook. Indeed, as argued in Chapter 2, designing the optimal tax system for any country in fact requires the adoption of such an instrumental perspective to a considerable extent. A danger with this approach, however, is that one may become so engrossed with some particular end that one forgets that any specific tax measure as a rule affects not one but many ends.

Advocates of wealth taxation are commonly accused of making precisely this error by those who oppose such taxation. They are said to be seeking "equity" at the expense of "economic growth." Those who argue this way often appear to think that merely raising this possible conflict is sufficient to make their point. Such is not the case, however. There is no reason to expect a simple "trade-off" between these two vaguely defined goals of "equity" and "growth." As suggested in Chapter 1, the two are interdependent in a complex fashion that cannot be satisfactorily analyzed without at least the implicit quantification of all relevant goals and of the effects of various tax (and other) instruments on their attainment.[4]

Even the formal solution of such problems at present generally lies far beyond the capacity of public finance economists, except under the most stringent (and unrealistic) conditions. The value of approaching the design of tax structures in this way lies not in the answers it yields but rather in the perspective it provides on the proper task of public finance research. In the case of wealth taxes, as in many other instances, as Shoup (1969, p. 480) says, "the conflicts usually cited arise not because the goals are inherently incompatible but because the instruments assumed available are too few, or their values too constrained, or their effectiveness zero or negative for certain ranges of their values." One task of would-be wealth tax reformers is to eliminate or reduce this apparent conflict of goals, either by inventing new tax instruments—and in no field have more novel taxes been designed, at least on paper[5]—or, more realistically, by putting the appraisal of wealth taxes in the context of the tax system as a whole.

Within this general framework, the broad goals usually assigned to wealth taxes include the following: (1) to complete the income tax system;[6] (2) to tax wealth in its own right; (3) to achieve certain social goals; (4) to achieve certain economic goals; and (5) to produce revenue.

Wealth and Income Taxes

Wealth taxes may be viewed as complements to income taxes in two senses: administratively and structurally. No income tax is perfectly administered, and, as emphasized in Chapter 7, most are particularly deficient with regard to taxing income from capital. Even the best-run and most comprehensive income taxes do not tax accretions to wealth (capital gains) as they accrue, and most income taxes do not tax accrued gains if the property is held until death. Some substantial wealth holders also report such low incomes that subjecting them to income taxes alone may not be sufficient.[7]

Some taxation of wealth may thus be justified to make up for recognized but practically unavoidable defects in income taxes.[8] An annual tax on net wealth, taxes on inheritances and gifts, and even such a crude gross wealth tax as the real property tax have all been supported at times on these grounds—the last-named, for example, as a means of making all those with "a stake in the community" (as measured by their property holdings) contribute to the support of public functions, particularly at the local level (see Chapter 12).

A more refined argument is that an income tax that treats income from all sources equally, as a true "global" income tax is supposed to do, is unfair because income earned by labor is less "pure" (or net) than income earned from capital (e.g., because of the lack of explicit provision for the costs of acquiring and maintaining "human capital"). Furthermore, income from wealth is compatible with leisure in a way income from labor clearly is not, and it also has more "lasting power" in the sense that it does not depend on the continued ability of the taxpayer to put forth effort. As mentioned in Chapter 7, this line of thought has led to preferences for earned income in some countries. The same arguments may also be used to support an annual tax on the stock of capital.

The possession of wealth, it may be argued, carries with it a degree of security, independence, influence, and social power that is not adequately measured by the flow of realized money income to which it gives rise. Income and wealth are not simply alternative ways of measuring the same reality (with different time subscripts). The taxation of income—always in practice a partial tax, if only because leisure is excluded from the tax base—cannot adequately substitute for the taxation of wealth. Wealth constitutes, at least to some extent, an independent tax base that is appropriately tapped by an annual tax on net wealth.

The Social Case for Taxing Wealth

Most arguments both for and against wealth taxes focus on the alleged relation of these taxes to other social and economic goals. It is in this larger arena that most of the verbal battle over such taxes takes place, with proponents touting their social and economic virtues and opponents denigrating them. Economists are not well suited to sit as judges in this battle, because most players on both sides base their cases on value judgments rather than on empirical evidence or economic theory.

The existing distribution of assets in a country at any point in time is largely the outcome of historical accident, as condoned by the state and frozen in law. The result of this pattern of distribution of initial wealth is that many of those successful in life stand not on their own feet but on the shoulders of their fathers.[9] "Equality of opportunity" is admittedly a rather fuzzy concept (Klappholz, 1972), but its attainment, however attenuated in practice, is a legitimate goal of public policy in all democratic countries. Life may be a lottery, and it is well known that people accept the legitimacy both of there being big winners in a lottery and of the need for big prizes to keep people participating. But those who take part in lotteries must believe they are fairly run. One role of the state is to improve the fairness of the lottery of life; and one way to do so is through direct taxation of inherited wealth.

The best tax instrument for this purpose might be a virtually confiscatory tax levied when accumulated wealth is passed from the original accumulator to someone else by gift or bequest. The tax should be levied on the heir (or donee), not on the estate as such. It should also be graduated in accordance not only with the amount transferred on any one occasion but also with the total amount of such transfers received by any individual throughout his or her life. In other words, it should be some form of "accessions tax" (Andrews, 1967; Sandford, Willis, and Ironside, 1973).

Furthermore, there seems no reason for any favoritism at all to close relatives. On the contrary, since relatives are the recipients of most gratuitous transfers, they should be reached, in the name of increased equality of opportunity, by this tax. Even full taxation of bequests and gifts under the income tax cannot achieve this goal. Indeed, high income taxes may be perverse in their effects if they are considered to replace taxes on inherited wealth as such. Since income taxes make it harder for new entrants to breach the charmed circle of the already wealthy, they tend to perpetuate rather than diminish existing inequalities.

The other major social argument for wealth taxation leads to rather different conclusions about the optimal design of wealth tax structure. Wealth is more concentrated than income in all countries. This concentration of wealth in relatively few hands may be considered socially undesirable for a number of reasons. Great inequality may be considered unlovely in itself. Or it may be thought to represent an actual or potential danger to the economic or political system—for example through the ability of a few rich families to export capital in economic crises or to extend massive financial support to politicians or officials sympathetic to their interests.[10] The oft-mentioned fact that spreading the wealth of the few among the many would, given the relative numbers of the two groups, have little effect upon the well-being of the latter, is irrelevant. The social goal of wealth taxation is to make the rich less powerful, not the poor richer. The case for direct taxation of wealth rests on the desire to mitigate the undesirable political and social effects of the distribution of wealth arising from the system of private property.[11]

The ideal way to deal with problems arising from the undue concentration of wealth might be to reallocate wealth directly through such devices as confiscation or a true capital levy.[12] Since such drastic steps have been ruled out in most countries, the relevant question for policy designers becomes: what fiscal instrument, short of confiscation, will best reduce the (presumably) excessive concentration of wealth? One such tax would be a death tax levied at high rates on large estates, even when left entirely to close relatives. The tax base is determined not by how much is left to any one person but by the size of the total estate.

The possible alternative of an inheritance tax with steeply graduated rates according to the size of the legacy is less desirable because most of the alleged evils of concentration remain even when formal legal title is divided among a number of heirs. The root of the problem is the size of the estate itself, so it is that which must be taxed. Annual net wealth taxes, capital gains taxes, and taxes on capital income may also of course have a role to play in diminishing the build-up of such large masses of wealth in the first place. But short of a revolution the only feasible fiscal instrument that can be aimed explicitly at wealth concentrations in most countries is a high-rate estate tax.

This line of discussion usually gives rise to two sorts of objections: philosophical and economic. The more important is the philosophical. To some people, the inequality of wealth (and income) is an ugly, unnecessary, and undesirable accretion on the social and economic system. To others, it is a reflection of the inevitably unequal abilities of men and of the just distribution of rewards in the market economy (Wagner, 1977). Put another way, some believe that property is, in the final analysis, a creation of the state—a privilege granted by the community, not a natural right (Pigou, 1947). Others believe that the possession of property is a natural intrinsic right of man and that family wealth is a dynastic trust, the perpetuation of which is in the national interest. There is no easy way to reconcile these opposing views. There are no simple answers to the age-old question of what is a just or equitable distribution of income and wealth, although it is, in the end, this question that governs what a society does to achieve such possible social goals as reducing the concentration of wealth.

Economic Aspects of Wealth Taxation

The only arguments vaguer and more nebulous than those used to support wealth taxation on social and equity grounds are those used to attack it on economic grounds. Undoubtedly, the most politically potent argument against wealth taxes, especially in developing countries, is that they deter private saving and investment.

Many think the freedom to dispose of one's property is a necessary incentive to the accumulation of capital. Restricting this freedom through taxing wealth, even at death, will, it has been argued, deter saving and investment tremendously. This is at best a highly oversimplified view. The desire to accumulate wealth springs from many sources—desire for power, fame, or income, for example, or the desire to accumulate for the sake of accumulation, or to pass on wealth to one's heirs, or to maintain and increase the family fortune. All these motives are at play simultaneously. Analysis of the effects of wealth taxes on economic behavior is even more obscure and difficult than the analysis of income taxes, but the consensus appears to be that wealth taxes—whether low-rate taxes levied annually or high-rate taxes levied at death—are unlikely to have much effect on the work/leisure choice, the savings/consumption choice, or the choice of what sorts of assets to acquire.[13]

In particular, wealth taxes are likely to have less adverse effects on incentives than income taxes of equal yield paid by the same people.[14] Indeed, since wealth taxes constitute a heavier burden on low-yielding than on high-yielding assets, they should in principle act as a stimulus to utilize assets more productively. This idea has been exploited extensively in the literature on agricultural land taxes (and to a lesser extent with respect to the pervasive underutilization of industrial equipment in developing countries), though again there is no empirical evidence worthy of the name in any country.[15] Nevertheless, it is safe to say that there is as good (or bad) an economic case for, as there is against, wealth taxes.[16]

Two other economic aspects of wealth taxation often give rise to concern: the first is their effect on small family-owned businesses and the second is their effect on international capital flows. The alleged effects of death taxes on family businesses seem greatly overstated.[17] Moreover, what death taxes "destroy" is not productive capital but the maintenance of family fortunes through the generations. Family ownership often means family management, and there is little reason to believe that entrepreneurial genius is genetically derived. Indeed, from the point of view of a country, it might be a good thing if death taxes forced changes in the management and ownership structure of more companies than seems likely.[18]

A common feature of the structure of taxes on wealth transfers is the differentiation of rates in accordance with the relationship between donor and donee. Invariably in such systems the rates applied to spouse, children, and other immediate family members are much lower than those applied to more distant relatives and strangers. The result is that the more an estate is left concentrated in the hands of direct descendants, the lighter the tax will be—an outcome which is directly contrary to the reasons for taxing such transfers in the first place. Since the natural propensity of people is to leave most of their wealth to their direct heirs anyway, such provisions reduce the effective tax rate to very low levels on most transfers.

One rationale for thus emasculating this important part of the wealth tax system may be that policy-makers agree with the dynastic concept of the family. Another may be to recognize adequately the contribution and needs of the spouse and minor children—although this does not explain tax-free transfers to children who have reached the age of majority. A final possible rationale is that the tax is intended to tax "windfalls," that is, accretions to wealth which, because of their unexpected nature (e.g., a bequest received by a distant relative or a stranger) are considered to reflect a particularly high degree of "ability to pay." Presumably the idea is that because the bequest was unexpected, the incentive effects of taxing it will be minor—although it is not clear that this argument holds for the testator also.[19] In any case, the "windfall" argument, despite its apparent influence on tax structures in many countries, is weak.

The other economic aspect of wealth taxes mentioned above as giving rise to concern is their effect on capital flows. This is indeed a potentially serious problem. Any tax on capital may in theory induce internationally mobile domestic capital to migrate (and foreign capital to stay out) until the overall rate of return on capital has risen by enough to offset the tax—in other words, until the tax has been shifted to consumers or less mobile factors of production such as workers. This argument presumes that a uniform rate of return on capital is set by international market forces, a considerable oversimplification of reality, and depends on other restrictive assumptions common to general equilibrium models. Nevertheless, there is some truth in the view that wealth taxes may affect international capital flows in an undesired fashion.

Although such effects are likely to be small in the context of all the factors affecting such flows in any country and could presumably be offset if desired (e.g., by marginal exchange rate changes), this problem precludes imposing drastic wealth taxes in the absence of an effective exchange control system. Indeed, wealth taxes, like those on capital income, have often been lowered on these grounds to what may be labeled an internationally competitive or "least common denominator" level. The increasing interdependence of today's world limits the role of redistributive fiscal policy by encouraging the establishment of such "least common denominator" tax systems which press lightly on capital and on the well-to-do, who have more avenues of escape than the less mobile sectors of the economy.[20]

The Revenue Dimension

A final goal of wealth taxation is to produce revenue. In most countries, as already stated, taxes on personal wealth do not produce much revenue. This fact, used by some as a reason to argue these taxes might as well be abolished, has been turned into a virtue by others who have argued that this small revenue yield means that even the most drastic effects of such taxes on saving, investment, and other aggregate economic magnitudes will be so small as to be invisible in the larger picture. Moreover, the revenue yield of these taxes is irrelevant to their presumed main purposes—that is, to supplement the income tax and to regulate the distribution of wealth. Indeed, if heavy death taxes were successful in breaking up large estates, no revenue would be collected from them at all.

What has been less often noted, however, is the potential importance of the contribution to total tax progressivity of even small wealth taxes which, however defective their administration, are paid almost exclusively by the richest groups in society. A study of Bolivia, for example, found that even the very weak death taxes in that country collected a significant amount of revenue from the top 1 or 2 percent of the population and that this tax constituted a significant fraction of the total personal taxes paid by this select group (Musgrave, 1981).[21] Taxes on personal wealth, even though their aggregate revenue yield is usually small (and inelastic), may constitute an important part of the total taxes paid directly by the wealthiest people in a country. Insofar as the task of the tax system is to make the rich relatively poorer, wealth taxes in principle (and sometimes even in practice) have an important role to play even in the poorest countries.

The Administrative Constraint

In all countries the easiest component of personal wealth to tax—and thus the component that is in reality the most heavily taxed, even under allegedly general wealth taxes—is real property. There are essentially two administrative problems in wealth taxation: the first is to locate the assets and the second is to value them.[22] On both grounds real property is the easiest asset to deal with. All other assets—personal property, assets abroad, securities, cash, family businesses—tend to be much harder to locate and (usually) to value, once located. Even when such assets as automobiles and (non-bearer) securities are registered, it is a formidable administrative task to bring together the information bearing on a particular taxpayer in one place.

The viability of net wealth and death taxes thus rests on the existence of an adequate and up-to-date real property valuation system.[23] In one sense, the taxation of real property should be relatively easy, since the object of taxation is not only visible but immovable. In another sense, however, such taxation is extremely difficult because of the problems in valuing it satisfactorily: no two parcels are identical; for many classes of property there are relatively few transactions, and they are often not very representative; owners have a direct financial interest in undervaluation, which makes reliance on either self-assessment or official assessment risky—the latter because of the susceptibility of (usually low-paid) assessors to corruption. Even when well and honestly run, real property valuation is as much an art as a science.

Despite such problems, it is, as many countries have demonstrated, perfectly feasible to operate a satisfactory tax on real estate provided the tax is relatively low-rate and uniform, without sharp differences in effective rates among and within classes of property (Fitch, 1965). The weaker the administrative apparatus, the simpler the tax must be if it is to operate successfully. As stressed in Chapter 15 below, complex taxes run by poor administrations tend to produce inequitable, and often allocatively undesirable, results. For this reason, a recent study concluded that the road to more effective land taxes in developing countries lies in simple, even crude valuation techniques and tax structures rather than the more complex taxes often proposed (Bird, 1974). This advice does not necessarily preclude such relatively simple structural devices as the exemption of low-valued properties (Holland and Follain, 1985), but it does suggest that very refined proposals (e.g., to deter land speculation through carefully structured land taxes), stand little chance of success (Smith, 1977).

Beyond real property, the most important administrative component of a wealth tax system is the development of a small core of experts to deal with such complex problems as the valuation of closely held businesses. Even if the limited technical resources available in most developing countries could be most profitably directed to such activities, however, in practice most wealth taxes will amount to little more than an additional "personalized" tax on real property. To say this is not to denigrate the potentially real value, social and economic, of such taxes; but it does suggest, in line with the earlier discussion, that it is a mistake to strive for undue refinement in the design of a tax structure that at base affects only a limited class of assets.

Conclusion

This chapter has covered, admittedly superficially, a vast area. In the first place, there is a strong case in most developing countries on social and equity grounds for taxing wealth. In fact, different arguments support all of the separate levies on wealth found in the world: the annual net wealth tax (equity); taxes on inheritances and gifts (equity and social); and even the real property tax (revenue).[24] Both the place of wealth taxes in the tax mix and the various forms of wealth tax seem adequately justified in terms of various objectives usually assigned to tax policy. This conclusion is not much altered when the economic objectives of tax policy are taken into account.

There are, however, two important constraints on wealth taxes: their possible adverse effects on international capital flows and the difficulty of satisfactorily assessing wealth. The first of these constraints counsels caution in pushing wealth taxes very hard—though not as much caution as most countries have shown. The second constraint suggests that restraint in designing elaborate tax structures is the better part of wisdom.

The most severe deficiency in the wealth tax system of most countries is the inadequate structure of their death taxes. Higher rates on larger estates and less favorable treatment of bequests to close relatives are needed if the tax is to achieve its alleged ends. Such changes seem unlikely not only for obvious political reasons but also because few issues arouse emotion so out of proportion to their importance as death taxes, perhaps because of the conjunction of two events that no one could anticipate with pleasure.[25] Despite the curious general dislike of death taxes, however, there is little question that of all taxes on wealth, death taxes are the most abused, least understood, and—from an economic as from a social point of view—most underutilized in all countries.

When substantial revenue is produced through wealth taxation, it is invariably through relatively low-rate gross taxes on real property. When wealth taxation effectively supplements the income tax as a way of allocating taxation "fairly" (in accordance with ability to pay), it is generally the net wealth tax that does the job. But the only tax that even aims at the "higher" social objectives of achieving some degree of equality of opportunity and reducing the concentration of material wealth in most countries is the death tax. Despite its inevitable deficiencies in administration, its (largely unnecessary) deficiencies in structure, its invariably small revenue yield, and its allegedly pernicious economic effects, death taxation thus remains a subject worthy of much more study and attention than it has received in most developing countries.

Local Government Finance

11   Intergovernmental Finance and Local Taxation

The structure of government in any country largely reflects its history. Countries that were once a part of a colonial empire typically have governmental structures that bear a strong resemblance to those in the former imperial power. Countries that have experienced significant regional unrest tend to be either highly centralized or quite decentralized, depending on the outcome of the resulting political upheavals.[1] Countries in which the more lucrative revenue sources have historically accrued to the central government tend to be more centralized, as do countries that have had strong centralist political regimes in power at some time in their history. Many other factors peculiar to each country affect the extent and structure of governmental institutions so that it is usually difficult, if not impossible, to detect any clear relationship between the degree of decentralization—assuming this elusive concept can somehow be pinned down quantitatively (Bird, 1986a)— and such other characteristics as the size of government and the level of per capita income.

Despite this complexity, however, virtually every country shares several important characteristics in common with respect to governmental structure. First, there is almost invariably more than one level of general government, as well as a number of more specialized governmental agencies and enterprises at each level. Intergovernmental relationships, both vertical (between levels) and horizontal (within levels), are therefore matters of concern to anyone interested in the efficient and effective operation of the public sector—although of course the relative importance of the intergovernmental dimension varies greatly from country to country.

Second, the key issue in intergovernmental relations is the same everywhere. Viewed from the perspective of the economist's concern with the efficient and equitable delivery and financing of public-sector activities, this issue may be described in terms of the assignment of functions and finances to the different levels (and instrumentalities) of government (Hartle and Bird, 1972). This way of looking at things implicitly assumes that the assignment decision is made by some benevolent higher authority in pursuit of the highest possible level of well-being for the people in the country concerned. Seen from a more politically oriented perspective, essentially the same process may be described as the allocation of the authority and responsibility for public-sector decisions among different (and possibly conflicting) power centers.[2] How questions of governmental structure are resolved in practice in any country reflects both the resolution of the myriad of political forces currently at play in that country and its past history.

A third common characteristic is that money is at the heart of intergovernmental matters in all countries. Moreover, the general nature of intergovernmental fiscal relations is also surprisingly similar across a wide range of countries. Almost invariably, countries assign more expenditure functions to subnational governments than can be financed from the revenue sources allocated to those governments (if seldom fully under their control). The result of this mismatching of functions and finances—sometimes referred to as "vertical imbalance"—is that subnational governments are generally dependent upon transfers from higher levels of government, and that dependence increases in relation to the significance of the expenditures with which they are charged.[3]

Yet another pervasive characteristic of intergovernmental relations is the problem of "horizontal balance," or the need to cope with the reality that all subnational governments are not created equal. In every country, even the smallest, there are big cities and small cities, urban municipalities and rural municipalities, rich regions and poor regions. Designing fiscal institutions to cope with this complex reality is nowhere an easy task, and it is often severely complicated in practice by historical rivalries and by such political imperatives as the need to treat even the most disparate regions uniformly.

Some countries have tried to resolve some of the resulting problems by creating a proliferation of small geographical general governments, others by dividing governmental structure more along functional lines at either the national or local level or both, and still others by interposing a third level of government and becoming more or less "federal" in structure. Each of these solutions in turn creates problems: fiscal competition (horizontal or vertical), functional fragmentation unresponsive to the wishes of the population served, and the perpetuation of spatial inequities in the provision of public services. Still more ingenuity is then called for to construct elaborate transfer mechanisms to attain an acceptable level of equity and efficiency.[4]

Even this brief catalog of some of the factors entering into the design of governments makes it unsurprising that a final common characteristic of most intergovernmental fiscal systems is that there is considerable confusion and obscurity as to exactly who is responsible for what and precisely how various important public services are delivered and paid for.[5] The complexity of governmental structure may well be inherent in the nature of the problem, but the lack of transparency commonly found in intergovernmental relations is both unnecessary and undesirable. Public-sector activities are unlikely to be efficiently provided or to be responsive to the wishes of those served unless the lines of responsibility and accountability are clearly established. Given the strains on national budgets everywhere, countries concerned to get the most for what resources they have are well advised to reconsider both the present intergovernmental assignment of finances and functions and also the way in which they bridge the resulting gap through fiscal transfers.

The Case for Local Government

Public finance economists often divide the economic functions of government into three categories: stabilization, distribution, and allocation. The stabilization function is usually considered to be inherently national in nature owing to the openness of local economies and the lack of macroeconomic policy instruments at the local level (Oates, 1972). Although concern is occasionally expressed that "perverse" local fiscal actions may offset national policy initiatives, the relatively small size of the subnational sector in most countries makes this possibility remote. Even in countries where lower-level governments are important spenders, they are usually so dependent on the national level for finance that it makes more sense to think of them in this context as part of the national government rather than as independent actors (Bird, 1980b). Only in a few federal countries with constitutionally mandated diversion of a substantial share of national revenues to lower levels might the existence of a multilevel governmental structure give rise to difficulties in macroeconomic management—and even there, as experience in developed country federations shows, there is little evidence that serious problems are likely to arise.[6]

Although distribution policy too is fundamentally a national concern, local governments have a more important role to play in this respect in part precisely because tax and expenditure policies in many countries are largely imposed from above. If a local government tax is applied in the same way and at the same rates throughout a country, as is often the case, it is really a national tax. The openness of local economies and the sparsity of the policy instruments at the disposal of their governments may afford little scope for independent local redistributive policies, but local government actions may nonetheless constitute an important part of overall national policy. Indeed, as noted in Chapter 5 above, whether and how local governments deliver basic services, and how such services are financed, may have an important impact on the level of well-being of poor people.

The basic economic argument for local government, however, rests on the inherent inability of central governments to deliver many public services efficiently. Since people have different preferences for public services—some may be more concerned with good roads and others with good schools, for example—and since many services—including roads and schools—are consumed in a spatially differentiated pattern, the most efficient allocation of public-sector resources can be secured only if such services are provided (and paid for) by governments responsible to those most directly affected (Tiebout, 1956). Economic analysis, like democratic theory, thus provides a rationale for the establishment of local governments that are responsive to the wishes of their citizens instead of being simply the instrumentalities of central planners.

Unfortunately, the strength and simplicity of this conclusion quickly dissipates when other considerations, economic and political, are taken into account. The existence of benefit and cost "spillovers" from one jurisdiction to another, for example, suggests that larger governmental units are needed to internalize such externalities. Moreover, the unit cost of collecting revenues from most lucrative tax sources is much less for national than for local governments. Offsetting these factors is the fact that the cost of political decision-making (in terms of the nonsatisfaction of preferences) rises as the population covered expands. The extreme variation in the spatial dimension of every governmental function and subfunction makes it even more likely that the "optimal" government structure is likely to be as complex in theory as it is in practice in most countries (Hartle and Bird, 1972).

The observed complexity of intergovernmental structure, however, is unlikely to be what theory suggests. State and local governments exist in the form they do and with the finances and functions they have neither to maximize democratic access to government nor to provide public services as efficiently as possible but as a result of many complex historical and institutional factors. In many countries the role played in the public finances by local governments reflects less local autonomy than the extent to which central governments have chosen, for reasons of administrative efficiency or political choice, to utilize such governments as taxing and, especially, spending agents (Bird, 1980b).

The Special Case of Federalism

Many countries have not one but two subnational levels of government. Sometimes the intermediate state or provincial level plays a more important role in the public finance picture than the municipal or local level (as in Brazil); sometimes it is less important (as in Colombia). The countries in which the state level is more important are often countries that are at least nominally "federal": examples are India, Brazil, Papua New Guinea, Argentina, and Nigeria. In such countries, most transfers from the central government go at least in the first instance to the states, and the states often have a tutelary or supervisory role with respect to the municipalities.

Such formal similarities, however, obscure the wide range of structures and relations found within federal as well as within the group of nominally unitary countries. Indeed, the difference between a "tight" federation such as Malaysia and most unitary countries is probably less than that between Malaysia and "looser" federations such as India and Brazil in which state governments have more power to act independently with respect to expenditure and taxing patterns. What matters is not the constitutional label so much as the reality of the workings of the myriad of intergovernmental relations that constitute the essence of the public sector in all countries.[7] If, as is usually the case in developing countries, the central government in the end controls the actions of subnational governments, those governments may for most purposes be considered to be more agents of the central government than independent actors.

On the other hand, where there are real geographic differences in a country there is always a certain degree of local "autonomy" in practice even if the constitutional structure is formally unitary. Central governments must work with the local governments they have. Even if the central government is ultimately responsible for the size, structure, and functioning of local governments, it is not usually possible to change these characteristics in any but an incremental fashion.[8] Since the essence of the federal finance problem is how to adjust intergovernmental fiscal transfers to achieve tolerable results in the face of a clearly nonoptimal assignment of functions and finances, the intergovernmental problem in every country is in this sense "federal" to some extent. It is only in the few "true" federations that this constraint is long-term in nature, however. In most developing countries, a closer approach to an efficient public sector can and should be attained over time by judicious and feasible restructuring of functions and finances along the lines sketched below.

Restructuring Government Functions

Few countries can contemplate a "clean slate" approach to the assignment of functions and finances to different levels and agencies of government, but almost every country can gain from reviewing the assignment question. Some countries, such as India, have institutionalized mechanisms (the Finance Commission: see Chelliah et al., 1981) which periodically reconsider important aspects of intergovernmental fiscal arrangements. Others, such as Pakistan and Papua New Guinea, have provisions for such reviews but do not in fact appear to utilize them. Still others, such as Nigeria and Colombia (Bird, 1984), have employed occasional commissions to carry out such reviews of varying scopes.

Such reviews may be useful in facilitating the adjustment of historically determined governmental structures so that they can deliver services efficiently in the changed circumstances of today. At the very least, periodic review casts light upon the often obscure and confusing labyrinth of intergovernmental finance. But even the best study can have little impact in the absence of effective implementation, and there are few countries in which central governments have an adequate informational and institutional structure to monitor what subnational governments do in their ongoing day-to-day activities, let alone to de-sign and implement significant structural changes affecting the out-come of those activities.

The first step needed to improve the allocation of scarce resources in the local government sector of most countries is thus to improve the information basis available to public-sector managers. In many countries no one has any consistent idea of the size, structure, and trends of the subnational sector, let alone of its diversity. Such igno-rance is an expensive luxury when governments everywhere are under increasing pressure to make better use of the limited resources avail-able. Not only is special study needed to provide an initial data base, but provision must also be made to have it periodically updated (often on a sample basis) as part of the regular work of national data collec-tion. Until this essential step is taken, most discussion of subnational and intergovernmental finance will continue to be conducted in an informational vacuum.

Once at least a roughly accurate picture of current reality is ob-tained, the next step is to decide what can and should be done to improve matters. Should some functions be reallocated on a geo-graphic rather than a functional basis? Should some functions be real-located to higher or lower levels of government, or the responsibility divided between them in some different way? For example, it may make sense to delegate more of the responsibility for providing urban infrastructure to local governments while making public health a na-tional rather than local function. Should a number of small local gov-ernments be consolidated into a larger unit, or should some or all of their functions (such as spatial planning and refuse disposal) be taken over by a higher-level unit? To what extent should functions be de-volved differently to different-sized cities or to urban and rural areas? Questions such as these can be answered by drawing on the relevant theoretical and empirical literature in light of the specific circum-stances and policy objectives of the country in question.[9] But such questions cannot even be posed properly in the absence of detailed and specific knowledge of how the existing governmental system is structured and works.

Finally, even if the needed information is assembled, the right ques-tions asked, and acceptable answers obtained, there remains the most difficult part of all: implementation. Particularly if it is decided to de-centralize some functions to some degree, it is essential to provide adequate institutional support—for instance, in the form of staff train-ing, operational manuals, technical assistance and support, financial support, and performance monitoring. Decentralization alone, whether it takes the form of allocating more expenditure responsibility, more fiscal resources, or both to local governments must be backed up in such ways if the results are to be socially and economically beneficial.[10]

This plea for adequate institutional support of local government should be distinguished from the view that local governments should always do what central governments want. In some countries, decentralization has been motivated in part by the desire to improve the coordination between different national government agencies operating in a particular geographic area and hence the efficiency with which they achieve national policy objectives. In others, decentralization has been motivated in part by the belief that local people should have more say in the services they receive. These two motivations are incompatible unless the locality is identical in all relevant respects to the nation as a whole—in which case the only rational motive for decentralization in the first place is to improve administrative efficiency (Bird, 1983a).

Even if, as suggested above, local governments in most developing countries can be considered agents of national policy, to the extent that such governments have access to either fiscal transfers or taxes they collect themselves, they inevitably have some degree of freedom in deciding what to do—and they are not likely always to do exactly what the central government might prefer. Such "slippage" is simply part of the inevitable price of decentralization and is presumably offset by the economic or political advantages that led to decentralization in the first place. Nonetheless, it is a matter of real concern in most countries to ensure that local governments do not stray too far out of line.

One way of dealing with this problem is, as already mentioned, to monitor their performance. School inspectors, state public works engineers, auditors, and similar officials constitute the essential front line of this effort, supported by a well-informed central ministry charged with this supervisory role and an institutional structure (municipal development funds, training schools, and technical support facilities) designed to enable local governments to carry out their assigned roles efficiently and effectively. Unfortunately, this essential infrastructure is often either missing completely or sadly neglected, with the result that the task of ensuring that the resources under the control of local governments are not wasted (at least from the central government's point of view) generally falls by the wayside.[11]

Restructuring Government Finances

Whether "own" resources or transfers are considered, the basic conclusion that emerges from reviewing the structure of intergovernmental finance in any country is invariably the same: local governments need to be given access to adequate resources to do the job with which they are entrusted, but they must also be held responsible to those who provide these resources for what they do with them.

The simplest case, at least in principle, concerns local own-source revenues. Local governments should not only have access to those tax (and nontax) sources that they are best equipped to exploit—such as real property taxes and the valorization tax (see Chapter 12)—but they should be both encouraged and permitted to exploit these sources as fully as possible. The encouragement may be provided in part by a properly designed system of intergovernmental fiscal transfers (Bird and Slack, 1983). As in the case of improving local government expenditure performance, however, infrastructural and institutional support in the form of training, central assistance with, for example, property valuation, and so on are also required. That such support is sadly lacking in most countries is not surprising, given the many demands on scarce national public sector resources. But one cannot expect undertrained, understaffed, undermotivated local authorities to perform miracles in the absence of at least a modicum of support and encouragement from above.

The situation is even worse than this in many countries. Local governments are often actively discouraged from trying to exploit local fiscal resources adequately by a wide variety of central checks, controls, and hindrances on everything from local short-term borrowing to even out cash flow to utility tariffs and local tax rates (Bird, 1980b). When local planning decisions, changes in bus routes, water charges, property revaluations, and almost everything else that affects local budgets are either mandated by, or require explicit prior approval from, some higher authority, it should not occasion surprise that little evidence of local initiative or effort is to be found. Unless local governments are given some degree of freedom, including the freedom to make mistakes for which they are accountable to their paymasters—local taxpayers or the central government, as the case may be—the development of responsible and responsive local government will remain an unattainable mirage.

There are of course dangers other than political embarrassment in permitting local authorities even limited freedom, particularly in the absence of the monitoring and supporting infrastructure mentioned earlier. One such danger is that they will attempt to extract revenues from sources for which they are not accountable, thus obviating the basic efficiency argument for their existence. To counter this inevitable tendency, the central government should deny or limit access to taxes that fall mainly on nonresidents: examples are most natural resource revenues, corporate income taxes, pre-retail stage sales taxes and, to some extent, nonresidential real property taxes (McLure, 1983). The possible overexploitation of such politically less painful revenue sources may, somewhat paradoxically, at times be offset by economi- cally motivated underexploitation, as localities competing for mobile tax bases enter into rate-reducing competition, but this outcome too is not particularly desirable in developing countries starved of public services.

The best solution to both problems in the context of most countries is to establish a uniform set of tax bases for local governments (per- haps different for different categories—such as big cities, small towns, and rural areas), with a limited amount of rate flexibility being permit- ted in order to provide room for local effort while restraining unpro- ductive competition and unwarranted exploitation.[12] It is especially important to provide adequate flexibility to exploit "good" tax bases in order to avoid the pattern seen in many countries, where the only degree of flexibility available to cope with budgetary pressure is by exploiting such economically undesirable, but available and largely unregulated, taxes as the octroi (Indian municipalities), pre-retail sales taxes (Indian states), or archaic "industry and commerce" taxes (Col- ombia before 1984). The answer to such developments is not, as in Bangladesh, to replace the undesirable octroi by a grant which then fails to expand over time (Schroeder, 1987), but rather, as in Colombia after 1984, to redesign the tax base to provide the needed flexibility in a more tolerable fashion.[13]

Whatever is done to improve the quality and quantity of local own- source resources, the reality is that most subnational governments in most countries will continue to be heavily dependent for their suste- nance on fiscal transfers from above. Unfortunately, in practice such transfers often seem ill-designed to achieve their principal objectives. These objectives may usually be summarized as permitting recipient governments to carry out their assigned expenditure functions, while encouraging fiscal effort to the extent possible and ensuring at least a reasonably even level of public service provision throughout the coun- try. Too often, those governments get most which do least to help themselves, which need the funds least, and which waste them most flagrantly. Countries concerned to make the best use of the increasingly scarce resources available for the public sector cannot afford to tolerate such inefficient transfer systems.

While the precise design of an appropriate system of fiscal transfers for any country requires a good deal of knowledge of the particular circumstances of that country, a few general principles may be stated. In the first place, if functions and finances are properly assigned, there should be no need for any general budgetary support transfers to the richest subnational governments, since they should be capable of financing their expenditures themselves, and should be required (and permitted) to do so. What this means in most countries is that the largest cities should be made to stand on their own fiscal feet as far as providing basic urban public services is concerned, as argued in Chapter 12 below.

Less wealthy localities will of course need some general budgetary support from the transfer system. Ideally, the total amount of such transfers would be determined as the amount needed to provide a "basic" service package at average unit costs less the average contribution to be expected from local fiscal sources, if exploited with average efficiency (Bird and Slack, 1983). The extent to which the central government monitors local governments to ensure they deliver the services thus financed is obviously up to it. Countries also have a good deal of discretion as to what services are included in the package to be financed, how average unit costs and average own-source contributions are calculated, the precise extent and manner in which specific local factors affecting costs or needs (e.g., area and population density) and contributions (e.g., tax base and effort) are taken into account in distributing the total among different recipient governments, and so on.

In principle, the correct assignment of functions and finances solves the vertical balance or fiscal gap problem mentioned earlier, and a basic grant system along the lines just sketched solves the horizontal balance or regional equity problem. Since these problems lie at the core of the intergovernmental fiscal dilemma in all countries, progress in these directions is essential to ensure the optimal mobilization of public-sector resources and to improve the efficiency with which those resources are allocated within the public sector as a whole.

This is by no means the end of the tale, however. As emphasized earlier, for many purposes local governments can best be considered to be acting in effect as agents implementing national policies. To some extent, the "basic local public service" package approach to general grants suggested above fits within this framework. In addition, there are a wide range of other policy areas in which local governments, either alone or in conjunction with national governments or decentralized agencies, may have an important role to play in terms of delivering public services. Education, health, and other "people" services afford illustrations in the many countries in which, for instance, local governments are supposed to maintain schools or local public health centers. In other instances, local governments are required or expected to carry out segments of such things as national transportation plans.

If local expenditure is essentially to carry out a national project, the cost might be fully reimbursed, provided there are no significant purely local benefits. Indeed, given the financial stringency of most local governments, they would probably not be in a position to undertake such work in the absence of prior funding. At the other extreme, if there are significant local benefits and little spillover, so that in effect the national government is nudging the local government into doing something its citizens presumably want anyway, any national financial assistance should take the form of a matching grant, that is, one in which the national government provides, say, $1 for each $1 provided locally. The precise matching rate might, if information is available, be varied to take into account the extent of national interest and perhaps also the fiscal capacity of the locality in question.[14]

In other instances, where projects can be expected to generate increased fiscal revenues, the most appropriate form of finance might be a loan rather than a grant, with the terms of the loan subject to similar modifications. While there is no end to the refinements and variations that may be thought of with respect to such matters, it is, as always, important not to overburden the scanty administrative resources available in most countries with overly perfect designs that are more likely to come crashing down of their own weight than to produce the desired outcomes.

Basic Principles of Reform

What individual countries choose to do with respect to reforming intergovernmental fiscal relations and subnational finances is up to them. Whatever reform is carried out, however, four basic principles might usefully be kept in mind: transparency, stability, flexibility, and incrementalism (Bird, 1983a).

To the extent possible, the obscurity and confusion endemic in intergovernmental finance in many countries should be replaced by as open and transparent a system as possible. A key characteristic of underdevelopment is the lack of information; in no area is this more true than with respect to intergovernmental finance. The short-run political advantages to those in the (partial) know about what is going on are in the long run outweighed by the social benefits of making it clearer to all participants what the rules are, and especially who is paying how much for what. In the absence of such information, attempts to improve the efficiency of the public sector in many countries are doomed to perish in the swamp of misinformation.

Second, not only should the rules be clear, they should be as stable as possible. It is not possible for anyone in the public sector to operate effectively and efficiently if he or she does not know from day to day how much money is on hand, what they can expect to get next week, exactly how their use of these funds will be assessed, and so on. Yet this is the situation in which local officials continually find themselves.[15] As noted earlier, periodic reviews of intergovernmental fiscal relations, followed by the establishment of a stable grant system for a period of time, can do much to alleviate this problem—provided, of course, that the grants thus determined are actually paid.[16] Another essential ingredient of a successful decentralization program is not only the provision of adequate technical support and supervision, as stressed earlier, but also the establishment of a central agency charged with the responsibility of monitoring local government action and needs as a whole.[17]

Rules and institutions should be stable over time. At the same time, however, perhaps somewhat paradoxically, the way in which rules are applied and institutions operate should be flexible both to respond to changing external circumstances—droughts, foreign exchange crises, etc.—and especially to cope with the complex nonuniformity that characterizes subnational governments in most countries (Bird, 1984). A capital city of three million people is not the same as a rural village of two hundred, and there is no point in pretending to treat them the same way. Similarly, two cities of equal size and wealth may be quite different in that one is well managed, while the other is a disaster. Such realities must be allowed for in the design and operation of an efficient intergovernmental finance system. Provision should exist to give more leeway to better-run localities (perhaps through special "contracts" allocating them more functions and finances with less controls), to provide the needed tutelage to laggards, to require more fiscal effort from richer areas, and so on. Flexibility in these respects within a stable framework is the hallmark of a successful system, one that can adapt to changing circumstances and make the best use of existing resources.

Finally, in most countries it may seem to be a long way from where matters now are to some of the ideals briefly sketched here. Experience shows, however, that one can sometimes get there from here, provided the attempt is made in a deliberate, planned, and incremental fashion, building on what now exists and taking into account the historical and institutional realities that explain why things are the way they are, rather than trying to leap to the brave new world of rational, ordered, and effective local government all at once. The redesign of intergovernmental finance structures, like the reform of tax systems, will never be either a glamorous or an easy task; but it is a worthwhile one for all those concerned with the effective use of public sector resources in developing countries.

12   Financing Urban Development

The growth in urban population in developing countries has meant a continued need for expansion of such traditional municipal services as protection, street lighting, and garbage removal. Larger urban concentrations require larger expenditures on such costly infrastructure as water and sewerage systems and transport networks. The massive public expenditure required to accommodate and channel urban growth does not come cheap, particularly in the larger cities, where per capita costs are higher than in smaller cities. Cities everywhere are pressed to spend more and more in satisfying the needs and demands of their increasing populations.

In developing countries the interdependence of national economic policies and urban growth patterns is clear (Linn, 1983). Policies that make urban life relatively more attractive, as do many "development" policies, may result in such an inrush of migrants as to destroy any possibility of planned and rational urban growth. National policies on population, migration, and industrialization patterns are crucial determinants of urban growth and hence of urban problems. On the other hand, the way in which urban structures develop internally may itself be a powerful determinant of national policies. A dispersed urban development pattern, for example, may require much more national investment in the provision of urban infrastructure.

The problems of urban growth in many developing countries have been exacerbated by the adoption of technologically disruptive consumption patterns (especially the automobile) from more developed countries—patterns that are increasingly being called into question even in their countries of origin. A similar phenomenon exists with regard to public services, such as water supply, housing, and many others, to which inappropriately high standards of provision, derived from the more developed countries, are applied.[1]

This upward pressure on expenditures, combined with the dominant control of revenues by the central authorities in most countries, means (as noted in Chapter 11) that local governments everywhere have become more subject to central influences both through intergovernmental fiscal transfers and controls over local borrowing and local investment decisions and through the effects of central policies on the local economy and on local expenditures and revenues. Cities have been expected to do more, and more different things, while at the same time becoming more dependent on central largess and more subject to central control.

The result has been, in almost every country, that urban governments find themselves year after year facing rising expenditures and more slowly rising revenues, particularly revenues from sources under their own control. Even if local resources happen to match local expenditures at a particular moment, the changing times which characterize development invariably again throw urban revenues and expenditures out of balance.

Conventional Solutions

Since urban managers in developing countries tend, despite their different circumstances, to see their problems in the same way as their colleagues in more developed countries, the solutions they usually put forth are also rather similar. The main solution propounded, unsurprisingly, is almost always for a greater infusion of financial resources at the municipal level. However, in the face of the strong centralizing tendencies of most national governments in developing countries (Bird, 1980b), greater transfers from the central government are usually requested rather than greater direct access to tax sources.

In contrast to the situation in the 1970s in more developed countries, where urban managers tended to ask for more tax sources and get more conditional transfers (Bird, 1977), when municipal officials in developing countries ask for more transfers, they do not usually get them—or at least not with any degree of regularity or certainty (Schroeder, 1987). Instead, what has happened in recent years in many developing countries has been a persistent upward shift of governmental functions to higher levels of government. Often this shift has taken place via a proliferation of special national autonomous agencies whose purpose is to provide various urban public services.[2]

The principal response to the perceived urban fiscal crisis in many less developed countries has thus been increased centralization (or, better, "demunicipalization")—albeit often "secret centralization" through the agency of autonomous central organizations.

An Alternative Diagnosis

Central governments in developing countries generally do not have as many degrees of freedom as those in more affluent countries. They often act less from choice than necessity. It is understandable that urban governments which must depend upon the generosity of poverty-stricken parents are likely to be disappointed. What is not so understandable, however, is the almost universal reluctance of urban managers to seek, or central governments to grant, more local autonomy with respect to raising local resources for local purposes, particularly in the largest cities.

The case for increased reliance on local effort and know-how is strong in developing countries (Lewis, 1967; Bird, 1980b). In fact, in all but the smallest countries increased reliance on local governments is less a matter of choice than necessity. The last thing the overworked central governments of developing countries need, or should want, is still more responsibility for detailed local budgetary decisions. Such governments neither have, nor have any realistic possibility of obtaining, the information needed to make such decisions intelligently, nor do they have the human resources to cope with the information even if they could get it. Furthermore, the common problem of inappropriately rigid uniformity resulting from undue centralization is more important in many developing countries than in developed countries. Recourse to local knowledge, and reliance on local responsibility, constitutes an essential part of any comprehensive attempt to cope with the problems of urban growth in the developing countries.

Big cities in developing countries should be essentially self-financing (Bird, 1984). The great bulk of the wealth and resources of most countries is concentrated in the major urban areas. If these areas cannot finance their own expansion, who can? Even recognizing the dependence of the central government in most developing countries on the same tax base, it still seems reasonable to urge that the expansion of urban services in the principal cities receive no direct financial support from the national government (other than perhaps "bridging" loans through special credit institutions for urban development: see World Bank, 1988).

Such a self-financing policy has several virtues. In the first place, it reduces the drain on scanty national resources which arises from the need to finance from the central budget expensive urban infrastructure, often to the direct benefit of a relatively small number of people. When people have to pay directly for what they get, they are less likely to want (or "need") as much as they do when they get it for (apparently) nothing. In addition to thus cutting the demand for scarce public resources, a properly structured urban self-financing policy may also add to the total amount of resources available to the public sector since, as discussed below, the more direct connection of taxes to expenditures from which they derive direct and observable benefits may lower taxpayer resistance.

Such virtuous outcomes cannot be expected to result from a simple increase in the wildly inequitable and cumbersome revenue structures with which most urban areas are now saddled. A restructured urban fiscal system—such as should accompany and underpin a restructured urban government anyway—could not only achieve these results but aid in implementing a national land management plan. The ingredients for such a system exist in bits and pieces around the world—valorization taxes in Colombia (as discussed below), vehicle taxes in (say) Singapore (Watson and Holland, 1978), local income and sales tax surcharges in some countries, urban property taxes in others (Bahl, 1979), and some forms of public utility financing in various other countries (Bahl and Linn, 1991). Such experiences may be drawn upon and adapted to particular local circumstances, given a minimal commitment of administrative resources and political will. No country has as yet really managed to get a firm grip on the problems arising from rapid urban expansion, but some countries have had successes which deserve to be more widely emulated.

While a restructured urban government system and a more genuine partnership of urban and national governments are key ingredients in any attempt to grapple with urban development, any viable approach in developing countries will also have to include substantial expansion in the revenue-raising powers of at least the bigger cities as a rule, for two main reasons. The first is simply that the hard-pressed national governments in most developing countries do not have the resources either to take on urban development themselves or to provide the needed amounts to local governments. Greater reliance on local efforts to solve local problems is not a luxury but a necessity. Secondly, and fortunately, both the human and fiscal resources to do whatever can be done can in any case best be tapped at the local level, without significantly detracting from national efforts.

Benefit Taxation and Local Self-Finance

Many cities in developing countries have been growing for decades at rates seen only in boom periods in developed countries. This rapid urbanization has put a tremendous strain on municipal finances: heavy investments in roads, sewers, aqueducts, street lighting, parks, and schools are needed if cities are to remain suitable for human existence, but there is generally no capital market from which funds can be borrowed, and national governments cannot provide adequate assistance to finance capital investments.[3]

The rapid growth of cities in developing countries arises both from their development of dynamic manufacturing and commercial sectors and from the increasing importance of education, health, and other activities that are most efficiently carried on in urban areas. The public capital requirements for creating efficient cities with "satisfactory" social services are high, but domestic saving is generally low, and there is a shortage of capital. City growth in developing countries today, for example, is usually based on transport by urban buses. For efficient transportation, the narrow streets of old central cities must be widened and new streets opened. On the edge of the growing city, streets must be extended rapidly to new factories and new housing, often single-family homes being developed slowly from original squatter settlements by owners lacking the organization, financing, and technical capacities to build more compact multifamily structures even if they wanted to do so (de Soto, 1990). If a city is to be a location of low-cost production, it needs these streets to provide transportation. It also needs adequate water and sewerage systems to protect public health, and street lighting, parks, and schools for training and social betterment. All these investments require large amounts of capital, yet they must be provided if the city is to fulfill its potential for economic development. Such investment may be desirable not only for the benefits that it yields in better living conditions and more efficient production in the city but also because it requires a great deal of unskilled labor, thus helping to ease the always heavy urban unemployment in developing countries. In addition, such public-works investment generally uses few imported materials and puts less pressure on the balance of payments than most other types of investment.[4]

In most developing countries there is no organized capital market where domestic funds can be borrowed for long periods at low interest rates to meet these heavy capital requirements. At best, a few improvements may be financed by borrowing from international lending agencies, but such funding is invariably sporadic and inadequate. Some investment funds may be provided from central government subsidies, but these are likely to be inadequate, given the usual fiscal difficulties of the central government in a developing country. Nor can cities rely heavily on the ordinary local property tax, for property assessments are usually out of date and inequitable and administration and collection weak.[5] Finally, cities cannot usually call on private enterprise to finance these investments through subdivision laws which require the urban developer to provide streets, water, sewerage systems, and so on at his own expense.[6] Workable subdivision laws in developing countries must permit new subdivisions lacking street pavement, complete water services, and sewerage connections if the people flocking to the cities are not to be forced into already overcrowded existing housing or else forced to set up shantytowns without any urban controls (or services) at all (de Soto, 1990).

The same factors that lead to the financial difficulties of rapidly growing cities in developing countries—the large influx of population and the rapid growth of modern industrial, commercial, and service sectors—also result, however, in a rapid rise in property values. This fact can be used to advantage to finance a major part of the needed municipal investment through taxing this increase in value.

A rapidly growing city in a developing country generally has many potential projects with such high social productivity that the benefits to land values may greatly exceed the costs of the project itself. In theory, taxation can recover an amount equal to the entire increase in land values, but in practice a less ambitious target seems preferable, given the desirability of securing payment of the tax before the investment is made and the uncertainties of estimating the ultimate increases in site value. Even allowing an ample margin for error in estimating benefits, however, taxation can often recover the investment and operating costs of the public agency without exceeding the realizable benefit to any individual landowner from the increased site value of his property. This presumption has in fact worked out well in the case of the "valorization" tax in Colombia.[7]

The Valorization Tax in Colombia

The valorization tax appears to have been most successful in Colombia where the greatest efforts have been made to put it on a true benefit basis, as in the city of Medellín. To do this seems to require the following elements: (1) freedom from any fixed formula for distributing the tax among property owners; (2) careful study of projects at the initial stage to determine those that will create increased site values equal at least to the cost of the project; (3) participation of property owners in the planning and execution of projects without giving them obstructionist or veto powers; (4) careful costing of projects; (5) prompt construction of projects; (6) prompt and complete collection of all taxes assessed on the property owners while the project is being built; (7) extensive publicity; and (8) a general statement of the rules for hardship cases permitting, but not requiring, reduction in tax or delayed payment in certain circumstances.

The development of a valorization system is a matter for careful planning; experience indicates the importance of starting with small projects that can be completed quickly and with certainty and thus earn taxpayer trust. Preserving popular identification between the tax and the benefits is important. If one believes Abraham Lincoln's dictum that "you can't fool all of the people all of the time," the valorization tax over the long run must have approached a benefit basis in fact as well as in belief.

There is little reason to exempt any property from the valorization tax. Exemptions of government property in Colombia, for instance, have given windfalls to private-interest public groups such as pension funds.[8] Failure of other governments to pay assessments has at times seriously hurt the financial soundness of valorization in the city of Bogotá. Exemption may be justified for small landowners who are illiquid and cannot raise the cash to pay their assessments, but this problem can usually be solved in practice by giving small landowners longer periods to pay (in effect requiring them to pay less, especially in inflationary periods) and by making special arrangements in hardship cases. Valorization may force improvements on some owners that they do not want, leading them to sell out and move elsewhere. In theory, however, they should be able to sell out at a profit and suffer no financial harm (although there may be some loss of consumer surplus from valorization, as from any change in supply and demand conditions).

As noted in the next chapter, public finance textbooks tend to condemn earmarked taxes like the valorization tax because they limit the flexibility of budgeting, glutting some activities with too much revenue while other activities starve. This problem can be avoided, however, if the rate of the earmarked tax is changed regularly to bring it into line with actual revenue needs, as is the case with the valorization tax. Further, the financing of investments from the earmarked valorization tax gives an added incentive to examine the prospective benefits of projects more closely than would otherwise be done and hence promotes good budgeting and project appraisal procedures.

It may be argued that activities which can be financed on a benefit base will receive too much support at the expense of other activities which cannot be benefit financed.[9] Too much emphasis on benefit taxation may also limit the scope for income redistribution through taxation. The force of such criticisms is lessened to the extent that benefit taxes can be shown to be an addition to other taxes rather than substituting for other more general taxes. On the basis of the available evidence, the valorization tax does seem to constitute a net addition to public financing in Colombia (Rhoads and Bird, 1967; Doebele, Grimes, and Linn, 1979). As argued in Chapter 13, the need in most developing countries is for additional technically sound benefit taxes to expand the public sector, not for less use of those now existing.

Moreover, the valorization tax is probably a progressive tax, since property ownership is more unequally distributed than income in almost all countries. Viewed another way, the tax is neutral, for all taxpayers receive benefits equal to or greater than the payment. Compared with alternative ways of financing public improvements if valorization is not used, the valorization tax probably favors the poor over the wealthy.[10] All in all, the valorization tax and similar devices to recoup the costs of public investment seem to have a useful but limited role to play in financing urban expansion in developing countries.

The form of tax employed in Colombia may be contrasted on the one hand with a traditional property tax assessed on site value and on the other with a special capital gains tax on increases in site value. A property tax assessed on site values may, in theory, collect the entire net rent of the land: it may be viewed as taking away from the landowner the net revenue from all unearned increments in the site value of his property. A capital gains tax on increments in site values can also recover the total increment in site value, although payment usually takes place only when the increment in value is realized by sale. The practical difficulties of taxing unrealized gains on an accrual basis are well known (Smith, 1977). Moreover, neither site value taxes nor gains taxes on increments in site value are designed to raise the revenues to provide the public investments that will lead to an increment in site value.

Another difference between site value taxation and valorization taxation is that, in theory, a valorization tax recovers only those benefits from direct public investment that enhance the value of the land, while site value taxation also reaches increases in private site values that may arise in a large, heavily populated urban area from the external economies of face-to-face contact and of the mobilization of an efficient work force. The present value of maximum valorization taxes in a growing city is thus lower than the present value of the maximum site value tax.

Unlike most other taxes on land, however, the valorization tax has the political advantage that it is clearly on a benefit basis. The taxpayer is making no sacrifice, for the value of his property will rise by at least the amount of the tax he must pay. This is an important consideration where political resistance to paying taxes is high, as in most developing countries. In practice, since the tax is paid before the investment takes place and before site values increase, the estimates of the increase in value must be sufficiently accurate, or the upward trend of land values because of urban growth so rapid, that the forecast of benefit exceeding tax will be true in almost all cases. In effect, the increment in site value from rapid urban growth and (assuming some money illusion) inflation provides a cushion in case the increment arising from the public investment alone turns out to be inferior to the valorization tax paid.

A valorization tax will be successful only if the urban area is growing rapidly. The main use of valorization taxes in Colombia, for example, has been to provide new and improved streets in urban areas. If improved transportation provides more rapid access to the central business district from some outlying areas, however, site values in both the center and other fringe areas will fall as a result (Wingo, 1961; Alonso, 1964). Since for valorization taxation to be successful there must be an obvious connection between costs and benefits to taxpayers, it would be difficult to use such taxes in a static or slow-growing city unless the improvement in transportation lowered production costs sufficiently to attract new economic activity to central areas and new population to the city, thus supporting property values throughout the urban area and making the taxes more acceptable. The relationship between public investment and improved site values may be indirect in this instance, but property owners will still know from experience that better streets increase the value of land. They may thus be willing to pay a valorization tax even though they cannot distinguish between the increases in site values resulting from particular public investments and those resulting from rapid urban growth in general.[11]

Conclusion

The relatively minor role played by valorization or special assessment taxes in the urban areas of developed countries, and the consequent neglect of the tax in public-finance literature, may be accounted for in part by the slower growth of cities in developed countries and the lesser connection visible between public improvements and increases in site values.[12] Other factors explaining the difference between the potential usefulness of the valorization tax in advanced and less developed countries are the existence of capital markets, so that public improvements may be easily financed and paid for out of regular revenues over time, and the existence of subdivision laws that force many public improvements to be made at private expense.

The valorization tax seems desirable in developing countries from the point of view of stimulating saving and investment. The proceeds of the tax are used almost exclusively for investment and the nature of the tax is such that if it is to be successfully used the investment must be highly productive and increase land values. In fact, the valorization tax may be considered a forced investment where the taxpayer benefits from the increased site value of his land resulting from the public improvement financed by the tax. Income distribution in developing countries is highly unequal, and much urban land is owned by the wealthy upper classes. While these groups could be major sources of saving, as noted in Chapter 4, they often consume a surprisingly large fraction of their income. Thus, the valorization tax generally falls heavily on a group which has the potential to increase its savings considerably and might do so to pay the tax (although since this group also has the best access to the credit markets they might instead borrow the existing savings of others).

The incentive effects of the valorization tax are also favorable to investment and development. As a tax on pure site values, the valorization tax does not penalize development of unimproved land. The payment of the valorization tax itself is probably a stimulant to investment. It is sometimes argued that in theory a tax on site values should have no incentive effects on land use since it does not affect the most profitable use of the land (Netzer, 1966). This statement, however, implicitly assumes that land is always an investment good. In fact, in developing countries much land is held idle not for speculative purposes, but to provide pleasure and prestige to its owners, so that it is in a real sense a consumer good. Under regular site value taxation, the income effect (there is no substitution effect) of site value taxation can be expected to lower consumption (since land is probably not an inferior good); land formerly used for consumption purposes may be put to productive use as a result of the tax. For the valorization tax the analysis is different, since payment of the tax is matched by an increase in the site value of the land. The improvements financed by valorization taxes increase the value of the land for productive purposes, not for prestige consumption, however, and as a result the valorization tax and public investment combined increase the opportunity cost of using land for consumption purposes, and the substitution effect in this case tends to more productive use of the land.[13]

The effect of site value taxes in forcing more intensive land use may depend most on the lack of liquidity and capital markets facing many landowners and on the common failure of landowners to calculate carefully the most profitable use of their land (Holland, 1966). When a valorization tax must be paid, landowners may either realize the opportunity cost of holding the land idle and hence put it to more profitable use, or they may have to sell it to someone else who will do so. Since the valorization tax is a relatively large tax assessed over a short period of time, its effect in forcing better land use through the liquidity and "attention-to-use" effects should be stronger than a regular site value tax, where the rate may be too low to threaten the liquidity or arouse the interest in land use of any but the largest landowners.

From an administrative point of view the valorization tax is also attractive in some respects in developing countries, for land cannot easily be hidden from taxation. As a rule, the tax is collected in relatively large amounts from a relatively small number of taxpayers, which may make enforcement easier. The crucial factor in administration, however, is that the tax and the public improvements go hand in hand. If poor administration leads to badly planned or executed projects, projects which are not executed promptly, or poor allocation of taxes among landowners, and if, as a consequence, a significant number of taxpayers find that the tax they have paid is more than the increase in the value of their property, the tax may be discredited and appear to be only an arbitrary and capricious capital levy.

In summary, the valorization tax in theory seems an attractive one for developing countries. It has a clear benefit justification to help muster political support for the tax. Its effects on saving should be at least neutral and may be positive. Its incentive effects should be favorable. It should be relatively easy to collect. However, it is suitable only for financing public investments that will be demonstrably productive, and it will require skilled administration if it is to work in practice as theory indicates. That this administration is not beyond the reach of an underdeveloped country is demonstrated by Colombian experience.

13   Earmarking Tax Revenues

The earmarking of revenues to specific expenditures is an ancient fiscal practice. Perhaps partly for that reason, it has often been condemned by modern analysts. Indeed, the number of such condemnations found in the literature may be exceeded only by the number of examples of earmarking found in most developing countries. As with many fiscal institutions, however, neither universal condemnation nor universal praise of earmarking seems warranted. Careful consideration of the costs and benefits of each particular case is necessary.

Concepts and Varieties of Earmarking

The practice of assigning the revenue received from a specific tax or taxes to the financing of a particular government activity is common, but there are many different varieties of earmarking. Conceptually, the proceeds of earmarked taxes may be considered to be paid into a fund out of which the specified expenditures are then financed. Such a "fund" may be administered (with varying degrees of formality) by the government, or the favored institution may receive the proceeds of the tax directly. Expenditures on the designated activities may or may not receive additional financing from other sources. All proceeds of the earmarked taxes may or may not have to be spent on the activity in question (sometimes within some specified time period). Additional variables include the length of time for which the assignment of revenues is made and the degree of flexibility in the rate and base of the tax (or taxes) assigned. Finally, and most importantly in analytical terms, there may or may not be any "benefit" connection between the tax levied and the activity financed.[1]

There are strong and weak forms of earmarking. At one extreme, the entire proceeds of the earmarked tax, which is levied on a specified base at a specified rate, and only those proceeds, must be spent for an indefinite time period on an activity which does not confer any particular benefit on those who are taxed. The level of expenditure on this activity will thus rise and fall strictly in accordance with changes in the yield of the earmarked tax. In contrast, in a weaker form of earmarking the amount of expenditure on a function is not necessarily reduced if the yield of the tax falls, nor is it necessarily expanded if tax proceeds rise. In the extreme, when the earmarked tax always contributes only a small part of the total revenue devoted to the activity, earmarking has no practical effect at all.[2]

Between these extremes many other variants of earmarking are possible. A particularly important variant analytically is where the tax is intended to approximate a price or user charge for the service provided, and the amount it yields is taken as a signal of the need to expand or contract the level of activity: this might be called the "rational" strong form of earmarking. As noted in Chapter 1, much of what the public sector does in most countries is to provide specific benefits to identifiable individuals or groups. Except when a clear distributive motive is obvious, the correct amount of such services will in principle be supplied only when recipients signal their preferences through their willingness to pay for the services. When correct prices cannot be charged for technical reasons (for example, in the case of road services), complementary taxes (for example, on fuel and vehicles) may be used as a proxy for prices, and the yield of such taxes dedicated to the provision of the relevant services.

A quite different approach to earmarking departs from the expenditure rather than the revenue side of the budget. For example, a fixed percentage of all expenditures (or revenues) may be earmarked for a particular function—to take two Colombian cases as examples, 20 percent of the national budget must be spent on education and 10 percent on justice.[3] There is no rational justification for such expenditure allocations. Indeed, other than as an expression of good intentions, nothing good can be said for such arbitrary rules. If the levels set are below established norms, such earmarking may be harmless. If the levels set are above past levels, however, such earmarking may be positively harmful, forcing significant distortions in expenditure patterns with no corresponding benefits in the form of more rational resource allocation or new revenues. It is clear why the direct beneficiaries of such measures (such as teachers or judges) favor them; it is quite unclear why anyone else should do so.

General revenue sharing between different levels of government in which a fixed share of the revenues collected by the central government must be transferred to subnational governments is similar in concept to such expenditure earmarking. It may be less pernicious, however, if the funds are less narrowly constrained to be spent on certain activities and if there are potential efficiencies to be gained through decentralized expenditure decisions.[4] Other forms of tax sharing, in which designated portions of particular taxes are transferred, are intermediate on the conceptual spectrum between such general revenue-sharing arrangements and the more usual forms of earmarking.

The establishment of decentralized institutions or public enterprises with the right to retain earnings and to dispose of them as they see fit (within limits) is another form of earmarking. Treating public enterprise profits as equivalent to earmarked revenues may seem surprising at first sight. Conceptually, there are two possible approaches to such profits. One view is that since the government "owns" all such profits in the first place, then if profits are left with an enterprise, this should be treated as a conscious decision to designate revenues to the place where they arise. Under such "implicit earmarking," it is exactly as though the profits were first transferred to the central budget (for example, through taxes) and then transferred back to the enterprise. The opposite view is that the enterprise "owns" these resources. A compromise view might lie between these extremes: for example, giving an enterprise first priority over any profits that it generates but requiring such profits to be flowed through central government bank accounts so that the government has the information that it needs to understand what is going on in the public sector. Enterprises may also be subject to income tax so that at least some of their profits are transferred to public purposes. "Implicit" earmarking of the sort described above characterizes the public enterprise sector in many countries.[5]

Earmarking thus simply means that there is some sort of defined relationship between particular revenues and particular expenditures. Unless the term is more precisely defined with respect to the various characteristics discussed above, generalizations as to the desirability of this practice are hard to make. Although it is common to discuss "earmarked revenues" as though they constituted a homogeneous set of practices, they most decidedly do not. In Colombia, for example, close to one-half of all taxes collected from the private sector in Colombia were earmarked in the early 1980s (Bird, 1984). Of this amount, a "benefit" rationale could be discerned for less than half, with most of the non-benefit earmarking going to support presumably worthy activities in the health and education fields.

The Case against Earmarking

The long-standing association of earmarking with old-fashioned fiscal systems has not done its reputation any good, particularly since the rise of modern budgeting with its emphasis on the need for a unified budget for both fiscal control and economic policy purposes. The conventional critique of earmarking may be summed up as follows:

1. Earmarking hampers effective fiscal management and budgetary control by removing some activities from periodic review and control.
2. Earmarking leads to misallocation of funds, since some functions receive too much finance while others are undersupported.
3. Earmarking makes the revenue structure inflexible in the face of changing needs and conditions.
4. Earmarking tends to remain in force long after the need for which it was established has passed.

What these arguments amount to is the assertion that earmarking undesirably hampers budgetary control and flexibility and therefore results in a misallocation of resources. The model underlying this criticism is one in which the budgetary process allocates funds so that the benefit received from the last dollar allocated to each activity is equal, and the marginal benefit of total public activity is precisely equal to the marginal loss suffered when the taxes financing that activity are paid.

Criticisms of earmarking similar to those noted above were made, for example, in a recent study of Colombia (Gomez and Gomez, 1979).[6] This study found that the existence of extensive earmarking not only distorted public expenditure but also meant that government had lost the capacity to orient its resources as it wished and thus had little flexibility to finance its development policies. The distortion of public expenditures resulting from earmarking in turn resulted in a serious lack of coordination of government policies. These arguments ring true to anyone familiar with budgeting in Colombia (Bird, 1982a), or, for that matter, in many other developing countries (Caiden and Wildavsky, 1974).

The force of such criticism depends, however, on the particular form and nature of the earmarking in question. Earmarking in developing countries indeed often takes inappropriate forms. A 1966 law in Colombia, for example, earmarked the gasoline tax to the National Road Fund at a rate of 1 peso per gallon. This rate determined expenditures on national roads in accordance with the number of gallons of gasoline sold. Such once-and-for-all stipulation of tax rates makes it impossible to adjust them according to changing needs, let alone inflation. If needs change, this inflexibility causes a discrepancy between the desired amount of expenditure and the actual amount the stipulated tax rate will yield.[7] As noted in Chapter 12 with respect to the valorization tax, however, if the rate of an earmarked tax is flexible, so that revenues can be adjusted to satisfy independently derived expenditure needs, such objections lose much of their significance.[8] More importantly, this line of criticism is weakest precisely when the case for earmarking is strongest, that is, when earmarked taxes are paid by those who benefit in some direct (if not precisely measurable) way from the services financed *and* when the taxes constitute an addition to the revenues which would otherwise be possible to raise, thus enabling the expansion of desired services.

The conventional critique of earmarking rests on two questionable assumptions, one empirical and one theoretical. The empirical assumption is that non-earmarked revenues and expenditures are in fact periodically reviewed and controlled in such a way that the results of unified budgetary process more or less accord with the equimarginal principle stated above. This assumption is far from an adequate depiction of reality in most developing countries (Caiden and Wildavsky, 1974).

The theoretical assumption is that there is a clearly defined social preference function for public services which can be effectively implemented through a process of periodic review of generally financed expenditures, and which is not implemented because it is thwarted by earmarking. This assumption too seems subject to severe question in developing countries. Substantial differences often exist both in preferences for public services between different groups of the population and in the extent to which those preferences are reflected in the political budgeting process.

The Case for Earmarking

The principal arguments *for* earmarking revenues are two. First, this practice may provide a means in certain circumstances to implement the benefit principle—a principle which, as noted in Chapter 1, is appealing on both equity and, especially, efficiency grounds as a link between government expenditures and revenues. Second, earmarking may induce the public to support new or increased taxes, to which they would otherwise object, by linking the taxes with the expansion of some government activity that they desire.

The potential political attractiveness of benefit-based taxation, and the case for earmarking as a means of expanding revenues accruing to the public sector (and also directing those revenues to items desired by the public) may be illustrated by comparing the property tax to the Colombian valorization tax discussed in the previous chapter. Increases in property taxes encounter resistance everywhere. Valorization taxes, however, which finance public works by levies on presumed beneficiaries, have been more successful in Colombia, and particularly in some Colombian cities, than almost anywhere else in the world. As noted in Chapter 12, studies that have been made of the valorization tax suggest that one of the principal reasons why this tax is acceptable is precisely because it is seen by those who have to pay it as being related to the benefits that they expect to receive from the public works financed by the tax. These studies also suggest that valorization revenues tend to be additional to other local revenues, not substitutes for them.

To the extent that earmarking increases the revenues accruing to government, the contribution of earmarking to resolving the basic problems of development finance may exceed any complications it introduces into the fiscal system. This argument carries particular weight because what is involved is not just an increase in revenues but an increase that can (within limits) be achieved only if taxpayers think the revenues are used efficiently.

A less praiseworthy reason for the growth of earmarking in many countries has been to enable favored recipients to escape from the messy, uncertain, and complex budgetary routine to which they would otherwise be subjected. The inefficiency of the budgetary process in many countries can be observed at almost every link of the long budgetary chain. The basic financial control system in most Latin American countries, for example, rests on the premise that everyone has to be distrusted. From this premise has evolved a complex process of budgetary "control" involving innumerable checks and counterchecks that are bothersome and time-consuming (as well as inadequate to achieve their purpose: Bird, 1982a).

Whether earmarked taxes are collected by the government and then distributed to an autonomous agency or other spending agency or whether they are collected directly by the spending agency in the first place, there is little accounting control over these taxes. The administrative supervision of disbursements of earmarked revenue is as a rule less detailed and controlled than for general budget revenue. The ability to escape much of the ineffective, time-consuming paper work that constitutes the budgetary system may be one of the major advantages of earmarked taxes for recipients.

Avoiding the inefficiencies of the central government financial system has an obvious short-run advantage for the recipients—and in a sense perhaps even for the system as a whole through ensuring adequate financing for certain projects. Interest groups may like earmarking because it gives them more security. Politicians may like it because it insulates pet projects from subsequent legislative distortions. Through lessening the pressure to improve the inefficient budgetary system, and to resolve other basic problems, however, in the long run such avoidance almost certainly has unfavorable implications for the efficiency of government.[9] Although as a general idea one should not postpone the possibility of achieving "good" results in the forlorn hope of someday achieving "perfect" results, on the whole this argument seems strong enough to constitute a conclusive point against earmarking in all but a few instances.[10]

As noted earlier, public-sector financing can most closely approach the allocative efficiency of correctly functioning private markets through earmarking. Linking specific revenues and expenditures has the virtue of compartmentalizing fiscal decisions, thus permitting in principle more rational choice on the part of decision-makers— whether they be voters, their legislative representatives, or the executive branch itself. Contrary to the conventional view underlying the earlier critique of earmarking, that centralized budgetary decisions are required for rational choice, *decentralized* decisions are more likely to be rational.[11]

One reason for this divergence in conclusions is that the conventional view assumes that there is a single identifiable preference function for government activities, while the pro-earmarking view assumes that individuals and groups are as likely to have different preferences for public as for private goods and services. Another reason is that there are different implicit assumptions about the availability of information on people's preferences at different levels of government (assuming one function or aim of politicians and bureaucrats is to satisfy such preferences, if only to increase their chances of staying in office).[12]

The simplified individualistic model implicitly underlying the theoretical argument for earmarking is remote from the real world of politics and administration. Nevertheless, it is useful in revealing the even more unreal nature of the strongly normative model of the budgeting process—sometimes called the "benevolent dictator" view—which underlies the conventional critique of earmarking (Eklund, 1972). This point is strengthened if one remembers that a key reason for earmarking in many developing countries is that it is often necessary to increase revenues in conditions in which many citizens are, for various reasons, hostile to expansion of the state. In such circumstances it makes little sense to criticize earmarking for budgetary rigidity: without it, there would be less budget to be rigid about. Insofar as the revenue which is earmarked is additional to that which is otherwise raised, its allocation cannot really be criticized for inflexibility.

Over time, of course, the allocations established by any particular form of earmarking will become unsuitable. Like all tax and expenditure legislation, earmarking thus needs periodic review, and probably occasional change, if it is to fulfill its primary function of providing politically desirable expenditures without leading to gross misallocations of resources. Again, however, there is little evidence that earmarking is a worse offender in this regard in the conditions of developing countries than a more centralized system, and against this cost must be set any gains accruing from the expansion of government activity that earmarking may make possible. Nevertheless, an important feature of any earmarked revenue should be that it is for a fixed period, say, five years. Such a "sunset provision" (as such temporary authorizations have come to be called) will not automatically ensure that the appropriateness of earmarking arrangements will be systematically and carefully reviewed. Without such a periodic reminder, grossly unsuitable arrangements are likely to persist longer than will be the case if the matter gets discussed in public once in a while.

Some forms of earmarking are less desirable than others. The specific earmarking of particular taxes to activities with which they have no logical benefit connection is, for example, undoubtedly much less desirable—and leads to much greater rigidities and inflexibilities over time—than does the assignation of a portion of general expenditures or general revenues to a particular activity. To take two cases from Colombian experience, the earmarking of a hotel tax to a tourist agency is more defensible than the diversion of a fixed proportion of a cigarette tax to finance sports activities. Each case of earmarking should be considered on its merits rather than simply condemning such a long-standing and popular practice out of hand. When a device such as earmarking remains in place despite numerous attacks on it, one may usually conclude that there are good reasons for its existence and that changing it will first require other changes (for example, in budgetary practices and public attitudes to taxation) which will be neither simple nor easy.

Conclusion

In short, earmarking may in some circumstances have much to be said for it; in others it may be badly out of place. Most revenue systems should probably include a mixture of benefit financing—all of which should be earmarked—and non-benefit financing—some of which may also be earmarked in certain circumstances without doing much harm and perhaps even some good. While direct prices or user charges are better on efficiency grounds than earmarking, the latter, when correctly designed, is often better than general-fund financing, contrary to what too many public finance textbooks still say. This conclusion by no means implies that any and all earmarking desired by particular interest groups is beneficial, but blanket condemnation of this practice is not justified.

The practice in many countries of earmarking odd bits and pieces of revenue to worthy social expenditures, for example, has no redeeming merit from any relevant point of view. In contrast, earmarked taxes on gasoline and motor vehicles (as well as the valorization tax) may in principle make a good deal of sense from most points of view. The taxes on motor transport in most countries could no doubt be improved in design, but the general idea of linking revenues from this source to road finance has much to be said for it.[13]

In every case, however, what is required before reaching a final decision on the appropriate structure of any earmarked tax is close and careful examination of the cost structure of the service in question and of the distribution and characteristics of beneficiaries. Where groups of beneficiaries, such as highway users or residents in a particular area, can be identified and direct pricing is too costly or otherwise infeasible to administer, the benefit tax approach may make sense.

Where it does, such revenues should as a rule be earmarked to finance the service in question. If the rate is set roughly in accordance with the incremental cost of providing the service, and kept flexible, fluctuations in the revenue yield of such charges over time may serve as a guide to the efficient deployment of public-sector resources. Even if such (rough) perfection is not achievable, this sort of earmarking, which in effect requires beneficiaries to pay for what they get—and ensures that they get what they pay for—has ample justification in terms of both equity and efficiency. On the other hand, earmarking intended to launch this or that worthy project or to insulate some favored activity from budgetary vicissitudes should be phased out where it now exists and should be introduced, if at all, only in very special and limited circumstances, and even then for limited periods only.

PART V Tax Reform and Tax Design

14   Tax Reform and Tax Design

Taxation in developing countries is now a sufficiently developed subject to be recognized as a specialty in public finance equivalent to, say, local government finance or cost-benefit analysis.[1] The considerable time and effort devoted to reforming tax systems in developing countries may as yet have borne relatively little fruit in terms of either practical results or new economic knowledge, but much has been learned in the course of these efforts about the process of tax reform (Gillis, 1989a).

Perhaps the most important rule for would-be reformers to learn is what may be called the *Rule of Results*. As argued in Chapter 2 above, what is important in appraising any tax change are its *effects* in the context of the particular country in question, not whether the change moves the tax system closer in some sense to some predetermined standard or other.

The ease with which economists sometimes fall into the trap of assuming that they have all the answers to the manifold problems of implementing an adequate revenue system in a particular country at a particular time is astonishing. Indeed, Feldstein (1976) felt it necessary to warn public finance theorists that the design of an optimal tax system in terms of economic efficiency was an exercise very different from—and in most ways much simpler than—reforming any actual tax system.[2] This warning was well taken, given the propensity of analysts to forget the qualifications in their premises when drawing conclusions.

A second important rule for reformers is the *Rule of Relevance*. Policy changes should be relevant not only in terms of results in the specific context for which they are proposed but also with respect to some policy objective. As all who have worked in this field know, it is in practice extremely difficult to articulate a meaningful set of concrete policy objectives in any context, let alone in a country with which one is really not very familiar. Most of us tend in practice to *assume* that whatever it is we care about (horizontal equity, efficiency, or whatever) is what really matters—or if it doesn't, it should. In developed countries it is often possible to forget that a tax structure constitutes a set of policy instruments, and to focus on such aspects of tax reform as internal consistency and equity in some vague sense. In developing countries, however, where the scope of the desired ends invariably far exceeds the available means, the instrumental nature of taxation can never be forgotten. The effort needed to accomplish any tax change should therefore be reserved for changes relevant to development objectives and not dissipated needlessly.

Any tax reform should also be designed to satisfy the *Rule of Robustness*, in at least two senses. In the first place, the probability that policy recommendations will produce the desired results should not depend upon such articles of faith as a certain assumed tax incidence or an assumed relationship between such unknown magnitudes as, say, the elasticity of factor substitution and the elasticity of labor supply. When the outcomes of a policy are very sensitive to variations in such largely unknown facts, the policy is not a good bet.[3] Our knowledge of the relation between instruments and outcomes is often disputable, to the point that basing policy changes on the authority of such knowledge is more an act of faith than of reason.

Two ways of dealing with this problem are, first, to propose only policies that do not depend to a significant degree on such uncertain factors and, second, to propose a number of ways to achieve particularly desired policy objectives. In view of the multiplicity of policy objectives in most countries, the second strategy—of not putting all one's water in one probably leaky bucket—seems more advisable, as well as more feasible. This advice may itself be put in the form of a subsidiary rule, the *Rule of Redundancy*. The appropriate tax policy for development thus generally requires the orchestration of many subtle fiscal instruments

A second and somewhat contrary sense in which policy measures should be robust is in terms of their administrative requirements. As stressed in the next chapter, developing countries invariably suffer from a scarcity of trained administrators. Policies that depend for their success on fine-tuning of any sort are generally doomed to failure, or at least to such perversion in the process of implementation as to produce results quite different from those intended. If the political hurdles to adopting any new policy can be overcome, the best policies are likely to be those that offer as little latitude as possible for officials further down the line to mess them up.

This administrative constraint is the best reason for adopting as few interventionist policies as possible. Even the inevitably necessary interventionist component of policy in all developing countries should be as general in nature as possible and should not depend on discretionary decisions on specific cases.[4] A good grasp of the nature and limitations of the tax administration charged with carrying out reforms is even more important to the would-be tax reformer than is knowledge of the crucial empirical parameters.

Finally, a *Rule of Resiliency* may be postulated as an auxiliary or instrumental way (like the Rule of Redundancy) of meeting the three basic rules of reform set out above—Robustness, Relevance, and, above all, Results. If an objective is important, and its attainment is uncertain, redundant instruments may help, as noted earlier. More importantly, all life is a learning process, and tax reform is no different. No change is engraved in stone, and policy-makers must stand ready to alter and adjust their policies to suit changing needs and circumstances. Ideally, therefore, a certain degree of institutionalization of the tax reform process is essential—in the form, for example, of a special unit concerned with the continual review and adjustment of the tax system (Bird, 1970b; McIntyre and Oldman, 1975).

Such a unit may prove particularly useful in planning and implementing the inevitable adjustments to cope with perceived transitional inequities that will be made to policy proposals as they move through the political and administrative process. The importance of such perceived inequities in blocking reforms has been stressed by Feldstein (1976a). He suggested two ways of overcoming the problem, through compensation of losers and postponement of the time at which changes take effect. Shoup (1972a) had earlier stressed another, much more common solution, that of trade-off or compromise. He distinguished compromise by exchange from compromise by sharing (i.e., "splitting the difference"), favoring the former because the latter too often resulted in internal inconsistencies in tax structure. Although

Shoup introduced these notions as alternative means of accommodating conflicts of interest, they seem equally relevant in the context of increasing the transitional acceptability of tax changes. Whatever the approach adopted, however, some such adjustments will prove necessary for most significant reforms. Only continued close scrutiny of the tax policy process and a resilient attitude to adaptation will ensure that what emerges at the end of the process bears some relation to what was initially intended.

A Case in Point: Inflation Adjustment

The significance of these rules—and the somewhat unconventional recommendations to which they occasionally lead— may be illustrated by a brief discussion of inflation adjustments in the rate structure of the personal income tax.

As noted in Chapter 7, the principal argument in favor of adjusting the tax rate structure to take account of inflation is simply that inflation has a significant effect on the effective tax rate applicable to any given level of real income, particularly at the lowest income levels, where the decline in the real value of the exemptions weighs most heavily.

If exemption levels and the bracket limits within which the rates are applied are multiplied by an appropriate price index, this gradual increase in real tax levels is offset, and the distribution of real tax burdens remains precisely the same as when the nominal exemption levels and rates were established. The case for adjusting the structure of personal income tax to inflation is therefore essentially to retain both the same level of collections in real terms through the income tax *and* the same distribution of those collections by income class in the face of an inflationary increase in prices and incomes.

Even this brief account makes it clear that inflation provides good reason for considering an increase in personal exemptions and rate brackets. Nevertheless, there may be equally good reasons for *not* indexing income tax rates in developing countries to inflation.

The income tax became a mass tax in most industrial countries—admittedly often in wartime conditions—through the growth of income (real or nominal) on the one hand and the effective use of withholding on the other. Developing countries too may take advantage of these factors by allowing inflation and growth to move people into and up the income tax structure and by effectively withholding tax from that income. Leaving personal exemption and rate brackets at present levels will clearly accelerate this process.

The arguments made for adjusting exemption levels and rate brackets to inflation seem less applicable in many developing countries. The effects of deviations in income tax burdens as a consequence of price level changes should be judged in terms of results, not in accordance with their conformity to some ideal tax on real net income. The fact that exemptions (in real terms) bear increasingly less resemblance to those established in the past, or to those expenses needed to maintain a family in reality, is in principle less important than the *consequences* of raising the level of exemptions: remember the Rule of Results stated above.

In these terms, an important reason for keeping exemption levels and rate brackets at current levels in some countries, despite the ravages of inflation, is that the alternatives to doing so are all less palatable. Although, as stressed in Chapter 7, not all upper-income recipients are income taxpayers, income taxpayers generally belong to the upper-income strata in developing countries. For this and other reasons, the income tax, despite its deficiencies, is by most standards the fairest of all taxes in most countries. If income taxes are lowered, either other (less fair) taxes have to be raised, expenditures cut, or inflation accentuated. Any minor equity benefits derived from lightening income tax burdens on the relatively favored few seem unlikely to offset the costs, economic and social, of these alternatives, particularly since those who fall within the income tax structure are often better able to protect themselves against the adverse effects of inflation in any case. It is also hard to see how indexing will aid in achieving such common goals of reformers as a fairer tax system, a more redistributive tax system, or a more elastic domestic tax system—all of which generally require the income tax to take a larger, not a smaller role.

The alternatives to keeping the present tax structure unchanged in nominal terms involve either taxing even poorer people more, or else taxing the same people in ways that are inherently less equitable in terms of individual circumstances. The main argument in developing countries for adjusting income taxes to inflation through exemption and bracket adjustments is probably the important one of improving (or maintaining) the political acceptability of the tax in the relevant constituency (see Chapter 16). Against this, the case for nonadjustment rests basically on the desire to raise the importance of personal taxes in the tax mix and thus to increase the equity and responsiveness of the system as a whole (see Chapter 7). While it would no doubt be better to raise income taxes explicitly, the real choice is often whether it is better to do it implicitly, or not at all. The ideal way to *design* a tax system may have little to do with how best to *reform* it.

Conclusion

As has been emphasized throughout this book, policy recommendations need to be geared specifically to the circumstances of particular countries. It is often harder to do this than to develop an applicable analytical model. In this, as in other fields of development economics, policy-minded economists are continually driven back to first principles, namely, that one must know a country before one can prescribe for it. As mentioned earlier, historical, institutional, and statistical studies may prove more useful for this purpose than conventional economic analysis.

Too often, an advisor who continually stresses such eternal verities as better administration, paying more attention to local circumstances, and cutting one's suit to fit the available cloth, feels like a salesman of secondhand looms faced with the competition of the people who gave us the emperor's new clothes. The demand for magic gadgets—computerization, investment incentives, value-added taxes, etc.— that will resolve fiscal problems without painful political and economic restructuring is comparable to the demand for painless diets. Repeated failure in both cases seems to make little difference to true believers, whether sellers or buyers of panaceas. Nevertheless, it cannot be said too often that there is no panacea, just as there is no single optimal tax system for developing countries (though there may be one which is feasibly "best" for a particular country at a particular time).

Tax reform is a more difficult and challenging task than tax design. It calls on all the economic knowledge we can muster, and much more besides. It is also as a rule inherently messy and institutional rather than elegantly analytical. No doubt, the professional prestige derived from engaging in this activity—and the success ratio of those who do—will never be very high. Nevertheless, the challenge is great, and the more that able scholars are willing to turn their minds to such policy-oriented activities the better it will be for the discipline and also, although less certainly, for the policy outcomes with which we have to live.

15   The Administrative Dimension of Tax Reform

The importance of good administration has long been as obvious to those concerned with taxation in developing countries as has its absence. Over thirty years ago, Stanley Surrey (1958, pp. 158–59) noted that "the concentration on tax policy—on the choice of taxes—may lead to insufficient consideration of the aspect of tax administration. In short, there may well be too much preoccupation with 'what to do' and too little attention to 'how to do it.'" Although Surrey's paper has been frequently cited, and presumably read, there is little evidence in the hundreds of articles, books, and reports on tax reform written over the last few decades that this warning has been taken sufficiently seriously.[1] It thus seems time to sound the alarm again, before we launch into another thirty years of misguided attempts to reform tax structure while largely ignoring tax administration.[2]

The administrative dimension should be placed at the center rather than the periphery of tax reform efforts. As Casanegra (1990, p. 179) put it; "tax administration *is* tax policy." The most rewarding approach to tax reform in most countries is to design a tax system that can be acceptably implemented by the existing weak administration. Miracles being always in short supply, any other course of action is, in the end, unlikely to prove successful.

The Importance of Administration

Limited administrative capacity is a binding constraint on tax reform in many developing countries. Studies of tax evasion in different developing countries show that it is not uncommon for half or more of potential income tax to be uncollected (Richupan, 1984). Matters are not much better with respect to most other taxes (Bird, 1989).

The scanty quantitative evidence accords with the common perception that there is widespread tax evasion in most developing countries. Moreover, even when there is not outright evasion, the tax structure in these countries is often designed, administered, and judicially interpreted in such a way as to ensure the emergence of a huge gap between the potential and the actual tax base. Sometimes this result is achieved crudely, as through the continued use in Guatemala after a major devaluation of values converted at the old exchange rate for purposes of customs duties, thus forgoing the main budgetary benefit of devaluation (Bird, 1985). Sometimes it is achieved through more subtle (and usually peripherally legal) exploitation of the peculiarities of banking and tax laws, perhaps particularly with respect to the widespread availability of tax "incentives" (McLure, 1982). And sometimes it is achieved by the functioning—or nonfunctioning—of the appeals system. However it is accomplished, whether at the legislative, administrative, or judicial levels, the result in most developing countries is that there is a great discrepancy between what the tax system appears to be on the surface and how it actually works in practice.

The effects of this discrepancy are more important and pervasive than seems generally to be recognized. Not only is revenue lost but the elasticity of the tax system is also reduced—particularly, of course, in inflation when administrative lags alone will usually suffice to yield this result (Tanzi, 1977). Additional revenue must continually be secured through a series of discretionary ad hoc rate increases and new taxes. The patchwork character of the tax system of many developing countries arises in large part from their inability to administer the taxes they legislate, resulting in the continual need to legislate new tax changes.

The incidence and effects of the tax system are as sensitive to how it is administered as is its yield. Tax evasion inevitably undermines the horizontal equity of the tax system. Recipients of equal income, like consumers of similar products and owners of similar properties, are not taxed alike in practice, whatever the law may say. As argued in Chapter 7, the income tax in most developing countries is a schedular tax, with the effective tax rate depending largely on the source of the income and almost always being heavier on wage than on self-employment or capital income. Taxes on property are even more sensitive to administrative interpretation, with old buildings being favored over new, and so on (Bahl and Linn, 1991). Even in the case of sales and excise taxes, in practice the products of small firms are usually favored (Cnossen, 1977, and Chapter 6 above).

Most divergences between law and reality undermine the vertical equity of the tax system. It is the well-to-do who can most readily arrange for the law to contain convenient loopholes in the first place, and to exploit them once they are there with the aid of the "rent-seeking" skills of tax accountants and lawyers (and the consequent waste of scarce resources). The same group receive much of their income in the forms that are hardest to track down. They may also more readily hold their wealth, and even spend it, in ways hard to detect (e.g., offshore). Finally, not only can they most readily bribe and subvert administrators but they have the most to gain from doing so. Since the incidence of a tax results from the interaction of statute law, the opportunities different groups have to evade it, and the rigor with which it is enforced—and the rich come out ahead on all three counts—taxation in developing countries is, as a rule, unlikely to cause much disturbance to the inhabitants of the upper ranges of the income distribution.

For similar reasons, the real incentive effects of the tax system may be quite different from those that may be surmised from the statute. The global progressive personal income tax established by law is in practice likely to amount to little more than at most a mildly progressive tax on wage earners in the modern sector (see Chapter 7).[3] The equally formidable-looking modern corporate income tax may turn out to be a crude gross receipts tax in practice.[4] Even an apparently general ad valorem sales tax may in practice amount to little more than a collection of specific excises on a small fraction of consumption.[5] In these circumstances, comparisons of the merits of general income or consumption taxes and lamentations about the heavy burden imposed on capital by nominally progressive income and corporate taxes represent more obeisance to current trends in the academic literature than serious analysis of tax reform.

Tax administration in any country inevitably reflects to a large extent the nature of the country itself. If the country is a sea of corruption, as some are, the tax administration will not be an island of incorruptibles, and it is foolish to pretend it is. If most traders in the country are illiterate and keep no written records, no accounts-based tax (such as income or general sales tax) can effectively be levied on them, and it is futile to pretend to be doing so. If land titles are in chaos or nonexistent in rural areas, no effective rural land tax can be levied. If officials are judged solely by the tax revenue they produce and little else—as was long the rule in the Western world (Webber and Wildavsky, 1986) and is still true in some developing countries—they are likely to get that revenue from the politically weaker sectors of the population (such as ethnic minorities), regardless of what the law says. If the only way for an honest official to make a living wage is to claim travel allowances, then he is forced to travel even if it is a complete waste of his time. If only the incompetent and the untrained are left to deal directly with taxpayers, as is the case in many administrative systems where advancement comes only in the form of being promoted to a desk job, then taxpayers will meet only the incompetent and the untrained. This catalog of woes is not easily remediable even in principle, let alone in practice.

In some developing countries, the honesty of both taxpayers and tax officials is suspect (Virmani, 1987). Governments have little control over officials, little information as to what is going on, and no easy way to get it. Even if the information were available, the problem is inherently complex: market structures (and hence adjustment costs) vary widely, as do risk and time preferences, so that the costs, probabilities, and benefits of detecting evasion and corruption vary widely. Administrative cost functions are discontinuous and hard to interpret (Bird, 1982b). Tax schedules, the interpretation of the law, the penalty schedule, and the appeals process all vary over time, as do enforcement efforts—and the reaction of taxpayers to such efforts.[6]

In the circumstances, it is not surprising that many tax analysts simply ignore the problem of tax administration—a problem epitomized in many countries in the phrase "All taxes are negotiable" (Gray, 1987)—perhaps in the hope it will go away on its own. Even those most aware of these problems have done this. In a perceptive piece on tax administration in Nigeria two decades ago, for example, Taylor (1967) began by saying these were only short-run problems which would undoubtedly be resolved in twenty or twenty-five years. An official report in Papua New Guinea (1971) similarly said of the income tax that doubtless, by the end of the decade, its reach will have extended throughout the population. Both these predictions, like similar ones made in other countries, have turned out to be wildly optimistic.

Many tax reform proposals in developing countries have not paid even such passing obeisance to the problem of tax administration.

Indeed, some reform proposals would make the life of administrators even more difficult. It is no wonder that tax administrators often view would-be tax reformers as little more than residents of an ivory tower, who descend after the battle is over to shoot the wounded.

One reason for this apparent disinterest in administration is that it is hard to go beyond platitudes on this subject. A more basic reason, however, has less to do with platitudes than with attitudes. As Witt (1987, p. 140), puts it: "Efficient and inefficient tax systems are not the result of some kind of 'happy' coincidence but of social and political power constellations." To put the point another way, if after thirty years of persistent criticism there has been so little perceptible improvement in important aspects of tax administration in many developing countries, the next thirty years are likely to mean more of the same.[7] Whether this administrative inertia shows that a society gets the tax administration it wants (or deserves)—perhaps because taxation reflects the reality of political power (Best, 1976)—or whether it shows that no administration can differ much from the society of which it is a part, is less important than the fact of its existence. Neither quick fixes nor head-on confrontations seem likely to change matters much in the foreseeable future in most countries. Tax administration will thus remain a binding constraint on tax reform. In these circumstances, what can be done?

Coping with Administrative Reality

Solutions to the administrative problems of tax reform may be divided into three groups: those that would change the environment, those that would change the administration, and those that would change the law.

CHANGING THE ENVIRONMENT

Academic economists discussing policy issues sometimes in effect advocate that the way the world works should be changed to fit the conditions assumed in their models. Tax reformers discussing the need to change the institutional context within which a tax system functions often sound equally futile.

It is common to hear, for example, that modern direct taxes depend on what is usually called "voluntary compliance." Such compliance is motivated less by civic conscience than by the fear of being caught. It is exceedingly difficult, perhaps impossible, to administer any tax if every hand is raised against it. One cannot put the entire population into jail. Equally, however, one cannot will into being a spirit of compliance that is not there. If the willingness of taxpayers to comply with their obligations depends upon their perception that the funds thus taken from them are put to good use and that they are treated fairly when compared to other taxpayers, the fiscs of many developing countries are in deep trouble indeed.[8] These conditions do not now prevail, and in many cases are not likely to prevail in the near future.

Several ways of attempting to remedy this serious "environmental" defect have been mooted. One is simply to undertake a campaign of "taxpayer education," to convince taxpayers that—in Justice Holmes's phrase—taxes are the price paid for a civilized society, that they live in such a society, and that the tax system is equitable. Such campaigns to encourage compliance are unlikely to do much good, however, if reality is too obviously different.

Words alone are unlikely to change basic attitudes. Deeds may do so, however, so another approach is obviously to turn government into something which people see as adding to their lives rather than a burden.[9] Thoroughgoing expenditure reform (Chapter 16), increased use of devices such as earmarking (Chapter 13) and benefit taxes which link taxes and expenditures in some believable way (Chapter 12), the devolvement of functional and financial responsibilities on local communities (Chapter 11)—such fundamental changes in the way government is conducted may lead to a change in the attitude to taxation over time, and hence make the work of the tax collector, if never pleasurable, at least acceptable.

The perceived fairness of the tax system may of course also be a factor in shaping attitudes (Chapters 7 and 9). Fundamental changes in such matters, however desirable, by definition cannot be made easily or quickly, so there is little immediate hope for relief from this source. On the other hand, one should not overdo the importance of securing any particular concept of equity in the context of the tax system. Most developing countries are at best limited democracies or constrained autocracies. Even in the most democratic countries, only limited groups are both tax-sensitive and politically significant. Most governments seem more concerned with the few who matter than with the burden on the many: the "horizontal equity" emphasized in tax reform discussions seems often to be viewed solely from the perspective of those sufficiently well-off to be subject to direct taxes. The treatment of the population as a whole sometimes seems to be considered primarily in terms of how to secure the necessary revenues with the least fuss. The "ability to pay" doctrine as it applies in some countries seems concerned more with the ability of the government to make people pay than with abstract notions of equity.

As suggested in Chapter 2, the only role for tax policy advisors in such circumstances is to trace as carefully and convincingly as possible the consequences of particular measures, leaving decisions about their acceptability up to the presumably responsible authorities.

CHANGING THE ADMINISTRATION

Another approach to relieving the constraints imposed on tax reform by administrative limitations is to tackle those limitations directly. Some proposals for administrative reform, however, seem to amount to little more than looking reality squarely in the eye and passing on. An example is the common suggestion that an elite corps of tax administrators should be created. This hoary chestnut deserves to be put aside once and for all.[10]

The tax administration is part of the public service generally. Consequently, it is a fantasy to think that it can for long be pulled out of the ruck of political favoritism, employment-generation, and the myriad other factors that account for the masses of low-paid, poorly trained, poorly motivated public servants found in most developing countries (Goode, 1981). Even if such an elite could be created, they cannot do the job properly without both good soldiers (the front-line clerks, tellers, and so on) and adequate tools (computers, communication system, etc.), neither of which is likely to prove easy to procure in developing countries, particularly for usually low-status revenue agencies.

An even more popular way of ignoring the administrative problem is to pretend it can all be handled by a small staff equipped with appropriately up-to-date computers. There is no doubt that in certain areas of tax administration good use can be made of computers and that, indeed, they may in some instances obviate the need to acquire the skills of many highly trained specialists (Hutabarat and Lane, 1990). On the other hand, the computerization of tax administration is a complex task that has as yet been successfully accomplished by few. Computers must be programmed and operated by people; they must rely on information obtained and inputted by other people; and their output must be acted upon by still other people. Since the motivations and incentives of all these people are unlikely to be altered by the introduction of new equipment alone, it is by no means obvious that the dawning of the computer age has significantly reduced the importance of the administrative constraint on tax reform in developing countries.

Indeed, it is not hard to find instances in which the inappropriate introduction and use of computer systems has even made matters worse. On the whole, computerization is clearly most useful where the tax administration is already well organized (Corfmat, 1985).

Too often, as was recently noted in India—sometimes thought to be among the best of all developing countries in this respect—the tax administration is "neglected" and "archaic," characterized by poor training, low status, poor salaries, and poor equipment (Archaya et al., 1985). An obvious remedy is to tackle these and other organizational and procedural problems head on: to see that the law is properly drafted and codified; that the administration is properly organized, staffed, and trained; that taxpayers are located, placed on the rolls, and their returns adequately examined and audited; that relevant information is obtained from other government departments and elsewhere and properly utilized; that controversies between taxpayers and the administration are satisfactorily resolved; that taxes due are collected; and that penalties are properly applied. This is the approach taken by Surrey (1958) in the seminal paper cited earlier. Unfortunately, necessary as such measures are (Chapter 8), they not only take much time and effort to carry through but also are politically unpopular and seldom attract sufficient support to be successful.

Perhaps the oldest means of dealing with the pervasive administrative problem is to "privatize" tax collection. "Tax farming," as this practice is known, has a bad name in view of the gross injustices to which it led. Nonetheless, it also had real virtues in many countries during the centuries when it was the dominant form of tax collection. In particular, it ensured a reliable and steady stream of revenue into state coffers (Webber and Wildavsky, 1986). The practice went out of favor in Europe when modern public administrative structures began to emerge in the seventeenth and eighteenth centuries.

No one would recommend the revival of tax farming today. Some important features of tax administration in many developing countries, however, are not dissimilar to tax farming in both their good and their bad aspects. Moreover, the recent adoption of what is in effect the private administration of important customs functions in countries such as Indonesia may signify a new legitimacy for this practice.

Not many developing countries have opted to hire foreigners, let alone local private firms, to collect their taxes (on a commission basis as opposed to the fixed fees characteristic of traditional tax farming).[11] In practice, however, some aspects of how tax administration works in many countries are not dissimilar. In some countries (e.g., Senegal), tax inspectors are rewarded in accordance with the amount of additional tax and fines they collect. The earmarked taxes common in Latin America are sometimes shared between the collecting agency and the state. The "third party" collection systems that are the backbone of most effective taxes in all countries (Chapter 8) also have a commission aspect since the collecting agent (the withholding employer, the sales taxpayer) has the use of the funds for a legally or customarily agreed period before remitting them to the government (Sandford et al., 1981). Finally, in all too many countries tax collectors are more or less expected to make up for their poor salaries by supplementary collections from taxpayers—collections that are not accompanied by a corresponding remittance to the government. In many such corrupt situations, indeed, there is a conventionally accepted level of private reward to the fortunate possessors of official positions which is regarded as no more criminal than the equivalent rake-off by a cook from the household budget.[12]

Yet another interesting variant of "official tax farming" which exists in some countries is to establish revenue targets for each auditor, tax official, or district tax office.[13] If such targets are used as the sole basis for evaluating performance, and if compliance with such targets is considered essential to ensure an adequate flow of revenue to the central authorities, clearly such a system has both the virtue (stable revenue) and the vice (a license for extortion) of traditional tax farming. Moreover, unless the targeting system is altered, tax changes intended to alter allocative and distributive outcomes will not have much effect in reality, however refined their design, since the basic incentive of officials will still be to meet their targets by collecting the most from those least able to resist.

In other instances "targeting" may be simply a relatively innocuous device used as one part of an array of measures intended to keep administrators up to mark. Indeed, one of the main purposes of such a system—and perhaps even its effect if there are adequate controls to restrain excessive zeal—may be to provide a higher degree of certainty to both the state and taxpayers. With respect to public as to private tax farming, full understanding of the possible merits and demerits of the practice requires a detailed examination of its context and effects.[14] Labels alone are not grounds for condemnation.

Many countries for many centuries have found it useful, even necessary, to thus employ private cupidity to serve public needs. Rather than outright condemnation of the desire of tax officials to feather their private nests, and pleas for the invention of "new model" men to replace the present unworthy vessels, one component of a realistic study of tax administration in developing countries should perhaps be to devise incentive systems, perhaps at times including financial rewards, that will lead to a better matching of public and private interests.

Should this risky advice be acted upon, it would of course be important to have an effective system of controls to ensure that tax administrators do not steal the state (and the taxpayers) blind. As Webber and Wildavsky (1986, p. 39) note, "a tax collector's very function tempts him to cheat." Much of their lengthy history of fiscal administration is devoted to detailing ways over the centuries that sovereigns have tried to restrain this natural impulse of their servants. Rewards for good performance and penalties for poor performance: overlapping, duplicative, and redundant administrative structures;[15] the division of functions among different officers, both to use each as a check on the other and to make it more difficult and costly to bribe them; the use of internal and external "spies" to check on the honesty of tax officials—such devices and others have long been employed for this purpose in different countries.

The most basic way to ensure that tax officials do what they are supposed to do, and no more, however, is (as stressed in Chapter 8) to reduce to a minimum the amount of discretion they have in dealing with taxpayers. The more room there is for negotiation between official and potential taxpayer, the more scope there is for bribery by the one, arbitrary exaction by the other, and collusion by both. The more the tax to be paid is based on some readily measurable, observable, and verifiable base, the less scope there is for such maneuvers. If tax administration is to be effective and seen to be fair in the context of many developing countries, it is thus necessary to apply clear, known, objective standards—however rough the ensuing justice—rather than leaving the application of a fine-sounding general statute to negotiations between taxpayers and officials.

CHANGING THE LAW

The best way to cope with the administrative problem is to design tax reforms for developing countries in full recognition of the severe limitations imposed by administrative realities. The administrative dimension is central, not peripheral, to tax reform. Without significant administrative changes, the alleged benefits of many proposed tax reforms will simply not be achieved. Too many tax reform efforts have regarded tax policy and tax administration as quite separate matters. The world is not like that. No policy exists until it is implemented, and it is the manner of its implementation which really determines its impact. Those who would alter the outcomes of a tax system must therefore understand in detail how it is administered, and adjust their recommendations accordingly if they want to do good rather than ill.

There are three ways to approach the question of modifying the legal structure to accord with the administrative realities of developing countries: the first, to develop some gadgetry to bypass the problem, is a false lead; the second, to provide an adequate legal structure for administration, is obviously important but in itself inadequate; while the third, to design the basic tax law properly in the first place, is in the end the only sensible procedure.

*Gadgets.*Many types of tax "gadgets" have been suggested to get around the administrative problem. The "lottery" approach, for instance, uses the cupidity (or gullibility) of taxpayers to make their interests congruent with those of the administration. An example of this approach is a scheme suggested by Hart (1967) to encourage customers to collect their sales receipts, so that they could enter them for lottery prizes.[16] The idea was to obtain more reliable information on both the gross receipts of business and the expenditures of taxpayers.

One problem with such schemes is that it is unlikely the probability of a prize is great enough to make it worthwhile for people to comply. Even if it is, the seller could easily offset this incentive by offering two prices, with and without receipt. Another problem is that there is no conceivable way most tax administrations in developing countries could use the information thus provided, since they are already swamped with usable but unused information. An example is the provision found in some countries permitting the deduction of professional fees only on the submission of appropriate receipts. The idea is to aggregate such receipts and match them with the declaration (or non-declaration) of the professional in question. Unfortunately, this never seems to happen.

For much the same reasons, the much-touted "self-checking" feature of the value-added tax has in fact amounted to little in most countries. This is one area where computerization in principle could be the answer, although it does not as yet seem to have amounted to much in the case of other "information return" reporting systems (such as bank interest in Canada and the United States). Korea, for instance, at first matched all value-added returns on the computer, although it seems unlikely that this elaborate exercise was more productive than a properly designed audit system would be (Han, 1990).

Another tax "gadget" is the tax amnesty. Recently there has been increased interest in this device as a result of some apparent success with this device in, of all places, the United States (Jackson, 1986). On the whole, however, there seems no reason to change the traditional view that this approach is of little use unless the tax in question will henceforth be fiercely and strictly administered. History suggests that such tightening seldom follows and that those who miss out on one amnesty can likely count on another one in the future.[17] For these reasons, tax amnesties will doubtless continue to be more popular with politicians than with tax analysts.

Legal framework. In contrast to the false hopes of gadgetry, there is clearly much to be gained by ensuring that the basic legal structure of tax adminstration is set out properly (Yudkin, 1973). This path too will not lead to Nirvana, however. In particular, while it is obviously important to have a correct,and enforceable, set of sanctions, the notion that all that is needed to deter evasion is a correct penalty structure is simply fantasy.[18] The one-off game between a rational tax evader and a two-instrument administration postulated in the theoretical tax evasion literature is too far removed from the real world to provide much useful guidance to tax designers or officials. So long as the probability of being caught is close to zero, as is the probability of being subjected to a severe penalty if one is caught, then even within the framework of this model there would seem to be little that penalty design can do to alleviate real-world problems. Why would anyone who can costlessly evade a 50 percent tax rate hesitate to dodge one of 30 or even 10 percent?[19]

Adapting the tax structure. As with earmarking and tax farming, schedular taxation has long had a bad press, much of which has been well deserved. As in the other cases mentioned, however, wholesale condemnation of the schedular approach is by no means justified. As Chapter 7 argued, not only is the income tax in every developing country schedular in practice, but this outcome is inevitable, no matter what the law may say. It is simply not possible to apply a strictly "global" income (or expenditure) tax in the circumstances of most developing countries.

As argued in Chapter 8, the administrative case for a properly designed set of presumptive taxes is strong in most developing countries. Obviously, such crude methods should not be applied in the more organized sector, from which most taxes are likely to be collected in any event. What can be done, however, is to concentrate the scarce administrative skills available in most tax administrations—the "detective" skills needed to uncover accounting fraud, for example—on those firms, seldom more than a few hundred in number, from which most taxes are collected, whether in the form of corporate income taxes, withheld personal income taxes, or sales, excise, and payroll taxes, rather than dissipating them uselessly across a vast sea of noncompliant small and medium traders (Muten, 1981). This may not be fair, but it is reality.

Scarce administrative resources should thus often be concentrated on ensuring that the larger taxpayers, who are generally already on the rolls, comply fully with their fiscal obligation.[20] In the case of the well-off (and notoriously elusive) "professional" class, whose noncompliance brings direct taxation into disrepute in so many countries, the best approach, as with small traders and farmers, is to impose as stiff a presumptive system as can be implemented, with the best officials being used to devise and adapt the standards rather than to deal directly with individual taxpayers.

The moral of this story is of course not that there is no place for an income (or other general direct) tax in any developing country. The moral is rather that those who would design a better direct tax system for such countries must realize that economic and administrative realities are usually such that what is really being done is to design a schedular tax.[21] The tax analyst who approaches his task in this way is unlikely to make the same reform proposals as one who does not take into account the way the world works.

16   Tax Reform in Developing Countries

Over a quarter of a century ago the well-known English economist Nicholas Kaldor (1963) wrote an article provocatively entitled "Will the Underdeveloped Countries Learn to Tax?" Kaldor's argument was twofold: first, that the *level* of taxation in most developing countries was simply too low; and, second, that the *structure* of such taxation as existed was quite inappropriate.

The level of taxation was, he thought, too low to enable the public sector to carry out in a noninflationary fashion the public saving and infrastructural investment needed to launch the poor countries on the road to development, as well as to provide the minimal level of essential public services to their growing populations. Around the same time, Sir Arthur Lewis (1966) independently estimated that the required minimal tax level for these purposes was perhaps 17 percent of national income, compared to the ratio of less than 10 percent then prevailing in a wide range of developing countries.

Since one of the most outstanding facts of the last twenty-five years is that the tax ratio has increased in almost every developing country to levels exceeding the target set by Lewis—in India, to cite only one important example, tax revenues as a percentage of GNP had approximately doubled by the mid-1980s compared to the early 1960s—the first part of Kaldor's question seems to have been answered satisfactorily: the underdeveloped countries have indeed learned to tax.

But have they learned to tax *properly*? Kaldor's concerns with the structure of taxation were essentially two: first, the tax system should help to redress the gross inequality found in most developing countries by levying effective progressive taxes on personal income and expenditure; and, second, it should also encourage the effective utilization of wealth, particularly of the extensive amount of wealth held in the form of agricultural land in most developing countries. To achieve the first of these objectives, Kaldor (1956) proposed an ingenious "self-enforcing" system of interlocking taxes on income, expenditure, and wealth.[1] Similarly, to encourage the fuller utilization of agricultural land, he proposed a tax on the presumptive (or potential) income that would be produced by such land if properly utilized.

These two themes, touching respectively on the distributive and pro-development allocative uses of taxation, were not only developed more fully in other literature of the era (e.g., Wald, 1959) but are still common. The continuing concern with the use of the tax system to redress inequality, for example, has given rise to a flood of academic papers purporting to measure such distributional effects, as well as to tax reforms in many countries with the avowed aim of increasing progressivity—although, as emphasized earlier, at best very modest success has been achieved in this respect. Nevertheless, both India and Sri Lanka introduced a truncated version of Kaldor's original "self-enforcing" scheme of personal taxation, albeit only for short periods (Goode, 1961). Moreover, several Latin American countries have at different times introduced variants of the presumptive income tax on agricultural land, although again with little evident success (Bird, 1974).

Were Kaldor to write his article now, therefore, it would need a different title, since his original concerns have clearly been dealt with, at least to some degree. Not only have the underdeveloped countries learned to tax—with a vengeance, some might say—but many of the ideas on tax structure reform proposed by Kaldor, Richard Musgrave (1971, 1981), Carl Shoup (1959, 1970), and other early writers on taxation in developing countries have clearly had some impact on tax policy in many such countries. Even a cursory glance at the large literature on taxation and tax reform in India, for example, suffices to demonstrate the influence of such ideas both on the content of the tax reform discussion and, to some extent, on the system itself.

Despite such apparent success, it is unlikely that Kaldor and the other scholars who in the 1950s and 1960s envisaged a brave new world of activist states financed by much larger taxes would be particularly happy with the present state of fiscal affairs in most developing countries. More importantly, governments themselves in many countries are clearly not too happy and are casting around for new solutions to the apparently endemic fiscal crises arising largely from the fact that expenditures have risen even more quickly than taxes.

At least some countries appear to think that they may find such a solution in so-called "supply-side" tax policies of the sort popularized, and to some extent implemented, recently in the United States. There is nothing new under the sun, however, so it should come as no surprise that recent advocates of supply-side taxation are largely repeating the advice offered to developing countries some twenty-five years ago by a contemporary of Kaldor, Peter Bauer (1957; Bauer and Yamey, 1957), whose advice differed from Kaldor's in almost every respect. Tax more, said Kaldor; tax less, said Bauer. Increase public spending to encourage development, said Kaldor; reduce public spending to encourage development, said Bauer. Tax the rich especially heavily, said Kaldor; tax the rich, if at all, with great care, said Bauer, who in this and other ways should perhaps be considered the modern father of supply-side taxation in developing countries.

The voice of Bauer, not that of Kaldor, seems to echo more strongly in many developing countries today. At a recent conference on supply-side taxation, for example, the association in India of reductions in the top marginal rate of income tax and a higher growth rate was cited in support of the validity of the supply-side approach (Rabushka and Bartlett, 1985). In fact, however, little analysis of the effects of these or similar cuts in other countries has been carried out. As noted in Chapter 4, such claims with respect to the connection between tax changes and growth rates should be scrutinized with care. There are few aspects of tax theory or policy which are *less* clear than the connection between taxation and growth, and those who pronounce on this complex matter with certainty should, as a rule, be viewed with some suspicion. There is little useful that can be said at this stage about the merits of the new religion of supply-side taxation except to express skepticism about the more exaggerated claims of new converts and interested parties.

Instead, this concluding chapter explores a few reasons why so little has resulted from many of the tax reform efforts that have been undertaken in a wide range of developing countries in recent decades. Some points emerge that require closer attention from would-be tax "reform-mongers" (to use Albert Hirschman's [1963] evocative term), whether their ultimate objective be along the lines set out by Kaldor or those sketched by Bauer.[2]

Taxation and Expenditure

It may seem a bit peculiar to begin a discussion of taxation with a discussion of expenditures. But just as it is meaningful to characterize the end of production as consumption, so is it meaningful to characterize the end of taxation as expenditures. Public finance specialists may at times view matters differently. As argued in Chapter 1, for example, the basic aim of taxes cannot be to raise money to finance government expenditures, since governments can always simply print any money they need. The purpose of taxes is rather to reduce inflationary pressure by taking money away from the private sector in as fair and efficient a fashion as possible. Nevertheless, in the eyes of most people, taxes are clearly intended to finance the expenditures of government.

How people feel about taxes at least to some extent therefore reflects how they feel about expenditure. Governments which enjoy widespread popular support and which most people think are doing a good job are more able to depend on a certain degree of public acceptance of the need for taxation than are governments in countries in which the popular belief is that nothing good comes from the capital city. When people are antagonistic to government, when they feel that it is wasting their money and not acting in their best interest, taxes are clearly likely to be even more unpopular than usual.

This argument should not be misunderstood. It does not rest on the common view that a good tax system is one in which there is a high degree of "voluntary compliance." As noted in Chapter 15, voluntary compliance in this sense is a myth. Even if every individual citizen fully supports all government expenditures and willingly accepts the resulting high tax level in principle, it will still be in his individual interest to reduce his share of the total tax burden, and he must be expected to take every reasonable measure to do so. Any effective direct tax system, as discussed in Chapter 8 above, thus rests more upon taking money away from people before it gets into their hands and scaring them into paying the balance than on their good will. The boundaries of what is considered "reasonable" in terms of tax evasion in any society are elastic, however, and how far they are stretched will depend at least in part upon how the government is perceived by its citizens.

A telling demonstration of this point may be found in a well-known study by Peacock and Wiseman (1967) of the growth of public expenditure in the United Kingdom. A central argument in this study is that the pattern of expenditure growth reflects changes in what they call the "tolerable" level of taxation. At any one time, the argument goes, there is an accepted level of taxation in any country which governs, within limits, the level of sustainable government expenditure. Only when this tolerable level of taxes is increased—as commonly happens in wartime, for example—can expenditure increase. After the war (or other emergency) passes, although the immediate need for expenditures is lessened, people are accustomed to a higher level of taxation, and politicians and officials seldom have difficulty in finding sufficient good things on which to spend to prevent taxes from falling back to their prewar level. The level of expenditure will thus, as a result of the "displacement" of taxes that occurred during the war, remain permanently higher than it would otherwise have been.

Studies for a number of other countries have demonstrated a similar linkage between tax and expenditure levels, to a greater or lesser degree (Diamond and Tait, 1988). The once-popular view of the need for an expanded public-sector development effort as in some sense morally equivalent to a "war" on poverty and economic backwardness may perhaps explain why some analysts have found this displacement hypothesis worthy of exploration in developing countries. While others have been more skeptical of both the underlying argument and the empirical tests to which it has been subjected (Bird, 1972a), countries in which the role of the public sector in development is taken seriously have amply demonstrated their ability to raise taxation, and hence expenditure, to what were once considered wartime levels. The case of India has already been mentioned. Even more dramatic is a case such as Nicaragua, in which a "state-minded" government—admittedly, one which also has a "defense" motivation—raised the level of taxation from 10 percent to 40 percent of (a declining) GNP in only six years (Bird, 1985).

Tax *increase*, whether in India, Nicaragua, or anywhere else, however, is not necessarily tax *reform* in the sense of a change in tax structure that improves both its distributive and allocative effects. On the contrary, the evidence is overwhelming that in almost every developing country in which taxes have increased significantly, the bulk of the increased revenues have come not from the direct taxes on income, expenditure, and wealth that have customarily been stressed by tax reformers but rather from a variety of indirect taxes on consumption—taxes which have equally conventionally been condemned as regressive and (in the forms they have generally taken in developing countries) inefficient. In both India and Nicaragua, for example, virtually the entire increase in tax revenues is attributable to such indirect taxes.[3]

Those versed in the rhetoric and literature of tax reform sometimes seem to find this result hard to understand, perhaps particularly in countries like Nicaragua where simplistic explanations in terms of the interests of the ruling class are not readily applicable (Best, 1976). The preponderance of indirect taxation, however, simply reflects the importance of the administrative constraint on tax reform stressed in Chapter 15.

The initial call for increased taxes by many analysts in the early postwar period rested on the belief that increased taxation was needed to yield the savings needed to finance the investment that was in turn needed to produce the desired rate of economic growth (see Chapter 4). Such calculations of the so-called "required" rate of taxation were at one time almost mandatory in developing countries and are still by no means uncommon. Nevertheless, even the first link in this chain of reasoning is highly questionable, as was first pointed out in a prescient article by Stanley Please (1967). As Please observed, increases in tax revenues in developing countries have often been matched, or more than matched, by increases in current expenditures, with the result that there has been no corresponding increase in public-sector saving. Empirical studies of this so-called "Please effect," like those of the displacement effect mentioned earlier, are by no means conclusive (Please, 1970; Heller, 1975; Chhibber, 1985). Nevertheless, there is enough evidence in enough countries to cast substantial doubt on the validity of the traditional chain of reasoning that development requires additional saving, that the public sector is the most efficient saver, and that increased taxation is the best way to secure the needed additional saving.

Indeed, this argument has been called into question on two distinct grounds. The first is the "supply-side" concern with the disincentive effect of taxes on private saving, a concern dating back at least to Bauer, as noted earlier. The second is the Please concern that increased taxes will be eaten up by increased current expenditure (often in the form of a higher public-sector wage bill) and hence yield no increase in public savings.[4] Of course if *both* of these bad things happened, as some suggest has occurred at times in some countries (e.g., Jamaica in the 1970s), the result of increasing taxes might be a net *decline* in savings, and hence perhaps a fall in the rate of economic growth. The Kaldor-Lewis vision of a world in which increased taxes fuel increased development is thus completely reversed in the Bauer-Please world, in which the opposite occurs.

Such an outcome is bad enough. But matters will clearly be much worse if the expenditure financed by the increased taxes is itself so structured as to do little good in developmental terms. The evidence in some countries that the structure of much government expenditure is at best misguided and at worst almost a complete waste from the point of view of development is stronger than the evidence underlying the attack on taxation as a means of generating public saving.[5] Almost every developing country could use substantial expenditure reform to accompany, support, and perhaps even to some extent replace tax "reform" insofar as the latter means, as it often does, tax increases.

Perhaps the most important conclusion of the modern analysis of public expenditure policy is that the process by which such policies are made bears little resemblance to the model implicit in much development literature, namely, that expenditure decisions are made by a rationally calculating, benevolent, all-powerful dictator whose sole object in life is not only to improve the economic welfare of his citizens but who also possesses the incredibly detailed knowledge that enables him to do so. The problem is not simply that the dictator is seldom that benevolent, although that too is true. The problem is more that even where there is a dictator (as there often is in developing countries), not only is his knowledge limited but so also is the span of his authority. Even the most absolute dictator's power is limited by his need to balance the interests of the conflicting groups that keep him in power. Such balancing acts are even more obvious in a democratic state.

Political scientists sometimes define the two principal functions of government as delivering services and managing conflict. Traditionally, economists have considered only the first of these objectives. Those who study public expenditure cannot similarly close their eyes to the reality of conflicting interests. Even the best-intentioned government can live up to its good intentions only if it is in power, and it can stay in power only if it can muster sufficient support. Some may support it because they agree with its intentions; others because they dislike its opponents even more. The evidence in all countries, however, is that some critically needed support comes from groups to whom, so to speak, government delivers the goods, often in terms of public expenditures favoring their interests—whether it be food subsidies to urban workers, irrigation projects in a particular region, new military equipment, or the subsidization of inefficient but employment-generating public enterprises.[6] Moreover, like tax policy, expenditure policy does not implement itself: it is implemented by a public bureaucracy which expects, and generally receives, its own substantial share of the public-sector pie.

There is, it must be emphasized, nothing evil about this process. In the real world, unlike Utopia, things get done by rewarding those whose support and cooperation is needed to ensure that they get done. The result of this natural process, however, is that it is excessively naive to expect that an extra dollar of tax revenue will necessarily provide an extra dollar of either public saving or benefit to whatever group or groups are the supposed target of public-sector policy at any particular time. Either a substantial fraction of the dollar will go to other, perhaps also worthy (but undoubtedly powerful) groups, or well over a dollar in taxes will be needed to deliver the promised dollar's worth of services to the target group. Increased taxes leading to increased spending on education—or whatever—may indeed provide more education in the end, although this is far from certain in many countries. What *is* certain, however, is that the result will be to provide more, and better-paid, jobs for teachers and those who staff the educational bureaucracy. Subsequent pleas for still more taxes to finance still more education may understandably be received with skepticism by those once burned.

It is probably more important in most developing countries to spend wisely than it is to tax more. Just as the need to invest huge sums in new sources of energy may be reduced by cheaper measures to curtail energy-inefficient activities, so the need for new taxes can be reduced by measures to curtail inefficient expenditure activities. Citizens in most countries seem to think that there are many such activities. They are right, even if they are seldom able to articulate clearly exactly where they think the money is wasted, and even if they always seem to be convinced that any expenditures directly benefiting them are fully justified.

The existing structure of expenditure (like that of taxation) in any country is, in a sense, the necessary result of its economic and political structure. Drastic changes in expenditure (or tax) patterns cannot be expected in the absence of similarly drastic changes in these underlying factors or exogenous events which alter the relevant costs at the margin of spending (or taxing) in one way or another (Hettich and Winer, 1988). It may therefore seem hopelessly quixotic to call for a serious attempt to reform public expenditures in developing countries to get more developmental impact for each tax dollar.

Such a conclusion is too pessimistic, however. Reforms in budgetary processes, in expenditure analysis, management, control, and appraisal systems are neither glamorous nor easy to accomplish. But experience in a number of countries shows that something can be done along those lines and that such changes can have some beneficial influence, at least at the margin (Premchand, 1983). Similarly, changes in transfer programs—whether to individuals or firms or sub-national governments—may, again with difficulty, be accomplished (Uchimura and Bird, 1989). Such changes may, over time, both reduce the need for more taxes to accomplish desired policy ends and perhaps, if the result is to induce a little more faith that something useful will result, lessen resistance to those increases that are necessary as well as increase accountability to citizens as to how the money is spent.

Directions for Tax Reform

Those concerned with promoting development in a fair and efficient way are thus well advised to pay more attention to expenditure. One key to meaningful tax reform may be precisely to link expenditures and revenues more explicitly than has usually been done either in practice or as advocated in the tax reform literature.

This linkage is sometimes discussed, often disparagingly, under the label of "benefit taxation." As noted in Chapter 1, the principle of levying taxes in accordance with the benefits received from the expenditures they finance is of course an old one, with a rationale well grounded in terms of both equity and efficiency. But few seem to realize the extent to which this approach can and should be applied in the modern world, particularly in developing countries which find it difficult either to raise taxes or to spend the proceeds efficiently.

One reason for the relative neglect of the virtues of the benefit tax approach may simply be that the virtues of the competing "ability to pay" approach to taxation seem so much more obvious in the context of countries in which inequalities are usually great, and sometimes growing. In many circumstances a moderately progressive direct tax structure, combined with soundly conceived public expenditure, would indeed appear in principle to be the best way to achieve any desired growth rate in an efficient and acceptable fashion. Nevertheless, in many countries the sorts of progressive taxes applied have been quite arbitrary in their impact and their impact has not been particularly progressive. Redistribution can be achieved through taxation only by taking from those who have—and they generally have, among other things, the power to block the effective implementation of such policies. Moreover, as just mentioned, there is little evidence in most countries that the money thus raised has been well spent.

The overenthusiastic application of the ability-to-pay principle manifested in the highly progressive direct taxes legislated in developing countries such as India—perhaps influenced by the generalized postwar flush of confidence in government's ability to accomplish any desired goal—has in the long run done such countries a positive disservice by bringing both progression and, to some extent, taxation into undue disrepute. It is time to consider new directions for tax reform. One such direction should be much closer attention to the possible use of benefit finance.

Benefit taxes have suffered from an unduly bad press—partly because there have often been clear misuses of the principle of linking taxes and expenditures, partly because of the mistaken view that charging for public services is inherently regressive, if not positively evil, and partly because of the implicit comparison with some nonexistent omniscient benevolent monarch busily equating at all margins and producing the optimal size and structure of public-sector activities. The last of these objections is sheer nonsense. In fact, as noted in Chapter 13, a good case can be made that one way to improve many expenditure programs is precisely to link their provision to demonstrated willingness to pay for them.

The distributive objection to charging for public services has merit in principle with respect to an important range of explicitly redistributive public services, just as other public services cannot, even in principle, be charged for, owing to their inherent "social good" character. Even in fields such as education and health, however, where the plea for the free provision of public services is commonly heard most loudly, studies suggest that the principal beneficiaries of such policies are often those who can most afford to pay (Bird and Horton, 1989).

In part, this result no doubt emerges because of the distorted nature of the services provided—heart transplants instead of primary health care and so on. But more importantly, such studies show clearly the importance of *access* to public services as the key to who benefits. If one result of providing services free is to restrict the expansion of such services, and hence to limit access to them, as Chapter 5 argued, the redistributive results of *not* charging are precisely the opposite of those asserted by the proponents of this policy.

The precise outcome of charging policies of course depends very much on the details of the particular expenditures and financing methods in question. As usual, generalizations are suspect. Nevertheless, probably the key place where more use needs to be made of benefit finance is with respect to the financing of urban public services, as argued in Chapter 12. Such infrastructure can and should be financed in one way or another primarily by the direct beneficiaries —a policy which, incidentally, would have the additional benefit of redressing at least marginally the incentives to overurbanization prevailing in most countries. It is important not to subsidize the urban middle/upper class at expense of both the urban and rural poor, which is what usually happens (Chapter 5). Similar things happen in rural areas, of course, with respect to irrigation schemes and the like. The major problem with proposals for reform in this area is, as always, political: it is extremely hard to take back benefits once bestowed. Nevertheless, more can and should be done along these lines in most countries.

Of course, even a well-designed benefit tax system with good political backing needs to be administered properly to be effective, which leads to a final major point. As argued in Chapter 15, neglect of the administrative factor has led to much of the futility evident in so many tax reforms in developing countries—and not just there, as shown in Christopher Hood's (1976) fascinating study of the limits of administration in attempting to tax gambling and to levy development charges in postwar Britain. There are some things governments just cannot do, or at least do well enough to be worth doing, and there are, inevitably, more such things in a developing country.

Taxes in developing countries must be designed so that they will work with a poor administration. Tax reforms must aim not at producing a finely tuned masterpiece that will work wonders if properly implemented but will fail or produce poor or perverse results if poorly administered—because such reforms will, in all likelihood, be poorly administered. Highly progressive income taxes, refined taxes on personal expenditure and wealth, unduly complex value-added taxes, elaborate taxes on the potential income of agricultural land—such clever ideas tend to come crashing to earth when put into place with the usual inadequate administration in poor countries. Moreover, since this is the way things are going to remain, no reform proposals that simply presume, implicitly or explicitly, that administration will be improved mean anything. Indeed, such proposals have too often been seized upon as a sort of panacea to enable governments to solve this or that problem *without* tackling the hard task of introducing the sort of technically competent, honest, and dedicated administration that such proposals usually assume already exists, or can readily be brought into being. One should also be clear that even competent, honest, and dedicated tax officials in most countries—and it is amazing how many of them there are, even in the most corrupt countries—can seldom do their jobs properly, for lack of adequate political support on the one hand and the minimal resources needed on the other.

Those proposing tax reforms must therefore understand thoroughly the existing administration and assess realistically the possibility of rapid improvement. Unfortunately, all too many reform proposals in developing countries would complicate, not simplify, the work of an already overloaded administration and hence are likely to fail.

As emphasized in Chapter 15, the solution to this problem is simply to try to design a tax reform that "works," that is, produces better results than the present system with an administration of the caliber of that which now exists, and is likely to continue to persist, in most developing countries. Complex proposals such as Kaldor's (1956) interlocking income, expenditure, and wealth taxes or his tax on the presumptive income of agricultural land should be shunned. Such schemes have not worked, and they will not work, in the conditions of most developing countries. Too often tax designers have been led astray by the futile search for the perfect fiscal instrument, not realizing that the perfect is often the enemy of the good, in the sense of a roughly acceptable tax system, that is, one that can be administered roughly and still produce acceptable results. In the income tax field, for example, the key to success is invariably a good withholding system supplemented by some sort of legally based presumptive assessment method on the hard-to-tax groups, as argued in Chapter 8 above. Both of these approaches work best if rates are not too high or steeply progressive. In the sales tax field, for some countries the best that can be done is a physically controlled excise system of varying dimensions—most revenues come from alcohol, tobacco, and fuel in any case—though some use of the value-added principle is both feasible and desirable within limits in many countries, largely to reduce cascading (Chapter 9 and Bahl, 1991). The many small, open countries with little domestic production and relatively low tariffs on most items may achieve much the same results by levying a uniform tariff on imports, while exercising due care to avoid fostering inefficient industrial development (Bird, 1989a). As for wealth taxes, simple flat-rate taxes on urban and rural property, coupled with the special assessments to finance urban public works discussed in Chapter 12, are about all that can be done in all but the most advanced developing countries (Bird, 1974).[7]

The "brave new world" of tax reform sketched in the previous paragraph may not sound either very brave or very new, but it is the world in which most developing countries live. Since he who would change the world must first understand it, starting from such a basis offers a better prospect of attaining a genuinely fair, generally efficient, tax system than the finest academic dream of perfection.

Conclusion

Three conclusions emerge with respect to tax reform in developing countries. First, since tax "reform" in such countries almost invariably means tax increase, such reform must be accompanied—or perhaps even replaced—by expenditure reform. Second, more attention should be paid to the benefit principle of finance, broadly conceived, both in the sense of charging for public services where feasible (and distributionally acceptable) and particularly in the sense of matching expenditures and tax responsibilities in at least the richer urban areas. And, third, as emphasized also in Chapter 14, whatever tax changes are carried out should be "robust" in the sense that they will produce the desired results however poorly they are administered.

None of these recommendations is easy to implement. The first requires a detailed and painful examination of expenditure policy and management and will undoubtedly encounter substantial political opposition from powerful beneficiaries. The same is true of the second, which in addition has to overcome a common philosophical hangup favoring the free provision of "public" services. And the third requires both, again, closely detailed examination of reality and, in all likelihood, the establishment of fairly modest "reform" goals. The lure of the new—computerization, value-added taxation, "cash-flow" taxes, "supply-side" incentives, or whatever—is always great. One can only hope that at least some governments will be strong enough, and wise enough, to cease chasing after fundamentally nonexistent panaceas to their fiscal problems and to begin paying adequate attention to such mundane but important concerns as those emphasized here.

Notes

Chapter 1: A Primer on Taxation and Development

1. This section to some extent follows a discussion in the Canadian Carter Report (Royal Commission on Taxation, 1966, vol. 1, chap. 1).

2. For a detailed treatment of this subject in the context of a developed country (Canada), see Bird (1976a).

3. See Musgrave and Musgrave (1989), chap. 4, for a careful exposition of this concept.

4. Tait and Heller (1982), for example, show the importance of essentially "private" public expenditures (such as most education and health expenditures) even in the poorest countries.

5. For an attempt to dislodge such prejudices with respect to both urban public service charges and property taxes, see Bird and Miller (1989), as well as Chapter 5 below.

6. The "urban bias" of much development policy is set out in Lipton (1976). The fiscal implications of rectifying this bias are discussed in the Colombian context in Bird (1984), as well as Chapter 12 below.

7. This was, for instance, the view taken by the Canadian Carter Commission cited in note 1 above.

8. For a recent review of government policy and the poor in developing countries, see Bird and Horton (1989).

9. In part for this reason, the tax structure has been called "quasi-constitutional" by Head and Bird (1983).

10. In recent years numerous attempts have been made to formalize such distributional judgments in the "optimal tax" literature (Ahmad and Stern, 1989). In the

end, however, equity inevitably lies in the eye of the beholder rather than in the terms of a formula.

11. For critical appraisals of such incentives in developed countries see Bird (1980) and Bosworth (1984). Similar criticisms may readily be applied to most tax incentives in developing countries.

12. Indonesia, convinced by such arguments, recently took the bold step of abolishing all income tax incentives (Gillis, 1985). This position may perhaps not be sustained too long in view of the competitive aspect of much incentive legislation, but the experiment should nonetheless be observed closely.

13. An extensive review of such arguments (e.g., in Gandhi, 1966) and a skeptical treatment of them, may be found in Bird (1974).

14. In this connection, however, note that there is almost no evidence that the *marginal* propensity to save of the rich is particularly high in any country: for further discussion, see Bird (1970a).

15. For a useful recent review of this literature, see Gandhi et al. (1987).

16. As shown in Bird and DeWulf (1973) and DeWulf (1975), however, their systems are not particularly regressive either.

17. A case in point is Pakistan, once praised (Papanek, 1967) for policies more or less like those sketched here. Subsequent events in that country have served to underline some of the dangers inherent in such inegalitarian policies. See also Chapter 4 below.

18. For exchange-constrained models, see Chenery and Strout (1966) and Vanek (1967). In a small, open economy all that policies inducing more private domestic saving generally do is to alter the ownership of the capital stock, not its size.

19. If the rich are savers, an almost quasi-Keynesian situation may perhaps prevail, in that *reducing* savings may increase employment and income!

20. The recent emergence of the "expenditure tax" literature (Kaldor, 1955; Institute for Fiscal Studies, 1978; Bradford, 1986) has cast some doubt on this proposition in the eyes of many younger economists. As yet, however, no country, developed or developing, appears to have accepted these new views to any significant extent.

21. The importance of such "unneutralities" is one of the main themes in Bird (1970b). The optimal tax approach (Newbery and Stern, 1987) makes neutrality the key policy goal but argues that nonuniform rates are generally needed to achieve this target. This approach neglects unduly the severe administrative and informational constraints that suggest uniformity as the lesser evil (Lindbeck, 1987; Slemrod, 1990).

22. This argument is elaborated in the Canadian context in Bird (1970c). In some circumstances, a more ambitious "package" approach of the sort carried out in the United States in 1986 may prove workable. For two recent developing-country examples (Jamaica and Indonesia), see Gillis (1985) and Bahl (1991). This question is discussed in more detail in Gillis (1989a).

23. See, for instance, the discussion of land tax design in Bird (1974).

24. *Ex ante* and *ex post* elasticity (or "buoyancy") are sometimes distinguished, with most emphasis being put on the former: for an early discussion, see Sahota (1961). However, the latter, which incorporates the "average" realized rate of dis-

cretionary change over time, seems the more relevant measure in most developing countries.

25. The more or less explicitly differential treatment of certain ethnic groups in Malaysia is a particularly obvious example (Snodgrass, 1974).

26. The distinction between tax reform and tax design is emphasized in Feldstein (1976); see also Bird (1977a) and Chapter 14 below.

27. See, for example, the discussion of "getting the prices right" in Bird (1982) and Chapter 6 below.

28. For more general arguments pointing in the same direction, see Hirschman (1963), Popper (1957), and Simon (1971). See also the discussion of this issue in Gillis (1989a).

Chapter 2: Analyzing Tax Policy

1. Kaldor (1965) proposed a tax on the potential output that land would yield if managed with average efficiency: for a critical evaluation of this proposal, see Bird (1974).

2. As noted in passing in Chapter 1, the optimal tax approach to reform set out in detail in Newbery and Stern (1987), while it does not posit an "optimal" system for all countries, is also as yet of relatively little use in practice both because of its failure to take administrative constraints adequately into account (Slemrod, 1990) and its impractical informational requirements. Nonetheless, as argued in Bird (1987), in the long run this approach may be more promising than the alternative approaches criticized in the text.

3. For an early attempt to live up to this demanding prescription, see Bird (1970b).

4. For surveys of earlier work, see Schlesinger (1965), Bird and Oldman (1968), and Andic and Peacock (1966). Matters have of course improved over the years, as the detailed analysis of various country experiences in Gillis (1989) demonstrates, but there are still many examples of the sort of work criticized here.

5. Economists, while perhaps willing to accept this view of equity goals, may bridle at the similar characterization of the well-established efficiency properties underlying the neutrality norm. Nonetheless, as Head (1968) argues, policy prescriptions based on welfare economics criteria—whether "new" or (as in the optimal tax literature) "old" welfare economics—are, in the end, no more persuasive than the number of relevant actors in the policy process who are persuaded. Quite apart from the fact that a neutral tax system may not be the best way to achieve allocative efficiency in the conditions of many developing countries, efficiency as the only or prime goal of policy does not seem to have won too many adherents in developing countries—or elsewhere!

6. The terminology used to describe the various approaches to tax policy is taken from Head (1968).

7. An example of an analysis along these lines is Bird (1970a). If the divergence of views between advisor and client is too great to be handled in this fashion, a principled advisor should resign.

8. For an extended argument along these lines (in the relatively stable and conservative context of Canada), see Bird (1970c).

9. This point is reinforced by many of the case studies reported in Gillis (1989), although see Gillis (1989a) for an extended (and different) discussion of the lessons to be drawn from these studies.

10. See, for example, the discussion of Colombian experience in introducing the sales tax in Bird (1968); the subsequent history of the sales tax set out in Perry and Cardenas (1986) reinforces the point.

11. Mention of the prolonged tribulations of trade policy in many countries—see, for example, Bhagwati (1978) and Krueger (1978)—may serve to make the point. As argued in Bird (1970b), chap. 6, the best (albeit idealistic) answer appears to be to "institutionalize" tax reform studies (McIntyre and Oldman, 1975) and to develop, so to speak, a "shelf" of tax reform projects to be implemented when crisis conditions require (and permit) change.

12. For a more extended discussion of tax reform in Colombia, see McLure (1989).

13. Ascher (1989) implies that carrying out a tax reform has almost become a symbol of "machismo" for governments in Colombia!

14. See Bird (1968a) for an early example.

15. See the recent discussion and evaluation in Perry and Cardenas (1986).

16. For a telling discussion along these lines, see the exchange between Radian (1979) and Ben-Porath and Bruno (1979); see also Radian and Sharkansky (1977) and Ben-Porath and Bruno (1977).

17. See World Bank (1988), pp. 102–3, for the striking case of Colombia's fifty years of tax reform and, more generally, the various cases discussed in Gillis (1989).

Chapter 3: Assessing Tax Performance

1. Perhaps the clearest example of this approach is Lewis (1966).

2. A more sophisticated version of the same position may be found in Musgrave (1969), where this is called "the only feasible approach" (p. 166).

3. For a similar argument, see Wolf (1988). Marsden's approach is deficient in some critical respects, as shown in Gandhi (1987), and more careful analysis of the relation between taxation and growth is much more equivocal in its results (Skinner, 1988).

4. For a recent example, see Lim (1987) and the comments in Bird (1988).

5. See Please (1967). This hypothesis has subsequently been reviewed and tested, with varying results, by such authors as Please (1970), Mikesell and Zinser (1972), Singh (1975), Heller (1975), and Bahl, Kim, and Park (1986). See also the discussion in Chapter 16 below.

6. This rationale is clearly stated, for example, by Bahl (1971).

7. For extensive discussion of this point in the context of a developed country, see Bird (1979, chap. 6).

8. A number of studies on this point are reviewed in Mikesell and Ziner (1972); see also Heller (1975).

9. See, for example, Singer (1965). This criticism is in fact generally mistaken: project aid (like intergovernmental conditional transfers) almost always stimulates

the aided project relative to other projects, although expenditure on the project out of *local* resources may fall (Bird, 1967a).

10. For strong critiques of this "leverage" approach to aid, see Hirschman and Bird (1968) and Bird (1981).

11. See, for instance, Advisory Commission (1971): this "representative tax" approach was applied to developing countries by Bahl (1972). For a recent review of formula-based intergovernmental transfers in developing countries, see Schroeder (1987); see also Bird (1986) on similar issues in developed countries.

12. Some years ago I was part of a team that made such an analysis of a Central American country for a private bank. "Country risk" analysts in big international banks today are engaged in essentially the same exercise.

13. One of the most important, if largely unsung, contributions to improved understanding of development finance in recent years has been the steady development and improvement of the International Monetary Fund's annual *Government Finance Statistics Yearbook*, an indispensable source of information for all interested in this subject.

14. For trenchant criticism of international fiscal comparisons, see Pryor (1967).

15. Some of the quoted statements come from an earlier study (Chelliah, 1971), itself cited by Chelliah, Baas, and Kelly (1975).

16. Among the early authors, Bahl (1971) recognized most clearly the limitations of this approach; see also Bolnick (1978).

17. For a similarly pessimistic assessment of our apparently endemic urge to quantify before thinking through just what it is we are doing, see the review of another large body of quantitative literature in Diamond and Tait (1988).

18. Of course, supply-side economists might well praise rather than condemn such countries!

19. Much the same result can be obtained simply by dropping those countries with a significant mining sector from the sample (Bird, 1976). Countries that can collect substantial revenues from natural resources often levy below average taxes on the rest of the economy.

20. See Tanzi (1987), who carefully refrains from drawing inferences of the sort criticized here, and the strong critique of tax ratio studies in Tabellini (1985), who shows that it is better to consider total current revenues than taxes alone but that total revenue measures are extremely sensitive to model specification.

21. For recent examples, see Lim (1987) and Wolf (1988).

22. This problem also comes up in some of the recent work relating expenditures, taxes, and growth. Even an author as careful as Skinner (1988), for example, slides into the error of assuming that the only alternative to taxes as a source of government finance is debt, ignoring completely the important question of nontax revenues emphasized by Tabellini (1985). He also fails to take into account the many conceptual and statistical problems with expenditure measures raised by Diamond and Tait (1988).

23. The widely used data of Summers and Heston (1984), for example, are clearly better than uncorrected data but are still subject to many serious problems.

24. For a classic critique of data quality even in developed countries see Mor-

genstern (1963); Whynes (1974) provides an excellent analysis of the problems of quantitative international comparisons.

25. See Kuznets (1966) in general, and Tanzi (1973) in particular with respect to tax studies.

26. It should also be noted that the usual international comparisons of tax "effort" assume implicitly that it is equally easy for a low-income country to raise an additional percentage point of national income in taxes as it is for a high-income country to do so. For a critique of this "proportionality standard," see Bird (1964) and Aaron (1965).

Chapter 4: Redistribution, Growth, and Tax Policy

1. The argument that consumption patterns, particularly their import-intensity, may be important determinants of the rate and pattern of economic growth is discussed in Cline (1975) and Berry and Soligo (1980).

2. This "two-gap" analysis is developed in, for example, Chenery and Strout (1966) and Vanek (1967). For a recent application, see Ize (1989).

3. See Chapter 16 below for the other side of this argument.

4. Cline (1975), and Chapter 6 below, however, take a somewhat skeptical view of this approach.

5. An important reason for restraint with respect to redistributive policy in small, open economies—not developed further in the present book—is the problem of capital outflow in response to tax differentials. Indeed, Bird and McLure (1990) have argued that this problem severely limits the effectiveness of highly progressive personal income taxes even in developed countries.

6. For a recent review of the (far from clear) evidence, see Ebrill (1987). The connection between income tax rates and growth is examined in detail in Manas-Anton (1987).

7. For further discussion of the cases mentioned, see Bird (1985) and Bahl (1991).

8. Unfortunately, de Soto's (1990) excellent study of the growth of the informal economy in Peru never considers the difference between *effective* and *nominal* tax rates, thus substantially reducing the utility of his attempt to consider the extent to which taxation is a factor explaining the growth of this "other" economy. The relevant effective rate is that applicable to marginal investments, as set out by King and Fullerton (1984) and applied to Colombia in McLure et al. (1990).

9. Wolf's (1988) otherwise excellent discussion of nonmarket failure is unfortunately marred by just this sort of argument, based largely on some very weak empirical evidence.

10. The most important contribution of Rabuska and Bartlett (1985) is not the undue emphasis on the connection between the top marginal rate of the personal income tax and growth but rather their pioneering discussion of the "implicit" taxes (and subsidies) resulting from government regulatory policies in developing countries. This topic is explored further in Bird (1991).

Chapter 5: Taxation and the Poor

1. A recent survey of this literature is Shoven and Whalley (1982). For an interesting early attempt at general equilibrium analysis in Malawi, see Minford (1970).

2. See, for example, Tanzi (1974), Meerman (1979), Toye (1981), and, for a recent survey, Bird and Horton (1989).

3. It is in part this consequence that underlies the strong case put forth by McLure and Thirsk (1978) for substantially reducing the importance of such "sumptuary" taxes in developing countries. See also the discussion in Chapter 9 below.

4. See, for example, the summary of three quite different studies of Jamaica over the years (Lovejoy, 1963; McLure, 1977a; Wasylenko, 1987) in Bird and Miller (1989a).

5. This point is developed at length in Bird and DeWulf (1973); for a recent similarly skeptical paper, see McLure (1990).

6. See, e.g., Bahl and Linn (1991), on the effects on property tax incidence of different administrative systems.

7. On the other hand, the same source shows that in thirty-eight of the fifty-five non-oil developing countries for which data are available central governments account for 95 percent or more of all tax revenue, and in only nine of the fifty-five is this proportion less than 90 percent. The explanation is that some of the larger developing countries are the most decentralized. In Brazil, for example, subnational governments collected 24 percent of all taxes in 1982, while in India the comparable figure was 30 percent.

8. Note, however, that there is not much case for levying progressive land tax rates in the first place (Bird, 1974). The main benefits can be achieved through more easily administered flat-rate taxes, although (as noted in the text) there may be merit in exempting *very* small properties. For an extended discussion of the incidence of property taxes in a developed country, see Bird and Slack (1978).

9. As Bird (1984) shows, the proportion of the urban population with access to public water varied widely in different regions of Colombia.

10. As is well known, such subsidization is in any case a second-best alternative to congestion pricing (Churchill, 1972).

11. At the time, a large subsidized urban public bus company provided most transit services, with the balance provided by a variety of private minibuses, often operating illegally. For an extreme example of the importance of private transit to the poor, see de Soto (1990).

12. Much the same result emerged in an earlier (unpublished) study of a similar point in the Philippines, where hair oil—an obvious "luxury"—turned out to be a basic consumption item of the lowest income groups. The Philippine example also points up the rather odd results that may emerge if tax rate classifications are determined on the basis of household surveys that classify as "essential" the most widely used goods—a practice commended by both Due (1970) and Asher and Booth (1983).

13. Incidentally, by far the most regressive tax on processed food turned out to be that on sugar, a finding that again suggests the danger of imposing a priori

views of what is, or is not, a basic necessity for the poor. A similar result was found for Pakistan in Ahmad, Leung, and Stern (1984). See also the discussion in Chapter 9 below.

14. This way of phrasing matters is based on the optimal tax approach, as set out, for example, in Ahmad and Stern (1989). It should be recognized, of course, that since most such foodstuffs are *not* consumed by the poor, exemption is not a particularly efficient way to help them. In the absence of an efficient transfer system, however, it is usually better than nothing.

15. Indeed, many common layman's questions on incidence ("is the tax system as a whole progressive?") can probably never be answered satisfactorily (Bird, 1980a). On the other hand, increasing familiarity with general equilibrium and other modeling techniques has made clearer how dependent the results of incidence studies are not only on data but also on our implicit models. To cite only one example, assuming the forward shifting of excise taxes in the face of trade restrictions, as is commonly done in quantitative studies (for an interesting exception, see Radhu (1965)), requires some strong, and rather strange, assumptions. For an interesting recent review of such questions, see Shah and Whalley (1990).

Chapter 6: Taxation and Employment

1. The rationale for postulating employment as a separate policy goal from income growth or a more equitable income distribution is that it has both an important instrumental value in relation to these other goals *and* an intrinsic value in its own right. While this matter is not pursued further here, a good discussion may be found in Jolly (1973); see also Squire (1981).

2. The failure to discuss tax effects on investment does not, of course, mean that this question is unimportant, even if one's policy concern is solely with increasing employment. Indeed, as noted later, one of the main problems in designing fiscal measures to create employment is to do so without unduly depressing the level of saving and the creation of new capital.

3. Technically, "indirect substitution" refers to the influence of factor prices on factor proportions through altering the output mix, but it is used here in a broader sense to encompass all influences of changing output mixes on factor use. An excellent survey of this literature is Cline (1975).

4. On the other hand, these studies (Cline, 1975) also suggest that even a radically different income distribution may affect savings rates only slightly, a finding in line with the argument in Chapter 4 above.

5. For an early discussion of this point, see Bird (1970b), chap. 4.

6. Of course, the inherent capital bias of the tax system may be offset by the effects of inflation (McLure et al., 1989) or by the implicit taxes levied on capital by financial and other regulatory policies (Bird, 1991).

7. A fourth possibility, that altering factor prices directly may lead to a fall in the prices of labor-intensive goods and hence to "indirect substitution" (see note 3 above), is not discussed separately here.

8. For influential early studies along these lines, see Little, Scitovsky, and Scott (1970) and Bhagwati (1978).

9. See, for example, the papers by Johnson and McKinnon reprinted in Bird and Oldman (1975) pp. 131–53; also Gillis and McLure (1971).

10. For an excellent brief summary of the fiscal aspects of this relationship, see two papers by Stephen Lewis reprinted in Bird and Oldman (1975), pp. 389–409. The broader aspects are thoroughly reviewed in Southworth and Johnston (1967).

11. This emphasis on a more disaggregated approach differs from the position taken in Chenery (1974), pp. 77–78, but generally agrees with the argument in Berry (1974), pp. 227–28. For a thorough discussion of agricultural tax policies, and of changing attitudes on the role of agriculture in development, see Bird (1974), esp. chaps. 1–2.

12. Taxes on products may in principle lead to changes in the process of production in an attempt to reduce pre-tax costs and thus hold the price line: this is the phenomenon that Seligman (1969) labeled "transformation." This point is most commonly raised when labor-intensive products are taxed, especially when the relative private cost of capital remains below its social cost, since the employment-depressing effect of such taxes is thus doubly guaranteed. Either demand will shift away from the taxed products because of the higher prices as a result of the tax, with output and employment in the industry falling, or price and output levels will be maintained in the face of the tax, at the expense of an employment-displacing change in the production process. The hope in an employment-oriented tax policy, of course, is that shifts in the other direction can be similarly induced. The probability of this occurring would seem to hinge largely on prior correction of the factor prices facing entrepreneurs, as stressed later in the text.

13. Peacock and Shaw (1973) cite these two industries in Indonesia.

14. On the other hand, *output* may go up or down; this important question is simply left aside here. For a classic discussion, see Stewart and Streeten (1973). (Note that the proposition in the text implicitly assumes a closed economy.)

15. It is presumed here, perhaps too optimistically, that the obvious adverse effects of such taxation of corporate saving can be offset by increased public saving. For further discussion, see Chapters 1 and 16.

16. This point is particularly important with respect to agriculture, where the greatest potential for productive labor-intensive employment lies in most developing countries: see, for example, Bottomley (1970).

17. The following discussion assumes that there is scope for tax policy measures to affect factor prices and that alterations in factor prices are felt uniformly throughout the economy. No account is taken of the effects of the tax measures discussed here on total revenues or on savings: it is implicitly assumed that any effects on these magnitudes considered to be detrimental can and will be offset through other measures—and that these other measures will not themselves affect relative factor prices. Nor is any attention paid to such other important policy objectives as growth and distribution.

18. For an early analysis along these lines, see Goode (1949). In recent years similar arguments have appeared as part of the explanation for the apparently growing "underground" economies even in developed countries: see Tanzi (1982). As de Soto (1990) argues, however, the principal barriers to entering the formal economy are more likely to be regulatory than fiscal in nature.

19. In the Philippines, for example, tuition paid to private high schools is de-

ductible for income tax purposes; special education deductions have also been allowed in Colombia.

20. The point made earlier in the text about the possibly offsetting effects on population growth of a payroll-financed social security system should also be kept in mind, of course.

21. Since its effects are therefore most unlikely to be similar to those of a general payroll tax, the *curiosum* that in some instances such a tax may not alter the wage-rental ratio (Samuelson, 1966) need not detain us. To mention another reason why this point is not worth further discussion, this result occurs only in a closed economy with no nonreproducible assets.

22. By levying an additional tax geared to the degree of value-added per employee (Peacock and Shaw, 1973).

23. Subsequently, however, the Philippines permitted a special deduction from taxable income (in addition to the normal deduction) by certain firms of direct labor costs up to 25 percent of export revenue. While the effectiveness of this scheme is limited—because, for example, it applies only to export production, and because the deduction also applies to local raw materials (which may be used by capital-intensive firms)—it marks a step in what might be the right direction. Further progress, however, would appear to depend on a more basic restructuring of the prevailing tax incentive laws, which impart a heavy bias in favor of capital.

24. Moreover, experience suggests that embodying such fine-tuned incentives in tax codes may have little effect in the context of most developing countries, where many firms do not even bother to claim depreciation and where in practice taxes are often negotiated between taxpayers and officials.

25. On further reflection, however, McLure (1980) suggested that incentives based on output may be beyond the administrative capability of most countries.

26. For an interesting preliminary effort along these lines, see Chenery et al. (1974), pp. 93–94.

Chapter 7: The Income Tax in Developing Countries

1. As noted in Chapter 1, an alternative concept of "fairness" is satisfied when taxes are allocated in accordance with the benefits taxpayers receive (or are assumed to receive) from government activity. The discussion in this chapter is confined to the problem of financing that large part of government activities which either cannot be related to benefits received by individuals or should not, for policy reasons, be so related.

2. The only other taxes that possesses the same attribute of "personalism" are taxes on personal wealth: see Chapter 10 below.

3. In practice, however, excessive progressivity may induce delinquency and evasion, particularly in inflationary conditions, so that the personal income tax is sometimes one of the *least* elastic revenue sources (Tanzi, 1977).

4. Although personal expenditure-based taxes (such as that advocated in Bradford [1986]) are not discussed in this study, much the same can be said of them.

5. The continued acceptance of the essential justice of income rather than expenditure taxation emerges clearly, for example, from the recent round of tax reforms in developed countries (Organisation for Economic Co-operation and De-

velopment, 1987). Much the same seems true in those developing countries with which I am familiar.

6. See, for instance, Aaron, Galper, and Pechman (1988). It may also be argued that expenditure-based taxes are more suitable for developing countries—particularly inflation-prone developing countries—than income-based taxes on administrative grounds (McLure et al., 1989), but this subject cannot be extensively treated here.

7. The international aspects of income taxation are discussed in Bird (1987a), though not from the perspective of a developing country. See also Oldman (1990).

8. For a rare exception, see Rezende (1976).

9. This appears to have happened, for example, in Bolivia in 1976 (see Musgrave, 1981).

10. The complex issues involved in devising such rules are discussed in Popkin (1973).

11. Farmers also are often taxed separately: see Lent (1973) and Bird (1974).

12. It should be noted also that the combination of the weak taxation of interest income received and the deductibility of interest for tax purposes may mean that the abolition of interest taxation (and deductibility) may actually *increase* revenue—a point emphasized by McLure et al. (1989).

13. A particularly interesting proposal of this sort is described in Bahl (1991). On the other hand, see Bird (1989a) for a case (Papua New Guinea) where a flat-rate tax (e.g. as recommended by Collins [1985]) would definitely be inadvisable.

14. As the lengthy literature on "tax expenditures" indicates, this role of a globalization standard should not be denigrated. See Maktouf and Surrey (1983).

15. An exhaustive discussion of corporate-personal tax integration may be found in McLure (1979).

16. The international aspects of corporate taxes are discussed more extensively in Bird (1987a); see also Bird (1980c) for further discussion of corporate taxation. In recent years, several countries have established taxes on corporate assets either to set a floor under corporate income taxes or to replace such taxes (Bird, 1992).

17. Indeed, Rezende (1976) argues that a revised form of schedular taxation would be more suitable for most developing countries than further moves toward ineffective globalization.

Chapter 8: Income Tax Reform and Administration

1. For a useful discussion and comparison of assessment systems, see Barr, James, and Prest (1977).

2. Systems along these lines may be found, for example, in Bolivia, Indonesia, and Papua New Guinea.

3. The rate applied to payments to nonresidents is often constrained by treaties, as discussed further in Bird (1988a).

4. An extensive system along these lines exists in Egypt, for example.

5. For one suggestion along these lines, see Bird (1970b), p. 62. Useful discussion of current payment systems may be found in Kelley and Oldman (1973), pp. 343–88.

6. The net worth method is discussed in United Nations (1967).

7. The Bolivian tax reform of 1986 was quite different in nature except for the "small taxpayers" discussed in the text. For further discussion, see Bird (1992).

8. The rationale for requiring some form of books and taxpayer filing was presumably largely to accustom taxpayers to the annual tax routine and to keep them aware of their fiscal obligations.

9. This terminology yields the rather unattractive acronym SAG. A later version partly implemented in Jamaica was more attractively labeled the "modified assessment program," or MAP.

10. There will of course likely be wide variation around these averages, however: for one instructive example, see the detailed study of small retailers in Sierra Leone in Isaac (1981).

11. The successful use of such an incentive in postwar Japan (the "Blue Return" system) is discussed in Kelley and Oldman (1973), pp. 221–29. A similar device has been employed in Korea.

12. The guide may also be used by officials as an initial starting point for the selective review of taxpayers who keep books in apparently satisfactory form. When the reported amounts differ widely from the averages set out in the guide, there is obviously something requiring further investigation.

13. This last point deserves special emphasis: it is this which distinguishes the estimated approach suggested here sharply from the *forfait* (negotiation) techniques widely used in some countries (e.g., in francophone Africa). See also Tanzi and Casanegra de Jantscher (1987).

14. Bird (1970b) contains an earlier discussion of presumptive techniques which is generally less favorable to their use outside of agriculture. Two more decades of experience around the world, however, have convinced me that there are really no alternatives.

15. For useful general references see Kelley and Oldman (1973), United Nations (1967), Surrey (1958), and DeGraw and Oldman (1985).

16. This statement is based in part on a study carried out in the Philippines in the early 1970s. On the other hand, the recent detailed work of Roy Bahl (1989) in Jamaica has emphasized the importance in that country of expanding the tax roll. As always, the best policy for any country at any particular time requires close examination of the circumstances.

17. This argument in part underlies the discussion in Chapters 11 and 12 below.

18. On the other hand, Cowell and Gordon (1989) have made a cogent argument for the superiority of random audits in at least some circumstances.

19. This characterization is taken from the important and stimulating study of tax administration by Radian (1980).

20. This characteristic can be added to the "rules for would-be reformers" set out in Bird (1977a); see also Chapter 14 below.

Chapter 9: A New Look at Indirect Taxation

1. See U.S. Treasury (1977), Institute for Fiscal Studies (1978), and Mathews (1984), for examples, although the first two references emphasize *direct* consumption taxes rather than the indirect taxes on which this chapter focuses.

2. For examples of each of these emphases, see McLure (1975), Cnossen (1978), and Stern (1984), respectively.

3. See, for some examples, Cnossen (1975, 1977), Asher and Booth (1983), and Due (1970, 1972, 1976, 1988).

4. All the preceding data are taken from International Monetary Fund (1984).

5. For another instance of a VAT gone wrong, see Bird (1989b) on Argentina.

6. A similar result was earlier reported by Cnossen (1977).

7. So has the related issue of the "optimal" tariff: see Due (1970), Greenaway (1981a), and Bliss (1980). Other useful discussions of the conflict between the revenue and protection uses of import taxes may be found in De Wulf (1980) and Tanzi (1987a).

8. The traditional argument may be found in Due (1970); for the other view, see Cnossen (1984). Due (1988) considers both approaches judiciously.

9. Such indexing should clearly be to a general price index and not to a special "commodity" index.

10. The traditional view is stated in Due (1970) and the "new view" in Kay and Keen (1982). See Due (1988) for an overview.

11. Parenthetically, it should perhaps be noted that taxing the *advertising* of alcohol and tobacco may be more appropriate than taxing the commodities themselves if one accepts the negative externality argument.

12. See also the useful recent review in Ferron (1986).

13. This conclusion is argued for the case of Papua New Guinea in Bird (1983a).

14. On these problems, see, for example, De Wulf (1975), Bird (1980a), and McLure (1990).

15. Note, however, that Cnossen (1978, 1981) has elsewhere favored explicitly differentiated specific-rate excise taxes on allocative grounds.

16. See Stern (1984) for a succinct introduction to this literature and Newbery and Stern (1987) for an extended application.

17. Food subsidies are unlikely to prove an adequate substitute given the administrative difficulties of such programs in most developing countries; see Bird and Horton (1989).

18. As Cnossen (1984) stresses, for instance, if nominally ad valorem rates are levied on administratively determined "constructive values" rather than market prices, they are conceptually identical to taxes levied at specific rates.

19. Although little has been said here on the relation between indirect taxes and economic growth, there seems no reason to urge developing countries to increase still more their heavy reliance on indirect taxes in order to encourage growth; see also Chapter 4 above.

20. For recent examinations of indirect taxation in two very different developing countries see Bird (1985a) on Jamaica and Bird (1989a) on Papua New Guinea. The first recommends a move to a (limited) VAT; the second concludes a VAT is neither feasible nor desirable. See also Shalizi and Squire (1990).

Chapter 10: The Case for Wealth Taxes

1. The most fully realized statement of this ideal remains the Canadian Royal Commission (1966). For a detailed analysis of what happened to this ideal on its

way to reality in Canada, see Bucovetsky and Bird (1972). Chapter 7 above discusses "globalization" as a goal of income taxes in developing countries.

2. See Institute for Fiscal Studies (1978), U.S. Treasury Department (1977), and Bradford (1986). Similar ideas were put forth thirty-some years ago by Kaldor (1955) and applied by him to India in Kaldor (1956); see Goode (1961) for a trenchant discussion.

3. "Wealth" as used here is identical to "property," that is, the legal ownership of assets. It therefore excludes "human capital" (the value of the capital an individual "owns" in the form of his own physical and mental capabilities at any point in time). There has been some theoretical discussion of the possibility and desirability of taxing such human wealth (Break and Turvey, 1964), but this chapter is concerned solely with the taxation of nonhuman wealth both because that is all that is now taxed anywhere and because it is all that should be taxed. As Goode (1976), p. 21, says: "I do not think that human capital can be measured with the degree of accuracy that is properly demanded for taxation. Furthermore, I see dangers of infringement on personal liberties in applying a tax on the present value of potential earnings: Would a person with great earning capacity who refused to work enough to earn the money to pay his tax be sent to jail?"

Moreover, in developing countries, one policy aim should probably be to favor the accumulation of human wealth. Despite the doubts cast on the efficacy of education as a redistributive agent in advanced countries in recent years, the distributional desirability of expanding education in most developing countries seems clear. See, for instance, Berry and Urrutia (1976), chap. 8, and Jimenez (1989).

4. An outstanding (and depressing) feature in most countries is the poor quality of the information available on the size and nature of wealth holdings, particularly toward the upper end of the distributional scale. This data deficiency makes explicit quantification almost impossible in this field. Nevertheless, what little information is available (mostly for the United States, Britain, and Canada) appears to support the general line taken here, namely, that the inequality of wealth distribution is a serious problem and that the tax system could do more than it now does to redress this problem. For a useful introductory discussion of the data, the issues, and possible reforms (in Britain), see Atkinson (1974).

5. See, for particularly interesting examples, Tait (1967), chaps. 10 and 11, on the Rignano plan and Vickrey's "bequeathing power" succession duty, and Institute for Fiscal Studies (1978), chaps. 15 and 16, on such esoteric forms of transfer and wealth taxation as the PAWAT (progressive annual wealth accessions tax).

6. Adequate wealth taxes are even more necessary to complete an expenditure tax system (McLure et al., 1989), but this aspect is not further discussed here.

7. Colombia's presumptive income tax, based largely on net worth data, in effect is an attempt to get around this problem; it is of course not a true income tax at all but rather a variant form of wealth taxation.

8. One danger of relying too heavily on this sort of argument to support wealth taxation is suggested by recent Canadian experience in which introduction of the constructive realization of capital gains at death was accomplished only at the expense of abolishing the federal death tax; the story is told in Bird (1978a).

9. The more fortunate members of society also benefit substantially from the human capital invested in them when they are young. Reducing initial disparities

in material wealth would do little to rectify this imbalance but it would at least prevent matters from being even worse. Even if taxing material wealth encouraged still more investment by the wealthy in (non-taxable) human capital, "the social gain from the rapid accumulation of human wealth could be an offsetting factor" (Brittain [1977], p. 7).

10. The existence of corporations has perhaps weakened the potential evils of highly concentrated personal wealth somewhat, especially in high-income countries, but it hardly eliminates the problem. As Okun (1975) has argued, societies concerned with the use of money to acquire power, particularly political power, can and should formulate and enforce specific rules to prevent money being spent in ways considered undesirable. Nevertheless, the importance of large blocks of wealth, whether spent or not, must not be underestimated, and it would seem wise to support such rules by taking away some of this potential power through wealth taxes.

11. The problem discussed here in part results from various state actions that created monopolies and privileged positions in the first place. The "first-best" approach is to alter these policies directly. In the nature of the policy process, however, the "first-best" is not always possible and one must fall back on such second-best policies as taxation.

12. Actually, as Tait (1967) discusses, many capital levies have not been "true" in the sense of one-time, unexpected levies—and those that have been surprises have often been inequitable in intergenerational terms.

13. See Bird (1972) for further discussion of this point; also Tait (1967).

14. This is especially true of death taxes, the revenue from which (even when poorly administered) may constitute a substantial fraction of the total direct taxes paid by the richest citizens (see text at note 21). Even if one thinks that the rich are rich because they work hard, it seems probable that an income tax is more likely to discourage them from so working than is the prospect of an equivalent tax at death.

15. See the discussion and references in Chapter 6 above, as well as Bird (1974) and Cnossen (1977), chap. 6.

16. This discussion does not attempt to deal with the incentive arguments against taxing capital (and capital income) developed in recent years by such writers as Boskin (1978). My general position on these arguments is (1) that some of the assumptions on how markets function are not very applicable to most developing countries and (2) that the taxes on personal wealth on which the present discussion is focused are so small in the total picture that any undesired impact on saving and growth can easily be offset by adjustments elsewhere. Clearly, however, these arguments require systematic evaluation for each country.

17. The Canadian evidence on this subject, which seems as bad (or good) as that in any other country, is reviewed in Bird (1972).

18. If one is worried about foreign takeovers of locally owned firms, more direct measures can and should be taken to deal with the problem.

19. Some of the literature seems confused on this matter. When discussing the effects of death taxes in general, for example, the disincentive to save for the testator (assumed to accumulate in order to leave an estate) is stressed while the incentive to save for the heir (owing to lower expectation of wealth) is ignored. On

the other hand, when discussing the structure of death taxes—the consanguinity rules mentioned in the text—the effects on heirs are stressed and those on the testator are ignored.

20. This argument is elaborated in Bird (1970c) and (1987a). See also Bird and McLure (1990), where this view is extended to cast doubt on the ability of even developed countries to maintain effective progressive taxes on capital income.

21. Although, as one might expect, the data were very weak, a comparison with the income tax data reported in Musgrave (1981), chap. 13, suggests that death taxes probably constituted a significant fraction of the total income and wealth taxes paid by the upper end of the taxpaying population.

22. A third administrative problem, of course, is to collect the taxes. It is assumed here, perhaps optimistically, that this can be done—although in reality the feasibility of collection no doubt itself depends in part on the political acceptability of the valuation process.

23. The link between net wealth taxes and property taxes came to the fore in Colombia in 1989, when revised valuations in Bogotá caused such a political uproar that the national government felt it necessary to abolish the long-established national net wealth tax.

24. Other arguments for taxes on real property are discussed in the next two chapters.

25. The curious Canadian history certainly confirms this statement (Bird 1978a), although Canada (like Australia) is an outlier among developed countries in having abolished death taxes.

Chapter 11: Intergovernmental Finance and Local Taxation

1. For an example of a centralized outcome see the analysis of Mexico in Bird (1963); for an example of a decentralized outcome, see the analysis of Papua New Guinea in Bird (1983a).

2. The "assignment problem" may be modeled in a number of other ways, as shown in Breton and Scott (1978) and some of the papers in McLure (1983), but this aspect is not further developed here.

3. For an overview of intergovernmental finance in developing countries, see Bird (1980b). A detailed discussion of similar problems in developed federations may be found in Bird (1986).

4. For an example of such a design, see Bird and Slack (1983).

5. This conclusion is based largely on two detailed examinations of very different countries—Bird (1983a) on Papua New Guinea and Bird (1984) on Colombia—as well as the review of developed federations in Bird (1986). (I also live in Canada, where public confusion as to who is responsible for what is endemic.)

6. See the discussion in Bird (1986). To some extent, however, Argentina has breached this rule in recent years (Bird, 1989b).

7. For a detailed analysis in support of this proposition (and that in the next paragraph) in developed countries, see Bird (1986).

8. This assumption underlies the analysis in Bird (1983a).

9. Again, for examples of such analysis, see Bird (1983a, 1984, and 1986)—and note the different conclusions reached in the different circumstances of different

countries. What these analyses suggest is, first, that a historical-institutional approach is not a frill to be tacked on, optionally, to a general theoretical model but an essential ingredient of any policy-relevant approach and, second, that such an approach requires very careful attention to detail and, on the whole, an incrementalist orientation.

10. This point is stressed especially in Bird (1990b) and in Uchimura and Bird (1989).

11. Uchimura and Bird (1989) discuss Colombia's decentralization from this perspective; see also Rojas (1989).

12. This is essentially the system proposed for Colombia in Bird (1984).

13. See Bird (1990b). As Uchimura and Bird (1989) note, however, Colombia has not really succeeded in this task.

14. As Feldstein (1975) has shown, an equalization element is needed in such grants in order to obtain equal outcomes in jurisdictions of different wealth.

15. Caiden and Wildavsky (1974) call this common practice "repetitive budgeting."

16. As Schroeder (1987) notes, this is not always the case.

17. As Uchimura and Bird (1989) note, the absence of such an agency is a major problem in Colombia.

Chapter 12: Financing Urban Development

1. See, for example, Mayo and Gross (1989) on housing.

2. For a particularly clear instance, see Bird (1984). The process is discussed generally in Bird (1980b).

3. In the countryside in many countries an analogous situation exists. With a rapidly growing population, agricultural development must take place at a rapid rate, often requiring heavy investment in transportation facilities to open up agricultural areas and in projects for drainage, flood protection, and irrigation to make more land productive. (For further discussion of rural government finance, see Bird, 1974).

4. For a forceful exposition of the position that rapid urbanization should actually be *promoted* as a means of accelerating economic and social development, see Currie (1966).

5. Of course, as Bahl (1979) and Bahl and Linn (1991) show, many improvements can be made in property tax administration in developing countries.

6. For an interesting variant of such laws, "land adjustment," which has proved successful in a few developing countries, see Doebele (1979). But see also de Soto (1990) for a strong condemnation of the barriers to rational development posed by land use regulations in Peru.

7. See Rhoads and Bird (1967, 1969), Doebele, Grimes, and Linn (1979), Bird (1984), and Pineda (1987) for detailed examinations of Colombian experience over the last twenty years.

8. The exemption of public property from taxation is sometimes justified on the grounds that such property has no commercial value. While this position may recognize the realities of political life, it has no base in economic analysis. The use

of land for public rather than other purposes has an opportunity cost equal to its highest value in alternative uses, and this cost should be recognized in making decisions on the location of public facilities.

9. Critics usually single out the inappropriateness of benefit financing for "redistributive" projects. As shown in Chapter 5, however, the fact is that in many developing countries such "free" (or subsidized) public activities seldom reach the poor.

10. For further discussion of the distributive effects of different local taxes and charges, see Chapter 5 above. Netzer (1966) favors a land-value-increment tax over the valorization tax recommended here; that is, he favors a tax assessed on benefits *actually* received as a result of the work to one on benefits that it is *presumed* will arise in the future. The valorization tax is preferable in developing countries, however, because of the lack of a capital market for financing public works, the more favorable attitudes of taxpayers to benefit taxes, and the growth-inflation cushion of rising property values.

11. Much the same favorable situation for valorization taxes may exist in the rural areas of developing countries. Large areas of rich land may be without any transportation, and construction of a road or railroad may have such dramatic effects on land values (by lowering transportation costs) that a large proportion of the cost of the new road or railroad can often be paid for through valorization taxes. In addition, projects to increase the value of agricultural land through dikes to prevent flooding or canals to provide drainage may have very high benefit-cost ratios in developing countries, so that financing them with valorization taxes may be feasible.

12. In the particular case of the United States, the non-deductibility of special assessments for income tax purposes may also play some explanatory role: see Bird and Slack (1983a).

13. This argument assumes that there is no "Veblen effect"; that is, it is not considered *more* prestigious to hold out of use land whose productive value has risen. Also, if the benefit exceeds the tax, the income effect will tend to increase all consumption, including that of land used for prestige purposes.

Chapter 13: Earmarking Tax Revenues

1. For a more detailed discussion of some of the points mentioned here, see Bird (1976a). The case for more reliance on "benefit" taxes is argued in Bird (1978b).

2. An obvious economic analogy is to a "supported" price set well below the market-determined equilibrium price.

3. For a detailed exploration of earmarking in Colombia, see Bird (1984). A related discussion of earmarking in Bolivia is Musgrave (1981).

4. For further discussion of intergovernmental fiscal transfers, see Chapter 11 above.

5. The extent of such earmarking has sometimes been exaggerated by comparing tax and similar receipts which accrue to general government to the *gross* re-

ceipts of public enterprises. Since these gross receipts are for the most part obtained from the sale of goods and services, they are more similar in nature to private enterprise receipts than to tax receipts. A more reasonable way of treating a public enterprise in public finance accounts is to include its proceeds only on a *net* basis, that is, to enter only such parts of enterprise earnings as are kept by the enterprise or paid over to the government in the form of taxes or savings. This treatment is not intended to deny that public enterprises may differ in important respects from private enterprises—see the discussion in Bird (1984)—but simply to make clear that the share of income and expenditures which flows through the public budget (and can therefore be used to provide public services and to pay for public investment, including that by public enterprises) is not well represented by figures on the gross receipts of public enterprises.

6. For more extensive discussion of the traditional criticism, as well as the alternative views mentioned below, see Bird (1976a).

7. In fact, in the Colombian case mentioned the tax rate was later changed to an ad valorem basis. Unfortunately, with the advent of the 1970s oil crisis, price increases intended to carry out the objectives of energy policy may then have resulted, quite inappropriately, in the construction of more roads (Bird, 1984).

8. Misallocation of resources as a result of earmarked revenues may be less likely if earmarked revenues contribute only part of the finance of the expenditure object to which they are destined—at least if one can assume that the general-revenue financed portion is allocated on a more rational basis. In this case, however, as noted earlier, it is not clear that earmarking serves any useful purpose.

9. In terms made familiar by Hirschman (1971), when the option to "exit" from the system is thus open, those best able to look after their interests will take it, thus reducing the pressure (through "voice") to improve the system—and leaving the weaker participants in the system to suffer its full rigors.

10. Another possible argument for earmarking is to establish worthy causes on a firm basis—sort of an "infant industry" argument. As with "infant industries" set up behind tariff barriers, however, infants with earmarked funding never seem to grow up.

11. Extensive arguments along these lines may be found in the modern literature on organization and administration: see, for example, Simon (1971). For an application to the theory of local government, see Hartle and Bird (1972).

12. When most expenditures come out of general taxes, voter-taxpayers may well suffer from a fiscal illusion to the effect that they are over-taxed (or under-taxed), with the result being under-(or over-) expansion of the public sector (Oates, 1988). It cannot be said which way the *mix* of public goods would change in any country with a change in the mix of earmarked and general financing, since the direction of change depends on the specific nature and distribution of preference functions. It can be said, however, that with a fully earmarked system and a functioning democracy—the last is far from an unimportant qualification, especially when discussing developing countries—the mix of services supplied by the public sector would surely be different from that which now prevails.

13. For further discussion, see Smith (1975, 1984), Linn (1979), and Prest (1969).

Chapter 14: Tax Reform and Tax Design

1. See, for example, the chapter on development finance in Musgrave and Musgrave (1989).

2. Note that Feldstein (1976a) in a way fell into the same error when he argued that only changes in taxes give rise to horizontal inequities. This conclusion follows impeccably from his premises. When markets (over time) function perfectly and individuals are free to choose their activities and expenditures, once behavior has been adjusted to the pre-existing tax structure any change will give rise to windfall gains and losses. The strength of Feldstein's apparent belief in the perfection and freedom of the market system considerably exceeds my own, however, certainly in the context of developing countries.

3. Another way to put this, as noted in Chapter 7 above, is that tax reformers should be risk-averse and avoid changes that may go very wrong.

4. Creative self-doubt about the validity of assumptions and the sensitivity of results to errors in data or analysis need not, however, lead to bland policies aimed at neutrality rather than conscious market intervention, as Brennan and MacGuire (1975) appear to imply. In the fragmented markets of developing countries, even a policy aimed at neutrality in fact requires a high degree of specific intervention, as the optimal tax literature illustrates in painful detail (Newbery and Stern, 1987).

Chapter 15: The Administrative Dimension of Tax Reform

1. Naturally, there are exceptions to this assertion, as to most of the more sweeping generalizations made in this chapter. The early report by Shoup et al. (1959) on Venezuela, for example, paid considerable attention to administration. The later Musgrave reports on Colombia (1971) and Bolivia (1981) are more typical in confining their concern with administration mainly to the vexed issue of the "hard-to-tax" groups. Even more characteristic of much tax policy work is the view epitomized by Kaldor (1980) that administrative deficiencies can and must be rectified to permit desirable policy changes. On the contrary, such problems will persist for a long time to come in most countries. To be successful, policy reform must take this reality into account.

2. Few studies have been made of the actual functioning of tax administrations in developing countries. Much of the best work by outside analysts is essentially nonquantitative (Joint Tax Program, 1965a; Wilkenfeld, 1973; Radian, 1980); the same is true of most of the better published country studies (India, 1960, 1969; Joint Legislative-Executive Tax Commission, 1961), although there is at least one interesting exception (Colombia, 1985). Most of the available literature is essentially prescriptive (Public Administration Service, 1961; United Nations, 1967, 1968; Nowak, 1970; Kelley and Oldman, 1973). There are few (if any) published empirical studies in developing countries of many of the key administrative issues touched on here: the costs and benefits of tax amnesties, the costs of rate differentiation and exemptions under sales taxes, administrative and compliance costs, the incidence and allocative effects of appeal procedures, the effects of revenue quotas and incentive systems, the costs and benefits of refund systems, audit selection

procedure, and so on. This research agenda obviously requires systematic exploration if the propositions asserted here are to be tested properly. For a useful beginning, see Yitzhaki and Vaknin (1989).

3. This is a good description, for example, of the situation in Bolivia a decade
ago (Musgrave, 1981). In 1986, however, Bolivia followed a path quite different from
that proposed by the Musgrave mission when it abolished the income tax and
replaced it by a set of consumption and asset taxes, calling the latter "presumed
income" taxes (American Chamber of Commerce, 1986; Bird, 1992).

4. The best description of this process at its extreme remains Hinrichs (1962).
To some extent, the alternative minimum taxes of some countries in francophone
West Africa as well as Colombia (where gross receipts were until recently an
alternative basis of presumption to net wealth) also work in the same direction
(Muten, 1982). The new Bolivian system mentioned in note 3 goes further, replacing
the business income tax by a tax on all companies at a rate of 2 percent on net
assets at the end of the year.

5. This is the characterization of the Jamaican consumption tax that emerges
from Cnossen (1984). As mentioned in Chapter 9, many so-called "general" sales
taxes in developing countries amount to little more than a levy on imports and a
few "excisables."

6. A particularly interesting discussion of this interaction is Boyd (1986), who
draws an analogy with the analysis of "predator-prey" relations. See also Mayshar
(1986), who takes a longer time perspective, referring to "a slow Darwinian process
of mutation and adaption."

7. The slow course of administrative improvement may be illustrated by referring to three studies of Colombia over the years (Caldwell, 1953; Bird, 1970b; and
McLure, 1982). There have clearly been substantial improvements in Colombian
tax administration over these three decades, but progress has been slow and episodic and there is still a very long way to go.

8. As Adam Smith put it: "In those corrupted governments where there is at
least a general suspicion of much unnecessary expence, and great misapplication
of the public revenue, the laws which guard it are little respected" (quoted in
Skinner and Slemrod, 1985, p. 353). This point is developed further in the next
chapter.

9. Governments should not, as some now do, burden even willing taxpayers
with such unnecessary discomforts as the need to stand in long queues to file
returns or pay taxes, needless requirements to submit numerous copies of returns,
and even charges for supplying returns in the first place.

10. A more promising approach may be to establish what is in effect a new tax
administration, for example, by contracting collection of export taxes to the central
bank or some other "reliable" organization, or by creating a new quasi-independent
revenue authority (such as the Revenue Board in Jamaica). Such measures may be
effective for a period, but over time the bad old ways are likely to creep in
again—unless, of course, the underlying factors creating the problems in the first
place have been corrected.

11. This change in the fee basis obviously obviates some of the worst problems
with tax farming. The basic problem with privatizing monopolies like revenue col-

lection, however, is to specify the terms of the contract. Indeed, if the contract is adequately specified, and compliance with it sufficiently monitored, it might be as efficient for the government to do the job itself!

12. Paying officials by a mixture of fees and bribes need not be inconsistent with those officials' doing a good job—although it is clearly a very dangerous practice. To take an historical example, Samuel Pepys has come down in history as one of Britain's greatest naval administrators; he was also, however, by modern standards an avid seeker and taker of bribes, gifts, fees, and commissions—as witnessed by countless references in his famous diary—and was, as the same source makes plain, acting entirely as expected.

13. This description is in part based on Indonesian practice in the early 1980s. (Until 1971, an explicit bonus was paid to those exceeding collection targets.)

14. In the case of Indonesia, for example, targeting may be condemned as arbitrary, inequitable, and discouraging administrative effort. Alternatively, it may be accepted as conforming to local standards of fairness and administrative probity while providing a modicum of oversight and not affecting administrative effort adversely (since close examination suggested that the effort tended to establish the targets, rather than vice versa).

15. Such devices may in practice often hinder the honest more than they deter the unworthy. A classic example is the Contraloria system in some Latin American countries (Bird, 1982a).

16. Such schemes are employed to various extents in some Latin American countries, Turkey, and Taiwan.

17. In fact, it might even be suggested that to the extent an amnesty successfully increases revenues, it often tends to *reduce* administrative efforts!

18. The theoretical literature on this subject has become so large that all that can be done here is to note that it started with Allingham and Sandmo (1972) and has since grown like wildfire. For three useful summaries by the IMF's Fiscal Affairs Department, see Sisson (1981), Richupan (1987), and Mansfield (1988). As Mansfield (1988) notes, the basic problem with this theoretical literature is that for the most part it ignores the constraints that permit the system to function at all. For useful reviews of tax sanctions, see Oldman (1965) and Gordon (1988).

19. For a formal argument suggesting that evasion is basically independent of the tax rate, see Yitzhaki (1986).

20. In Bolivia, for example, the main tax "gap" arose from the ineffective taxation of capital income rather than the failure to tap the self-employed (Musgrave, 1981). In Jamaica, however, the latter problem seems to have been greater (Bahl, 1989).

21. One reason surprisingly little attention has been paid to the weak taxation of capital income in many developing countries has been the influence of so-called "effective rate" analysis, as popularized by King and Fullerton (1984). For examples of such studies in developing countries, see Agell (1986), Pellechio (1987), and McLure et al. (1989). These analyses generally show, quite correctly, that *at the margin* the interaction of tax structure and inflation may result in a high marginal tax rate on prospective new investments. Such simulated calculations, however, assume (nonexistent) perfect tax administration. Moreover, as is true even in the

United States (Steuerle, 1982), these results are quite compatible with a situation in which virtually all capital income escapes personal income tax.

Chapter 16: Tax Reform in Developing Countries

1. This scheme seems unworkable, however, and has in any case not been taken seriously anywhere (Goode, 1981). Much the same fate has been suffered by the proposal for a "self-assessed" property tax (Harberger, 1965; Strasma, 1965), although in this case variants of such systems have in fact been employed in some countries, albeit without much success (Bird, 1984a). Once again, there seems to be no relief for the hard-pressed tax administrator in clever design. In the end, the only way to administer a tax is to do so.

2. See also the review of postwar tax reforms in developing countries in Gillis (1989).

3. The major exceptions are countries that have reaped revenue bonanzas from natural resource price increases: for an overview of this subject, see Gillis (1983).

4. Of course, not all "current" expenditure is bad nor "investment" expenditure good; nonetheless, in the present context, the simplification in the text seems acceptable.

5. For extensive discussion of one country see Bird (1984); see also World Bank (1988), chap. 5.

6. As pointed out in Bird and Horton (1989), the poor are most unlikely to be very influential in this process—a reality which goes far to explain the commonly noted failure of structural adjustment programs to protect the poor (Chhibber and Khalilzadeh-Shirazi, 1986).

7. In addition, as argued in Chapter 10, a surprisingly strong case can be made in many developing countries for even a relatively ineffective tax on personal wealth.

References

Aaron, H. J. (1965). "Some Criticisms of Tax Burden Indices." *National Tax Journal*, 17: 313–16.

——— (1975). *Who Pays the Property Tax? A New View.* Washington, D.C.: Brookings Institution.

———, ed. (1976). *Inflation and the Income Tax.* Washington, D.C.: Brookings Institution.

Aaron, H. J., H. Galper, and J. A. Pechman, eds. (1988). *Uneasy Compromise: Problems of a Hybrid Income-Consumption Tax.* Washington, D.C.: Brookings Institution.

Adler, J. H., E. R. Schlesinger, and E. C. Olson (1952). *Public Finance and Economic Development in Guatemala.* Stanford: Stanford University Press.

Advisory Commission on Intergovernmental Relations (1971). *Measuring the Fiscal Capacity and Effort of State and Local Areas.* Washington, D.C.

Agell, J. N. (1986). "Subsidy to Capital through Tax Incentives." In Shome (1986).

Ahluwalia, M. S. (1973). "Taxes, Subsidies, and Employment." *Quarterly Journal of Economics*, 87: 393–409.

Ahmad, E., and N. Stern (1983). "Effective Taxes and Tax Reform in India." Development Economics Research Centre, University of Warwick, Discussion Paper 25.

——— (1989). "Taxation in Developing Countries." In H. Chenery and T. Srinivasan, eds., *Handbook of Development Economics.* Vol. 2. Amsterdam: North-Holland. 2: 1005–92.

Ahmad, E., H-M. Leung, and N. Stern (1984). "Demand Response and the Reform of Indirect Taxes in Pakistan." Development Economics Research Centre, University of Warwick, Discussion Paper 50.

Allen, R.G.D. (1968). *Macro-economic Theory.* London: Macmillan.

Allingham, M. G., and A. Sandmo (1972). "Income Tax Evasion: A Theoretical Analysis." *Journal of Public Economics,* 1: 323–28.

Alonso, W. (1964). *Location and Land Use.* Cambridge, Mass.: Harvard University Press.

American Chamber of Commerce of Bolivia (1986). *Tax Reform Law: An Explanation of Its Contents.* La Paz.

Andic, S., and A. Peacock (1966). "Fiscal Surveys and Economic Development." *Kyklos,* 19: 620–39; excerpted in Bird and Oldman (1975).

Andrews, W. (1967). "The Accessions Tax Proposal." *Tax Law Review,* 22: 589–633.

Arango, S., J. Bueno, and F. Gomez de Arango, eds. (1979). *La estructura fiscal colombiana.* Bogota: Redactores Asociados.

Archaya, S. N., et al. (1986). *Aspects of the Black Economy in India.* New Delhi: National Institute for Public Finance and Public Policy.

Ascher, W. (1989). "Risk, Politics, and Tax Reform: Lessons from some Latin American Experiences." In Gillis (1989).

Asher, M. G., and A. Booth (1983). *Indirect Taxation in ASEAN.* Singapore: Singapore University Press.

Atkinson, A. B. (1974). *Unequal Shares.* Harmondsworth: Penguin Books.

Bahl, R. W. (1971). "A Regression Approach to Tax Effort and Tax Ratio Analysis." *International Monetary Fund Staff Papers,* 18: 570–608.

——— (1972). "A Representative Tax System Approach to Measuring Tax Effort in Developing Countries." *International Monetary Fund Staff Papers,* 19: 87–122.

——— (1989). "The Jamaican Tax Reform." In Gillis (1989).

———, ed. (1979). *The Taxation of Urban Property in Less Developed Countries.* Madison: University of Wisconsin Press.

———, ed. (1991). *The Jamaican Tax Reform.* Cambridge, Mass.: Oelgeschlager, Gunn, and Hain.

Bahl, R. W. and J. F. Linn (1991). *Urban Public Finance in Developing Countries.* New York: Oxford University Press, for the World Bank.

Bahl, R. W., C. K. Kim, and C. K. Park (1986). *Public Finance during the Korean Modernization Process.* Cambridge, Mass.: Harvard University Press.

Balassa, B. (1975). "Reforming the System of Incentives in Developing Countries." *World Development,* 3: 365–82.

Barr, N. A., S. R. James, and A. R. Prest (1977). *Self-Assessment for Income Tax.* London: Heinemann Educational Books.

Bauer, P. T. (1957). *Economic Analysis and Policy in Under-developed Countries.* Durham: Duke University Press.

Bauer, P. T. and B. S. Yamey (1957). *The Economics of Under-developed Countries.* Cambridge: Nisbet.

Becker, A. P., ed. (1969). *Land and Building Taxes: Their Effect on Economic Development.* Madison: University of Wisconsin Press.

Ben-Porath, Y., and M. Bruno (1977). "The Political Economy of a Tax Reform: Israel 1975." *Journal of Public Economics*, 7: 285–307.

——— (1979). "Reply to Dr. Radian." *Journal of Public Economics*, 11: 395–96.

Berry, R. A. (1974). "Factor Proportions and Urban Employment in Developing Countries." *International Labour Review*, 109: 217–336.

Berry, R. A., and R. Soligo, eds. (1980). *Economic Policy and Income Distribution in Colombia.* Boulder, Colorado: Westview Press.

Berry, R. A. and Urrutia, M. (1976). *Income Distribution in Colombia.* New Haven: Yale University Press.

Bertrand, T. (1969). "Rural Taxation in Thailand." *Pacific Affairs*, 12: 178–88.

Best, M. H. (1976). "Political Power and Tax Revenues in Central America." *Journal of Development Economics*, 3: 49–82.

Bhagwati, J. N. (1978). *Foreign Trade Regimes and Economic Development: Anatomy and Consequences of Exchange Control Regimes.* Cambridge, Mass.: Ballinger Publishing Co., for the National Bureau of Economic Research.

——— (1988). *Protectionism.* Cambridge, Mass.: MIT Press.

Bird, R. M. (1963). "The Economy of the Mexican Federal District." *Inter-American Economic Affairs*, 17: 19–52.

——— (1964). "A Note on 'Tax Sacrifice' Comparisons." *National Tax Journal*, 17: 303–8.

——— (1967). "Stamp Tax Reform in Colombia." *Bulletin for International Fiscal Documentation*, 21: 247–55.

——— (1967a). "A Note on the Influence of Foreign Aid on Local Expenditures." *Social and Economic Studies*, 16: 206–10.

——— (1968). "Sales Taxation and Development Planning—Colombia." in G. F. Papanek, ed., *Development Policy: Theory and Practice.* Cambridge, Mass.: Harvard University Press.

——— (1968a). "Coffee Tax Policy in Colombia." *Inter-American Economic Affairs*, 22: 75–86.

——— (1969). "Income Redistribution, Economic Growth, and Tax Policy." *Proceedings of the 61st Annual Conference of the National Tax Association.* Columbus, Ohio.

——— (1970). "Optimal Tax Policy for a Developing Country: The Case of Colombia." *Finanzarchiv*, 29: 30–53.

——— (1970a). "Income Redistribution and Tax Policy in Colombia." *Economic Development and Cultural Change*, 18: 519–35.

——— (1970b). *Taxation and Development: Lessons from Colombian Experience.* Cambridge, Mass.: Harvard University Press.

——— (1970c). "The Tax Kaleidoscope: Perspectives on Tax Reform in Canada." *Canadian Tax Journal*, 18: 444–78.

———— (1972). "The Case for Taxing Personal Wealth." In Canadian Tax Foundation, *Proceedings of Annual Tax Conference*. Toronto.

———— (1972a). "The 'Displacement Effect': A Critical Note." *Finanzarchiv*, 30: 454–63.

———— (1974). *Taxing Agricultural Land in Developing Countries*. Cambridge, Mass.: Harvard University Press.

———— (1974a). "Public Finance and Inequality." *Finance and Development*, 11: 2–4, 34.

———— (1976). "Assessing Tax Performance in Developing Countries: A Critical Review of the Literature." *Finanzarchiv*, 34: 244–65.

———— (1976a). *Charging for Public Services: A New Look at an Old Idea*. Toronto: Canadian Tax Foundation.

———— (1977). "Financing Urban Development: A Worldwide Challenge." *Habitat International*, 2: 549–56.

———— (1977a). "Tax Reform and Tax Design in Developing Countries." *Rivista di diritto finanziario e scienza delle finanze*, 36: 297–306.

———— (1978). "Perspectives on Wealth Taxation." *Bulletin for International Fiscal Documentation*, 32: 479–88.

———— (1978a). "Canada's Vanishing Death Taxes." *Osgoode Hall Law Journal*, 16: 133–45.

———— (1978b). "A New Look at Benefit Taxation." In H. C. Recktenwald, ed., *Secular Trends of the Public Sector*. Paris: Editions Cujas.

———— (1979). *Financing Canadian Government: A Quantitative Overview*. Toronto: Canadian Tax Foundation.

———— (1980). *Tax Incentives for Investment: The State of the Art*. Toronto: Canadian Tax Foundation.

———— (1980a). "Income Redistribution through the Fiscal System: The Limits of Knowledge." *American Economic Review, Papers and Proceedings*, 90: 77–81.

———— (1980b). *Central-Local Fiscal Relations and the Provision of Urban Public Services*. Research Monograph No. 30. Canberra: Australian National University Press, for the Centre for Research on Federal Financial Relations.

———— (1980c). *Taxing Corporations*. Toronto: Butterworths, for Institute for Research on Public Policy.

———— (1981). "Exercising Policy Leverage through Aid: A Critical Survey." *Canadian Journal of Development Economics*, 2: 366–85.

———— (1982). "Taxation and Employment in Developing Countries." *Finanzarchiv*, 40: 211–39.

———— (1982a). "Budgeting and Expenditure Control in Colombia." *Public Budgeting and Finance*, 2: 87–99.

———— (1982b). "The Costs of Collecting Taxes: Preliminary Reflections of the Uses and Limits of Cost Studies." *Canadian Tax Journal*, 30: 860–65.

———— (1983). "Income Tax Reform in Developing Countries: The Administrative Dimension." *Bulletin for International Fiscal Documentation,* 37: 3–14.

—— (1983a). *The Allocation of Taxing Powers in Papua New Guinea.* Discussion Paper No. 15. Port Moresby: Institute of National Affairs.

—— (1984). *Intergovernmental Finance in Colombia.* Cambridge, Mass.: Harvard Law School International Tax Program.

—— (1984a). "Put up or Shut up: Self Assessment and Asymmetric Information." *Journal of Policy Analysis and Management,* 3: 618–20.

—— (1985). "A Preliminary Report on the Guatemalan Tax System." Local Revenue Assistance Project, Metropolitan Studies Program, Syracuse University.

—— (1985a). "The Reform of Indirect Taxes in Jamaica." Jamaica Tax Structure Examination Project Staff Paper No. 24, Metropolitan Studies Program, Syracuse University.

—— (1986). *Federal Finance in Comparative Perspective.* Toronto: Canadian Tax Foundation.

—— (1986a). "On Measuring Fiscal Centralization and Fiscal Balance in Federal States." *Government and Policy,* 4: 384–404.

—— (1987). "A New Look at Indirect Taxation in Developing Countries." *World Development,* 15: 1151–61.

—— (1987a). *The Taxation of International Investment Flows: Issues and Approaches.* Wellington, New Zealand: Institute of Policy Studies.

—— (1987b). "Imputation and the Foreign Tax Credit: Some Critical Notes from an International Perspective." *Australian Tax Forum,* 4: 1–34.

—— (1988). "A Note on the Fragility of International Fiscal Comparisons." *Bulletin for International Fiscal Documentation,* 42: 199–201.

—— (1988a). "Shaping a New International Tax Order." *Bulletin for International Fiscal Documentation,* 42: 292–99.

—— (1989). "The Administrative Dimension of Tax Reform in Developing Countries." In Gillis (1989).

—— (1989a). "Taxation in Papua New Guinea: Backwards to the Future?" *World Development,* 17: 1145–57.

—— (1989b). "A Preliminary Appraisal of Tax Reform in Argentina." Unpublished; World Bank, Washington, D.C.

—— (1990). "Intergovernmental Finance and Local Taxation in Developing Countries: Some Basic Considerations for Reformers." *Public Administration and Development,* 10: 277–88.

—— (1990a). "Expenditures, Administration, and Tax Reform in Developing Countries." *Bulletin for International Fiscal Documentation,* 44: 263–67.

—— (1990b). "Fiscal Decentralization in Colombia." In R. Bennett, ed., *Decentralization, Local Governments, and Markets.* Oxford: Clarendon Press.

—— (1990c). "The Role of the Tax System in Developing Countries." *Australian Tax Forum,* 7: 395–410.

————, ed. (1991). *More Taxing than Taxes? Implicit Taxation in Developing Countries.* San Francisco: ICS Press.

———— (1992). "Tax Reform in Latin America: A Review of Some Recent Experience." *Latin American Research Review.*

Bird, R. M., and L. H. De Wulf (1973). "Taxation and Income Distribution in Latin America: A Critical Review of Empirical Studies." *International Monetary Fund Staff Papers,* 20: 639–82.

Bird, R. M., and S. Horton, eds. (1989). *Government Policy and the Poor in Developing Countries.* Toronto: University of Toronto Press.

Bird, R. M., and C. E. McLure (1990). "The Personal Income Tax in an Interdependent World." In S. Cnossen and R. M. Bird, eds., *The Personal Income Tax: Phoenix from the Ashes?* Amsterdam: North Holland.

Bird, R. M., and B. D. Miller (1989). "Taxation and the Poor in Developing Countries." In Bird and Horton (1989).

———— (1989a). "The Incidence of Indirect Taxation on Low-Income Households in Jamaica." *Economic Development and Cultural Change,* 37: 393–409.

Bird, R. M., and O. Oldman (1968). "Tax Research and Tax Reform in Latin America—A Survey and Commentary," *Latin American Research Review,* 3: 5–28.

————, eds. (1967). *Readings on Taxation in Developing Countries.* Rev. ed. Baltimore: Johns Hopkins University Press.

————, eds. (1975). *Readings on Taxation in Developing Countries.* 3rd ed. Baltimore: Johns Hopkins University Press.

————, eds. (1990). *Taxation in Developing Countries.* Baltimore: Johns Hopkins University Press.

Bird, R. M., and E. Slack (1978). *Residential Property Tax Relief in Ontario.* Toronto: University of Toronto Press.

———— (1983). "Redesigning Intergovernmental Transfers: A Colombian Example." *Government and Policy,* 1: 461–73.

———— (1983a). "Urban Finance and User Charges." In G. F. Break, ed., *State and Local Finance in the 1980s.* Madison: University of Wisconsin Press.

Bliss, C. J. (1980). "Optimal Tariffs to Raise Revenue." In G. A. Hughes and G. M. Heal, eds., *Public Policy and the Tax System.* London: George Allen and Unwin.

Bolnick, B. R. (1978). "Tax Effort in Developing Countries: What do Regression Measures Really Measure?" In Toye (1978).

Boskin, M. (1978). "Taxation, Saving, and the Rate of Interest." *Journal of Political Economy,* 86: S3–S27.

Bosworth, B. P. (1984). *Tax Incentives and Economic Growth.* Washington, D.C.: Brookings Institution.

Bottomley, A. (1970). *Factor Pricing and Economic Growth in Underdeveloped Rural Areas.* London: Cosby Lockwood.

Boyd, C. (1986). "The Enforcement of Tax Compliance: Some Theoretical Issues." *Canadian Tax Journal,* 34: 588–99.

Bradford, D. F. (1986). *Untangling the Income Tax.* Cambridge, Mass.: Harvard University Press.

Break, G. F. (1974). "The Incidence and Economic Effects of Taxation." In A. Blinder et al., *The Economics of Public Finance.* Washington, D.C.: Brookings Institution.

Break, G. F., and R. Turvey (1964). *Studies in Greek Taxation.* Athens: Center of Planning and Economic Research.

Brennan, G., and T. McGuire (1975). "Optimal Policy Choice under Uncertainty." *Journal of Public Economics,* 4: 205–9.

Breton, A., and A. Scott (1978). *The Economic Constitution of Federal States.* Toronto: University of Toronto Press.

Brittain, J. A. (1972). *The Payroll Tax for Social Security.* Washington, D.C.: Brookings Institution.

——— (1977). *The Inheritance of Economic Status.* Washington, D.C.: Brookings Institution.

Browning, E. K. (1978). "The Burden of Taxation." *Journal of Political Economy,* 86: 649–71.

Bruton, H. J. (1965). *Principles of Development Economics.* Englewood Cliffs, N.J.: Prentice-Hall.

Bucovetsky, M. W., and R. M. Bird (1972). "Tax Reform in Canada: A Progress Report." *National Tax Journal,* 25: 15–41.

Caiden, N., and A. Wildavsky (1980). *Planning and Budgeting in Poor Countries.* New Brunswick, N. J.: Transaction Books.

Caldwell, L. K. (1953). "Technical Assistance and Administrative Reform in Colombia." *American Political Science Review,* 47: 494–510.

Casanegra de Jantscher, M. (1985). "Chile." In *Adjusting for Inflation in Highly Inflationary Economies.* Deventer: Kluwer; excerpted in Bird and Oldman (1990).

——— (1990). "Administering the VAT." In Gillis, Shoup, and Sicat (1990).

Chelliah, R. J. (1971). "Trends in Taxation in Developing Countries." *International Monetary Fund Staff Papers,* 18: 254–331; excerpted in Bird and Oldman (1975).

Chelliah, R. J., and R. N. Lall (1978). *Incidence of Indirect Taxation in India, 1973–74.* New Delhi: National Institute of Public Finance and Policy.

Chelliah, R. J., H. J. Baas, and M. R. Kelly (1975). "Tax Ratios and Tax Effort in Developing Countries, 1969–71." *International Monetary Fund Staff Papers,* 22: 187–205.

Chelliah, R. J., et al. (1981). *Trends and Issues in Indian Federal Finance.* New Delhi: Allied Publishers.

Chenery, H. B., and A. J. Strout (1966). "Foreign Assistance and Economic Development." *American Economic Review,* 56: 680–733.

Chenery, H. B., et al. (1974). *Redistribution with Growth.* London: Oxford University Press, for the World Bank and the Institute of Development Studies.

Chhibber, A. (1985). "Taxation and Aggregate Savings: An Econometric Analysis for Three Sub-Saharan African Countries." CPD Discussion Paper, World Bank, Washington.

Chhibber, A., and J. Khalilzadeh-Shirazi (1988). "Public Finances in Adjustment Programs." Working Paper WPS 128, Country Economics Department, World Bank, Washington, D.C.

Churchill, A. (1972). *Road User Charges in Central America.* World Bank Staff Occasional Paper 15, Washington, D.C.

Clements, K. W. (1983). "Taxation of Alcohol in Australia." In J. G. Head, ed., *Taxation Issues of the 1980s.* Sydney: Australian Tax Research Foundation.

Cline, W. R. (1975). "Distribution and Development: A Survey of Literature." *Journal of Development Economics,* 1: 359–400.

Cnossen, S. (1974). "Capacity Taxation: The Pakistan Experiment." *International Monetary Fund Staff Papers,* 21: 127–69.

—— (1975). "Sales and Excise Systems of the World." *Finanzarchiv,* 33: 177–236.

—— (1977). *Excise Systems: A Global Study of the Selective Taxation of Goods and Services.* Baltimore: Johns Hopkins University Press.

—— (1978). "The Case for Selective Taxes on Goods and Services in Developing Countries." *World Development,* 6: 813–25; excerpted in Bird and Oldman (1990).

—— (1981). "Specific Issues in Excise Taxation: The Alcohol Problem." In K. W. Roskamp and F. Forte, eds., *Reforms of Tax Systems.* Detroit: Wayne State University Press.

—— (1982). "What Rate Structure for a Value-added Tax?" *National Tax Journal,* 35: 205–14.

—— (1984). "Jamaica's Indirect Tax System: The Administration and Reform of Excise Taxes." Staff Paper No. 8, Jamaica Tax Structure Examination Project, Metropolitan Studies Program, Syracuse University, Syracuse, New York.

Collins, D. (1985). *Designing a Tax System for Papua New Guinea.* Discussion Paper No. 18. Port Moresby: Institute of National Affairs.

Colombia (1985). "Diagnóstico operacional de la administracíon tributaria." In *Informe financiero.* Bogota: Contraloria General.

Corfmat, F. (1985). "Computerizing Revenue Administrations in LDCs." *Finance and Development,* 22 (3): 45–47; excerpted in Bird and Oldman (1990).

Cowell, F. A., and J. P. F. Gordon (1989). "On Becoming a Ghost: Indirect Tax Evasion and Government Audit Policy." Discussion Paper No. TIDI/127, Suntory-Toyota International Centre for Economics and Related Disciplines, London School of Economics, January.

Currie, L. (1966). *Accelerating Development: The Necessity and the Means.* New York: McGraw-Hill.

DeGraw, S., and O. Oldman (1985). "The Collection of the Individual Income Tax." *Tax Administration Review* (March), 35–48.

De Soto, H. (1990). *The Other Path.* New York: Harper & Row, Perennial Library.

De Wulf, L. H. (1974). "Taxation and Income Distribution in Lebanon." *Bulletin for International Fiscal Documentation,* 28: 151–54.

—— (1975). "Fiscal Incidence Studies in Developing Countries: Survey and Critique." *International Monetary Fund Staff Papers,* 22: 61–131.

—— (1980). "Taxation of Imports in LDCs: Suggestions for Reform." *Journal of World Trade Law,* 14: 346–51; excerpted in Bird and Oldman (1990).

Deyo, F. C., ed. (1987). *The Political Economy of the New Asian Industrialism.* Ithaca: Cornell University Press.

Diamond, J., and A. A. Tait (1988). "The Growth of Government Expenditure: A Review of Quantitative Analysis." IMF Working Paper WP/88/17, International Monetary Fund, Fiscal Affairs Department, Washington, D.C.

Doebele, W. A. (1979). "'Land Readjustment' as an Alternative to Taxation for the Recovery of Betterment: The Case of South Korea." In Bahl (1979).

Doebele, W. A., O. F. Grimes, and J. F. Linn (1979). "Participation of Beneficiaries in Financing Urban Services: Valorization Charges in Bogotá, Colombia." *Land Economics,* 55: 73–92.

Dosser, D. (1963). "Allocating the Burden of International Aid for Underdeveloped Countries." *Review of Economics and Statistics,* 45: 207–9.

Dowell, S. (1965). *A History of Taxation and Taxes in England.* New York: Augustus M. Kelly.

Downing, P. R. (1973). "User Charges and the Development of Urban Land." *National Tax Journal,* 26: 631–37.

Due, J. F. (1967). "Policy for Financing Economic Development." In United Nations, *Planning Domestic and External Resources for Investment.* New York; excerpted in Bird and Oldman (1967).

—— (1970). *Indirect Taxation in Developing Countries.* Baltimore: Johns Hopkins University Press.

—— (1972). "Alternative Forms of Sales Taxation for a Developing Country." *Journal of Development Studies,* 8: 263–75; excerpted in Bird and Oldman (1975).

—— (1976). "Value-Added Taxation in Developing Economies." In N. T. Wang, ed., *Taxation and Development.* New York: Praeger.

—— (1988). *Indirect Taxation in Developing Countries.* 2nd ed. Baltimore: Johns Hopkins University Press.

Ebrill, L. P. (1987). "The Effects of Taxation on Labor Supply, Savings, and Investment in Developing Countries: A Survey of the Empirical Literature." in Gandhi et al. (1987); exerpted in Bird and Oldman (1990).

Eklund, P. (1972). "A Theory of Earmarking Appraised." *National Tax Journal,* 25: 223–28.

Feldstein, M. S. (1975). "Wealth Neutrality and Local Choice in Public Education." *American Economic Review,* 65: 75–89.

—— (1976). "On the Theory of Tax Reform." *Journal of Public Economics*, 6: 77–104.

—— (1976a). "Compensation in Tax Reform." *National Tax Journal*, 29: 123–30.

Ferron, M. J. (1986). "Issues in Excise Taxation." In Shome (1986).

Finanzas Intergubernamentales en Colombia (1981). Bogotá: Departamento Nacional de Planeacíon.

Fitch, L. C. (1965). "Concepts and Administration of Taxes on Property." In Joint Tax Program (1965a).

Fluharty, V. L. (1957). *Dance of the Millions*. Pittsburgh: University of Pittsburgh Press.

Fry, M. J. (1987). *Money, Interest, and Banking in Economic Development*. Baltimore: Johns Hopkins University Press.

Galbraith, J. K. (1964). *Economic Development*. Boston: Houghton Mifflin.

Gandhi, V. P. (1966). *Tax Burden on Indian Agriculture*. Cambridge, Mass.: Harvard Law School International Tax Program.

—— (1987). "Tax Structure for Efficiency and Supply-side Economics in Developing Countries." In Gandhi et al. (1987).

Gandhi, V. P., et al. (1987). *Supply-side Tax Policy: Its Relevance to Developing Countries*. Washington: International Monetary Fund.

Gemill, G., and C. Eicher (1973). "The Economics of Farm Mechanization and Processing in Developing Countries." *RTN: A Seminar Report*. New York: Agricultural Development Council.

Gillis, M. (1983). "Evolution of Natural Resource Taxation in Developing Countries." *Natural Resources Journal*, 23: 619–48.

—— (1985). "Micro and Macroeconomics of Tax Reform: Indonesia." *Journal of Development Economics*, 19: 221–54; excerpted in Bird and Oldman (1990).

——, ed. (1989). *Tax Reform in Developing Countries*. Durham: Duke University Press.

—— (1989a). "Tax Reform: Lessons from Postwar Experience in Developing Nations." In Gillis (1989).

Gillis, M., and C. E. McLure (1971). "The Coordination of Tariffs and Internal Indirect Taxes." In Musgrave and Gillis (1971).

Gillis, M., C. S. Shoup, and G. Sicat (1990). *Value-Added Taxation in Developing Countries*. Washington: World Bank.

Gomez de Manrique, L., and H. J. Gomez (1979). "Las rentas con destinacíon espećifica." *Carta Financiera*, 43: 7–96.

Goode, R. (1949). "The Income Tax and the Supply of Labor." *Journal of Political Economy*, 47: 428–37.

—— (1952). "Reconstruction of Foreign Tax Systems." In National Tax Association, *Proceedings*. Sacramento, Calif.; excerpted in Bird and Oldman (1967).

—— (1961). "Taxation of Savings and Consumption in Underdeveloped

Countries." *National Tax Journal*, 14: 305–21; excerpted in Bird and Old-man (1975).

———— (1976). *The Individual Income Tax*. Rev. ed. Washington: Brookings Institution.

———— (1981). "Some Economic Aspects of Tax Administration." *International Monetary Fund Staff Papers*, 28: 249–74; excerpted in Bird and Old-man (1990).

———— (1984). *Government Finance in Developing Countries*. Washington: Brookings Institution.

Gordon, R. K. (1988). "Income Tax Compliance and Sanctions in Developing Countries: An Outline of Issues." *Bulletin for International Fiscal Documentation*, 42: 3–12; excerpted in Bird and Oldman (1990).

Gray, C. W. (1987). "The Importance of Legal Process to Economic Development: The Case of Tax Reform in Indonesia." Unpublished; World Bank, Washington, D.C.

Greenaway, D. (1981). "Taxes on International Transactions and Economic Development." In A. T. Peacock and F. Forte, eds., *The Political Economy of Taxation*. Oxford: Basil Blackwell.

———— (1981a). "Maximum Revenue Tariffs and Optimal Revenue Tariffs: Concepts and Policy Issues." *Public Finance*, 37: 67–79.

———— (1984). "A Statistical Analysis of Fiscal Dependence on Trade Taxes and Economic Development." *Public Finance*, 39: 70–89.

Han, S. S. (1990). "The VAT in the Republic of Korea." In Gillis, Shoup, and Sicat (1990).

Harberger, A. C. (1965). "Issues of Tax Reform for Latin America." In Joint Tax Program (1965).

———— (1977). "Fiscal Policy and Income Distribution." In C. R. Frank and R. C. Webb, eds., *Income Distribution and Growth in the Less Developed Countries*. Washington: Brookings Institution.

Hart, A. G. (1967). *An Integrated System of Tax Information*. New York: Columbia University School of International Affairs.

Hartle, D. G., and R. M. Bird (1972). "The Design of Governments." In R. M. Bird and J. G. Head, eds., *Modern Fiscal Issues: Essays in Honour of Carl S. Shoup*. Toronto: University of Toronto Press.

Head, J. G. (1968). "Welfare Methodology and the Multi-Branch Budget." *Public Finance*, 23: 405–24.

Head, J. G., and R. M. Bird (1983). "Tax Policy Options in the 1980s." In S. Cnossen, ed., *Comparative Public Finance*. Amsterdam: North-Holland.

Heller, P. (1975). "A Model of Public Fiscal Behavior in Developing Countries: Aid, Investment, and Taxation." *American Economic Review*, 65: 429–45.

Heller, W. W. (1954). "Fiscal Policies for Under-developed Countries." In United Nations, *Taxes and Fiscal Policy in Under-developed Countries*. New York; excerpted in Bird and Oldman (1967).

Heraty, M. J. (1980). *Public Transport in Kingston, Jamaica and its Relation* to *Low Income Households.* Crowthorn, Berkshire: Overseas Unit, Transport and Road Research Laboratory.

Hettich, W., and S. L. Winer (1988). "Economic and Political Foundations of Tax Structure." *American Economic Review,* 78: 701–12.

Hicks, U. K. (1965). *Development Finance: Planning and Control.* Oxford: Clarendon Press.

Hinrichs, H. H. (1962). "Certainty as Criterion: Taxation of Foreign Investment in Afghanistan." *National Tax Journal,* 15: 139–54.

——— (1966). *A General Theory of Tax Structure Change during Economic Development.* Cambridge, Mass.: Harvard Law School International Tax Program.

Hinrichs, H. H., and R. M. Bird (1963). "Government Revenue Shares in Developed and Less Developed Countries." *Canadian Tax Journal,* 11: 431–37.

Hirschman, A. O. (1963). *Journeys toward Progress: Studies of Economic Policy-Making in Latin America.* New York: Twentieth Century Fund.

——— (1968). "The Political Economy of Import-Substituting Industrialization in Latin America." *Quarterly Journal of Economics,* 82: 1–32.

——— (1971). *Exit, Voice, and Loyalty.* Cambridge, Mass.: Harvard University Press.

Hirschman, A. O., and R. M. Bird (1968). *Foreign Aid—A Critique and a Proposal.* Princeton Essays in International Finance, No. 69.

Holland, D. M. (1966). "The Taxation of Unimproved Value in Jamaica." In National Tax Association, *Proceedings of Annual Conference on Taxation.* Harrisburg, Pa.

——— (1979). "Adjusting the Property Tax for Growth, Equity, and Administrative Simplicity: A Proposal for La Paz, Bolivia." In Bahl (1979).

Holland, D. M., and J. Follain (1985). "The Property Tax in Jamaica." Staff Paper No. 16, Jamaica Tax Structure Examination Project, Metropolitan Studies Program, Syracuse University, Syracuse, New York.

Hood, C. (1976). *The Limits of Administration.* New York: Wiley.

Hutabarat, H., and M. Lane (1990). "Computerization and the VAT in Indonesia." In Gillis, Shoup, and Sicat (1990).

India (1960). *Report of the Direct Taxes Administrative Enquiry Committee, 1958–59.* New Delhi.

——— (1969). *Report of the Working Group on Central Direct Taxes Administration.* New Delhi.

Institute for Fiscal Studies (1978). *The Structure and Reform of Direct Taxation.* London: George Allen & Unwin.

International Monetary Fund (1984). *Government Finance Statistics Yearbook,* vol. 8.

Isaac, B. L. (1981). "Price, Competition, and Profits among Hawkers and Shopkeepers in Pendembu, Sierra Leone: An Inventory Approach." *Economic Development and Cultural Change,* 29: 353–74.

Ize, A. (1989). "Savings, Investment, and Growth in Mexico: Five Years after the Crisis." International Monetary Fund Working Paper 89/18, Washington, D.C.

Jackson, I. A. (1986). "Amnesty and Creative Tax Administration," *National Tax Journal*, 39: 317–23.

Jimenez, E. (1989). "Public Subsidies in the Social Sector: Equity and Efficiency." In Bird and Horton (1989).

Joint Legislative-Executive Tax Commission (1961). *A Study of Tax Administration in the Philippines*. Manila.

Joint Tax Program (1965). *Fiscal Policy for Economic Growth in Latin America*. Baltimore: Johns Hopkins University Press.

—— (1965a). *Problems of Tax Administration in Latin America*. Baltimore: Johns Hopkins University Press.

Jolly, R., et al. (1973). *Third World Employment: Problems and Strategy*. Harmondsworth: Penguin Books.

Kaldor, N. (1955). *An Expenditure Tax*. London: George Allen & Unwin.

—— (1956). *Indian Tax Reform*. New Delhi: Government of India Ministry of Finance.

—— (1963). "Will the Underdeveloped Countries Learn to Tax?" *Foreign Affairs*, 41: 410–19; excerpted in Bird and Oldman (1975).

—— (1964). "Economic Problems of Chile." In *Essays on Economic Policy*. Vol. 2. London: Duckworth.

—— (1965). "The Role of Taxation in Economic Development." In Joint Tax Program (1965).

—— (1980). *Reports on Taxation II. Reports to Foreign Governments*. London: Duckworth.

Katzman, M. T. (1978). "Progressive Public Utility Rates as an Income Redistribution Device in Developing Countries: The Case of Municipal Water." In Toye (1978).

Kay, J. A., and M. J. Keen (1982). *The Structure of Tobacco Taxes in the European Community*. London: Institute for Fiscal Studies.

Kelley, P. L., and O. Oldman, eds. (1973). *Readings on Income Tax Administration*. Mineola, N. Y.: Foundation Press.

King, M. A., and D. Fullerton, eds. (1984). *The Taxation of Income from Capital*. Chicago: University of Chicago Press.

Klappholz, K. (1972). "Equality of Opportunity, Fairness, and Efficiency." In M. Peston and B.Corry, eds., *Essays in Honour of Lord Robbins*. London: Weidenfeld and Nicolson.

Krauss, M. (1983). *Development without Aid: Growth, Poverty and Government*. New York: McGraw-Hill.

Krauss, M., and R. M. Bird (1971). "The Value-Added Tax: Critique of a Review." *Journal of Economic Literature*, 9: 1167–73.

Krueger, A. O. (1978). *Foreign Trade Regimes and Economic Development: Liberalization Attempts and Consequences*. Cambridge, Mass.: Ballinger.

Kuznets, S. (1966). *Modern Economic Growth*. New Haven: Yale University Press.

Lapidoth, A. (1977). *The Use of Estimation for the Assessment of Taxable Business Income.* Amsterdam: International Bureau of Fiscal Documentation.

Lent, G. E. (1967). "Tax Incentives for Investment in Developing Countries." *International Monetary Fund Staff Papers,* 14: 249–323.

—— (1971). "Tax Incentives for the Promotion of Industrial Employment in Developing Countries." *International Monetary Fund Staff Papers,* 18: 399–417.

—— (1973). "Taxation of Agricultural Income in Developing Countries." *Bulletin for International Fiscal Documentation,* 27: 324–43.

—— (1974). "Tax Policy for the Utilization of Labor and Capital in Latin America." *Rivista di diritto finanziario e scienza delle finanze,* 33: 3–23.

—— (1974a). "The Urban Property Tax in Developing Countries." *Finanzarchiv,* 33: 45–72.

Levin, J. (1971). "The Role of Fiscal Action in the Pursuit of Macroeconomic Objectives." *Public Finance,* 26: 573–85; excerpted in Bird and Oldman (1975).

Lewis, W. A. (1955). *The Theory of Economic Growth.* Homewood, Ill.: Richard D. Irwin, Inc.

—— (1966). *Development Planning.* London: George Allen & Unwin Ltd.

—— (1967). "Planning Public Expenditure." In M. F. Millikan, ed., *National Economic Planning.* New York: Columbia University Press.

Lim, D. (1987). *The Spending and Taxing Behaviour of Governments of Resource-Rich Countries: A Study of Papua New Guinea.* Discussion Paper No. 28. Port Moresby: Institute of National Affairs.

Lindbeck, A. (1987). "Public Finance for Market-Oriented Developing Countries." Discussion Paper DRD 212, Development Research Department, World Bank, Washington, D.C.; excerpted in Bird and Oldman (1990).

Linn, J. F. (1979). "Automotive Taxation in the Cities of Developing Countries." *Nagarlok,* 11: 1–23.

—— (1981). "Urban Finances in Developing Countries." In R. W. Bahl, ed., *Urban Government Finance: Emerging Trends.* Beverly Hills: Sage.

—— (1983). *Cities in the Developing World.* New York: Oxford University Press, for the World Bank.

Lipton, M. (1976). *Why Poor People Stay Poor: A Study of Urban Bias in World Development.* Cambridge, Mass.: Harvard University Press.

Little, I., T. Scitovsky, and M. Scott (1970). *Industry and Trade in Some Developing Countries.* Paris: OECD.

Lovejoy, R. M. (1963). "The Burden of Jamaican Taxation, 1958." *Social and Economic Studies,* 12: 442–58.

Mahler, W. R. (1970). *Sales and Excise Taxation in India.* Bombay: Orient Longman.

Maktouf, L., and S. S. Surrey (1983). "Tax Expenditure Analysis and Tax and Budgetary Reform in Less Developed Countries." *Law and Policy in International Business,* 15: 739–61; excerpted in Bird and Oldman (1990).

Manas-Anton, L. A. (1987). "Relationship between Income Tax Ratios and Growth Rates in Developing Countries." in Gandhi et al. (1987).

Mansfield, C. Y. (1988). "Tax Administration in Developing Countries: An Economic Perspective." *International Monetary Fund Staff Papers*, 35: 181–97.

Marsden, K. (1983). "Taxes and Growth." *Finance and Development*, 20: 40–43; excerpted in Bird and Oldman (1990).

Marshall, A. (1890; 1948). *Principles of Economics*. 8th ed. New York: Macmillan.

Marshall, M., ed. (1982). *Through a Glass Darkly: Beer and Modernization in Papua New Guinea.* Boroko: Institute of Applied Social and Economic Research.

Mathews, R. (1984). "The Case for Indirect Taxation," *Australian Tax Forum*, 1: 54–82.

Mayo, S., and D. Gross (1989). "Sites and Services—and Subsidies: The Economics of Low-Cost Housing." In Bird and Horton (1989).

Mayshar, J. (1986). "Taxation with Costly Administration." University of Wisconsin, Social Systems Research Institute 8616, Madison.

McIntyre, M., and O. Oldman (1975). *Institutionalizing the Process of Tax Reform.* Amsterdam: International Bureau of Fiscal Documentation.

McKinnon, R. I. (1973). *Money and Capital in Economic Development.* Washington, D.C.: Brookings Institution.

McLure, C. E. (1971). "Colombian Tax Incentives." In Musgrave and Gillis (1971).

—— (1975). "The Proper Use of Indirect Taxation in Latin America: The Practice of Economic Marksmanship." *Public Finance*, 30: 20–44; excerpted in Bird and Oldman (1975).

—— (1977). "Taxation and the Urban Poor in Developing Countries." *World Development*, 5: 169–88.

—— (1977a). "The Incidence of Jamaican Taxes, 1971–72." Institute of Social and Economic Research, University of the West Indies, Working Paper No. 16.

—— (1979). *Must Corporate Income Be Taxed Twice?* Washington, D.C.: Brookings Institution.

—— (1980). "Administrative Considerations in the Design of Regional Tax Incentives." *National Tax Journal*, 33: 177–88.

—— (1982). "Income and Complementary Taxes: Structure, Avoidance, and Evasion." Unpublished; World Bank, Washington, D.C.

——, ed. (1983). *Tax Assignment in Federal Countries.* Canberra: Australian National University, Centre for Research on Federal Financial Relations.

—— (1989). "Analysis and Reform of the Colombian Tax System." In Gillis (1989).

—— (1990). "Income Distribution and Tax Incidence under the VAT." In Gillis, Shoup, and Sicat (1990).

McLure, C. E., and W. R. Thirsk (1978). "The Inequity of Taxing Iniquity: A

Plea for Reduced Sumptuary Taxes in Developing Countries." *Economic Development and Cultural Change,* 26: 487–503.

McLure, C. E., et al. (1989). *The Taxation of Income from Business and Capital in Colombia.* Durham: Duke University Press.

Meerman, J. (1979). *Public Expenditure in Malaysia: Who Benefits and Why.* New York: Oxford University Press, for the World Bank.

Mikesell, R., and J. E. Zinser (1972). "The Nature of the Savings Function in Developing Countries: A Survey of the Theoretical and Empirical Literature." *Journal of Economic Literature,* 11: 1–26.

Minford, A. P. L. (1970). "A Model of Tax Incidence for Malawi." In Centre of African Studies, *African Public Sector Economics.* Edinburgh.

Morag, A. (1957). "Some Economic Aspects of Two Administrative Methods of Estimating Taxable Income." *National Tax Journal,* 10: 176–85.

Morawetz, D. (1974). "Employment Implications of Industrialisation in Developing Countries: A Survey." *Economic Journal,* 84: 491–542.

Morgenstern, O. (1963). *On the Accuracy of Economic Observations.* 2nd ed. Princeton: Princeton University Press.

Mueller, D. (1989). *Public Choice II.* Cambridge: Cambridge University Press.

Musgrave, R. A. (1963). "Growth with Equity." *American Economic Review, Papers and Proceedings,* 53: 323–33.

——— (1969). *Fiscal Systems.* New Haven: Yale University Press.

——— (1981). *Fiscal Reform in Bolivia.* Cambridge, Mass.: Harvard Law School International Tax Program.

Musgrave, R. A., and M. Gillis (1971). *Fiscal Reform for Colombia.* Cambridge, Mass.: Harvard Law School International Tax Program.

Musgrave, R. A., and P. B. Musgrave (1989). *Public Finance in Theory and Practice.* 5th ed. New York: McGraw-Hill.

Muten, L. (1981). "Leading Issues of Tax Policy in Developing Countries: The Administrative Problems." In A. Peacock and F. Forte, eds., *The Political Economy of Taxation.* Oxford: Basil Blackwell.

——— (1982). "A Cascade Tax by Any Other Name." *Public Finance,* 37: 263–68.

Myrdal, G. (1968). *Asian Drama.* 3 vols. New York: Pantheon.

Netzer, D. (1966). *Economics of the Property Tax.* Washington, D.C.: Brookings Institution.

Newbery, D., and N. Stern, eds. (1987). *The Theory of Taxation for Developing Countries.* New York: Oxford University Press, for the World Bank.

Nowak, N. (1970). *Tax Administration in Theory and Practice.* New York: Praeger.

Oates, W. E. (1972). *Fiscal Federalism.* New York: Harcourt Brace Jovanovich.

——— (1988). "On the Nature and Measurement of Fiscal Illusion: A Survey." In G. Brennan, B. S. Grewal, and P. Groenewegen, eds., *Taxation and Fiscal Federalism: Essays in Honour of Russell Mathews.* Sydney: Australian National University Press.

Okun, A. (1975). *Equality and Efficiency: The Big Tradeoff.* Washington, D.C.: Brookings Institution.

Oldman, O. (1965). "Controlling Income Tax Evasion." In Joint Tax Program (1965a).

———— (1990). "Taxation of International Income." In Bird and Oldman (1990).

Oldman, O., and R. M. Bird (1977). "The Transition to a Global Income Tax: A Comparative Analysis." *Bulletin for International Fiscal Documentation,* 31: 439–54; excerpted in Bird and Oldman (1990).

Organisation for Economic Co-operation and Development (1987). *Taxation in Developed Countries.* Paris.

Papanek, G. F. (1967). *Pakistan's Development: Social Goals and Private Incentives.* Cambridge, Mass.: Harvard University Press.

Papua New Guinea (1971). *Committee of Inquiry on Taxation.* Port Moresby: Government Printer.

Peacock, A., and G. K. Shaw (1971). *Fiscal Policy and the Employment Problem.* Paris: OECD.

Peacock, A., and G. K. Shaw (1973). "Fiscal Measures to Create Employment: The Indonesian Case." *Bulletin for International Fiscal Documentation,* 27: 443–53.

Peacock, A., and J. Wiseman (1967). *The Growth of Public Expenditure in the United Kingdom.* 2nd ed. London: George Allen & Unwin.

Pellechio, A. (1987). "Taxation of Capital Investment." Discussion Paper No. DRD 263, World Bank, Washington, D.C.

Perry, G., and M. Cardenas (1986). *Diez ãnos de reformas tributarias en Colombia.* Bogota: Fedesarrollo.

Petrei, A. H. (1975). "Inflation Adjustment Schemes under the Personal Income Tax." *International Monetary Fund Staff Papers,* 22: 539–64.

Pigou, A. C. (1947). *A Study in Public Finance.* 3rd ed., rev. London: Macmillan.

Pineda, F. (1987). "The Valorization System in Bogota: An Assessment of Recent Trends." Unpublished; World Bank, Washington, D.C.

Plasschaert, S. (1976). "First Principles about Schedular and Global Frames of Taxation." *Bulletin for International Fiscal Documentation,* 30: 99–111.

Please, S. (1967). "Saving through Taxation—Reality or Mirage?" *Finance and Development,* 4 (1): 24–32; excerpted in Bird and Oldman (1975).

———— (1970). "The 'Please Effect' Revisited." Working Paper No. 82, Economics Department, World Bank, Washington, D.C.

Popkin, W. D. (1973). *The Deduction for Business Expenses and Losses.* Cambridge, Mass.: Harvard Law School International Tax Program.

Popper, K. R. (1957). *The Poverty of Historicism.* London: Routledge & Kegan Paul.

Premchand, A. (1983). *Government Budgeting and Expenditure Controls: Theory and Practice.* Washington, D.C.: International Monetary Fund.

Prest, A. R. (1955). "Statistical Calculations of Tax Burdens." *Economica,* 22: 334–45.

——— (1969). *Transport Economics in Developing Countries: Pricing and Financing Aspects*. London: Weidenfeld & Nicolson.

——— (1971). "The Role of Labour Taxes and Subsidies in Promoting Employment in Developing Countries." *International Labour Review*, 103: 315–32; excerpted in Bird and Oldman (1975).

——— (1985). *Public Finance in Underdeveloped Countries*. 3d ed. New York: John Wiley & Sons.

Public Administration Service (1961). *Modernizing Government Revenue Administration*. Washington, D.C.: International Cooperation Administration.

Purohit, M. C. (1988). *Structure and Administration of Sales Taxation in India*. New Delhi: Reliance.

Rabushka, A., and B. Bartlett (1985). "Tax Policy and Economic Growth in Developing Nations." Unpublished; Agency for International Development, Washington, D.C.

Radhu, G. M. (1965). "The Relation of Indirect Tax Changes to Price Changes in Pakistan." *Pakistan Development Review*, 5: 54–63.

Radian, A. (1979). "On the Differences between the Political Economy of Introducing and Implementing Tax Reforms: Israel, 1975–1978." *Journal of Public Economics*, 11: 261–71.

——— (1980). *Resource Mobilization in Poor Countries: Implementing Tax Policies*. New Brunswick, N. J.: Transaction Books.

Radian, A., and I. Sharkansky (1979). "Tax Reform in Israel: Partial Implementation of Ambitious Goals." *Policy Analysis*, 5: 351–66; excerpted in Bird and Oldman (1990).

Rezende, F. (1976). "Income Taxation and Fiscal Equity." *Brazilian Economic Studies*, 2: 105–45.

Rhoads, W. G., and R. M. Bird (1967). "Financing Urbanization in Developing Countries by Benefit Taxation: Case Study of Colombia." *Land Economics*, 43: 403–12; excerpted in Bird and Oldman (1975).

——— (1969). " The Valorization Tax in Colombia: An Example for Other Developing Countries?" In Becker (1969).

Richupan, S. (1984). "Measuring Tax Evasion." *Finance and Development*, 21(4): 38–40.

——— (1987). "Determinants of Income Tax Evasion: Role of Tax Rates, Shape of Tax Schedule, and Other Factors." In Gandhi et al. (1987).

Rojas, F., et al. (1989). "Apoyo al proceso de descentralizacíon: Informe final—primera parte, síntesis de conclusíones y recomendacíones." Unpublished; Proyecto Col 86/010, Departmento Nacional de Planeacíon, Bogotá, Colombia.

Rosenstein-Rodan, P. N. (1961). "International Aid for Underdeveloped Countries." *Review of Economics and Statistics*, 43: 107–38.

Royal Commission on Taxation (1966). *Report*. 6 vols. Ottawa: Queen's Printer.

Sacks, O. (1982). *Awakenings*. New York: Vintage Books.

Sahota, G. S. (1961). *Indian Tax Structure and Economic Development.* Bombay: Asia Publishing House.

Samuelson, P. A. (1966). "A New Theorem on Nonsubstitution." In J. E. Stiglitz, ed., *The Collected Scientific Papers of Paul A. Samuelson,* Vol. 1, pp. 520–36. Cambridge, Mass.: MIT Press.

Sandford, C., J. Willis, and D. Ironside (1973). *An Accessions Tax.* London: Institute for Fiscal Studies.

Sandford, C., et al. (1981). *Costs and Benefits of VAT.* London: Heinemann Educational Books.

Schlesinger, E. (1965). "Tax Policy Recommendations of Technical Assistance Missions: Evolution, Pattern, and Interpretation." In Joint Tax Program (1965); excerpted in Bird and Oldman (1967).

Schroeder, L. (1987). "Intergovernmental Grants in Developing Countries." Unpublished; World Bank, Washington, D.C.

Seligman, E. R. (1929; 1969). *The Shifting and Incidence of Taxation.* New York: Augustus M. Kelly.

Selowsky, M. (1979). *Who Benefits from Government Expenditure? A Case Study of Colombia.* New York: Oxford University Press, for the World Bank.

Sen, A. (1980). "Labor and Technology." In J. Cody, H. Hughes, and D. Wall, eds., *Policies for Industrial Progress in Developing Countries.* New York: Oxford University Press.

Shah, A., and J. Whalley (1990). "An Alternative View of Tax Incidence Analysis for Developing Countries." WPS462, World Bank, Washington, D.C.

Shah, S., and J. Toye (1978). "Fiscal Incentives for Firms in some Developing Countries: Survey and Critique." In Toye (1978); excerpted in Bird and Oldman (1990).

Shalizi, Z., and L. Squire (1990). "Consumption Taxes in Sub-Saharan Africa: Building on Existing Instruments." In Gillis, Shoup, and, Sicat (1990).

Shaw, E. S. (1973). *Financial Deepening in Economic Development.* New York: Oxford University Press.

Shome, P. (1986). *Fiscal Issues in South-East Asia.* Singapore: Singapore University Press.

Short, R. P. (1984). "The Role of Public Enterprise: An International Statistical Comparison." In R. H. Floyd, C. S. Gray, and R. P. Short, *Public Enterprise in Mixed Economies.* Washington: International Monetary Fund.

Shoup, C. S. (1966). "Taxes and Economic Development." *Finanzarchiv,* 25: 385–97; excerpted in Bird and Oldman (1990).

——— (1969). *Public Finance.* Chicago: Aldine.

——— (1972). "Quantitative Research in Taxation and Government Expenditure." In *Public Expenditures and Taxation.* New York: National Bureau of Economic Research.

——— (1972a). "Tax Reform." In H. Haller et al., eds., *Theorie und Praxis des finanzpolitischen interventionismus.* Tubingen.

————— (1983). "Current Trends in Excise Taxation." In S. Cnossen, ed., *Comparative Tax Studies*. Amsterdam: North-Holland.

Shoup, C. S., et al. (1959). *The Fiscal System of Venezuela*. Baltimore: Johns Hopkins University Press.

————— (1970). *The Tax System of Liberia*. New York: Columbia University Press.

Shoven, J., and J. Whalley (1984). "Applied General Equilbrium Models of Taxation and International Trade: An Introduction and Survey." *Journal of Economic Literature*, 22: 1007–51.

Sicat, G. P. (1972). *Taxation and Progress*. Manila: National Economic Council.

Simon, H. A. (1971). "Decision Making and Organizational Design." In D. S. Pugh, ed., *Organization Theory*. Harmondsworth: Penguin Books.

Simons, H. C. (1938). *Personal Income Taxation*. Chicago: University of Chicago Press.

Singer, H. W. (1965). "External Aid: For Plans or Projects?" *Economic Journal*, 75: 539–45.

Singh, S. K. (1975). *Development Economics: Some Findings*. Lexington, Mass.: Lexington Books.

Sisson, C. A. (1981). "Tax Evasion: A Survey of Major Determinants and Policy Instruments of Control." Unpublished; International Monetary Fund, Washington, D.C.

Skinner, J. (1988). "Do Taxes Matter? A Review of the Incentive and Output Effects of Taxation." Unpublished; World Bank, Washington, D.C.

Skinner, J., and J. Slemrod (1985). "An Economic Perspective on Tax Evasion." *National Tax Journal*, 38: 345–53.

Slemrod, J. (1990). "Optimal Taxation and Optimal Tax Systems," *Journal of Economic Perspectives*, 4: 157–78.

Smith, A. (1776; 1937). *The Wealth of Nations*. New York: Modern Library.

Smith, R. S. (1974). "Financing Cities in Developing Countries." *International Monetary Fund Staff Papers*, 21: 329–88.

————— (1975). "Highway Pricing and Motor Vehicle Taxation in Developing Countries: Theory and Practice." *Finanzarchiv*, 33: 451–74.

————— (1977). "Land Prices and Tax Policy." *American Journal of Economics and Sociology*, 36: 337–50.

————— (1984). "Motor Vehicle Taxation in Jamaica." Staff Paper No. 10, Jamaica Tax Structure Examination Project, Metropolitan Studies Program, Syracuse University, Syracuse, New York.

————— (1990). "Factors Affecting Saving, Policy Tools, and Tax Reform: A Review" *International Monetary Fund Staff Papers*, 37: 1–70.

Snodgrass, D. W. (1974). "The Fiscal System as an Income Redistributor in West Malaysia." *Public Finance*, 29: 56–75.

Southworth, H. M., and B. F. Johnston, eds. (1967). *Agricultural Development and Economic Growth*. Ithaca: Cornell University Press.

Squire, L. (1981). *Employment Policy in Developing Countries*. New York: Oxford University Press, for the World Bank.

Stern, N. (1984). "Optimum Taxation and Tax Policy." *International Monetary Fund Staff Papers*, 31: 339–78.

Steuerle, E. (1982). "Is Income from Capital Subject to Individual Income Taxation?" *Public Finance Quarterly*, 10: 283–303.

Stewart, F., and P. P. Strecten (1973). "Conflicts between Output and Employment Objectives in Developing Countries." *Bangladesh Economic Review*, 1: 1–24.

Strasma, J. (1965). "Market-Enforced Self-Assessment for Real Estate Taxes." *Bulletin for International Fiscal Documentation*, 19: 353–65, 397–414.

Streeten, P. (1972). "Technology Gaps between Rich and Poor Countries." *Scottish Journal of Political Economy*, 19: 213–30.

Strout, A. M., and P. G. Clark (1969). *Aid, Performance, Self-Help, and Need.* Discussion Paper No. 20, Office of Program and Policy Coordination, Agency for International Development, Washington, D.C.

Summers, R., and A. Heston (1984). "Improved International Comparisons of Real Product and Its Composition: 1950–80." *Review of Income and Wealth*, 30: 207–62.

Sunkel, O. (1973). "Transnational Capitalism and National Disintegration in Latin America." *Social and Economic Studies*, 22: 132–76.

Surrey, S. S. (1958). "Tax Administration in Underdeveloped Countries." *University of Miami Law Review*, 12: 158–88; excerpted in Bird and Oldman (1975).

Tabellini, G. (1985). "International Tax Comparisons Reconsidered." Fiscal Affairs Department, International Monetary Fund, DM/85/34, Washington, D.C.

Tait, A. A. (1967). *The Taxation of Personal Wealth.* Urbana: University of Illinois Press.

Tait, A. A., and P. Heller (1982). *International Comparisons of Government Expenditure.* Washington, D.C.: International Monetary Fund.

Tait, A. A., W. Gratz, and B. Eichengreen (1979). "International Comparisons of Taxation for Selected Developing Countries, 1972–76." *International Monetary Fund Staff Papers*, 26: 123–56.

Tanzi, V. (1967). "Personal Income Taxation: Obstacles and Possibilities." *National Tax Journal*, 19: 156–62; excerpted in Bird and Oldman (1975).

——— (1973). "The Theory of Tax Structure Change during Economic Development: A Critical Survey." *Rivista de Diritto Finanziario e Scienza delle Finanze*, 32: 199–208

——— (1974). "Redistributing Income through the Budget in Latin America." *Banca Nazionale del Lavoro Quarterly Review*, 27: 65–87.

——— (1974a). "The Theory of Tax Structure Development and the Design of Tax Structure Policy for Industrialization." In D. Geithman, ed., *Fiscal Policy for Industrialization and Development in Latin America.* Gainesville: University Presses of Florida.

——— (1977). "Inflation, Lags in Collection and the Real Value of Tax Revenue." *International Monetary Fund Staff Papers*, 24: 154–67.

————, ed. (1982). *The Underground Economy in the United States and Abroad.* Lexington, Mass.: Lexington Books.

———— (1987). "Quantitative Characteristics of the Tax Systems of Developing Countries." In Newbery and Stern (1987); excerpted in Bird and Oldman (1990).

———— (1987a). "Tax Systems and Policy Objectives in Developing Countries: General Principles and Diagnostic Tests." *Tax Administration Review*, 3: 23–34.

Tanzi, V., and Casanegra de Jantscher, M. (1987). "Presumptive Income Taxation: Administrative, Efficiency, and Equity Aspects." DM/87/54, Fiscal Affairs Department, International Monetary Fund, Washington, D.C.

Taylor, M. C. (1967). "The Relationship between Income Tax Administration and Income Tax Policy in Nigeria." *Nigerian Journal of Economic and Social Studies*, 9: 203–15; excerpted in Bird and Oldman (1975).

Tiebout, C. (1956). "A Pure Theory of Local Government Expenditure." *Journal of Political Economy*, 64: 416–24.

Todaro, M. (1969). "A Model of Labor Migration and Urban Unemployment in Less Developed Countries." *American Economic Review*, 59: 138–48.

Toye, J. F. J., ed. (1978). *Taxation and Economic Development.* London: Frank Cass.

———— (1981). *Public Expenditure and Indian Development Policy, 1960–1970.* Cambridge: Cambridge University Press.

Uchimura, K., and R. M. Bird (1989). "Colombia: Decentralizing Revenues and the Provision of Services: A Review of Recent Experience." Unpublished; World Bank, Washington, D.C.

United Nations, Department of Economic and Social Affairs (1967). *Manual of Income Tax Administration.* New York.

———— (1968). *Manual of Land Tax Administration.* New York.

U. S. Treasury Department (1977). *Blueprints for Tax Reform.* Washington.

Usher, D. (1977). "The Economics of Tax Incentives to Encourage Investment in Less Developed Countries." *Journal of Development Economics*, 4: 119–48; excerpted in Bird and Oldman (1990).

Vanek, J. (1967). *Estimating Foreign Resource Needs for Economic Development.* New York: McGraw-Hill.

Virmani, A. (1987). "Tax Evasion, Corruption, and Administration: Monitoring the People's Agents under Symmetric Dishonesty." Discussion Paper No. DRD271, Development Research Department, World Bank, Washington, D.C.

Wagner, R. (1977). *Inheritance and the State.* Washington, D.C.: American Enterprise Institute for Public Policy Research.

Wald, H. P. (1959). *Taxation of Agricultural Land in Under-developed Countries.* Cambridge, Mass.: Harvard University Press.

Wasylenko, M. (1987). "The Distribution of Tax Burden in Jamaica: Pre-1985 Reform." Staff Paper No. 30, Jamaica Tax Structure Examination Project, Metropolitan Studies Program, Syracuse University, Syracuse, New York.

Watson, P. L., and E. P. Holland (1978). "Relieving Traffic Congestion: The Singapore Area License." Staff Working Paper No. 281, World Bank, Washington, D.C.

Webber, C., and A. Wildavsky (1986). *A History of Taxation and Expenditure in the Western World.* New York: Simon and Schuster.

Whalley, J. (1984). "Regression or Progression: The Taxing Question of Incidence Analysis." *Canadian Journal of Economics,* 17: 654–82.

Whynes, D. K. (1974). "The Measurement of Comparative Development—A Survey and Critiques." *Journal of Modern African Studies,* 12: 89–107.

Wilkenfeld, H. C. (1973). *Taxes and People in Israel.* Cambridge, Mass.: Harvard University Press.

Wingo, L. (1961). *Transportation and Urban Land.* Baltimore: Johns Hopkins University Press.

Winston, G. (1974). "The Theory of Capital Utilization and Idleness." *Journal of Economic Literature,* 12: 1301–20.

Witt, P.-C. (1987). *Wealth and Taxation in Central Europe.* Leamington Spa: Berg.

Wolf, C. (1988). *Markets or Governments? Choosing between Imperfect Alternatives.* Cambridge, Mass.: MIT Press.

World Bank (1988). *World Development Report.* New York: Oxford University Press, for the World Bank.

Yitzhaki, S. (1986). "On the Excess Burden of Tax Evasion." Discussion Paper No. DRD 211, Development Research Department, World Bank, Washington, D.C.

Yitzhaki, S., and Y. Vaknin (1989). "On the Shadow Price of a Tax Inspector." *Public Finance,* 44: 492–505.

Yudkin, L. (1973). *A Legal Structure for an Effective Income Tax Administration.* Cambridge, Mass.: Harvard Law School International Tax Program.

Index

Ability to pay principle, 6, 7, 194–95, 210–11; and income tax, 11, 85–86

Acceptability approach to tax reform, 20–21

Access to public services, importance of, 56, 211. *See also* Urban services

Accessions tax, 134. *See also* Death taxes

Ad valorem *vs.* specific rates, 122–23, 227n.18. *See also* Excises

Administration, tax: centralization, 115; constraint on reform, 11–12, 14–15, 25–26, 185, 189–201, 212; cost, 193; earmarked taxes, 177; expenditure taxes, 225n.6; income tax, 88, 98–118; land tax, 139–40, 192; legal structure, 115–16; lotteries, 199; politics and, 26, 193; property tax, 191; stability, 47; valorization tax, 169–70; wealth tax, 139–40. *See also* Appeals; Audit; Computerization; Identification of taxpayers; Information; Penalties

Advertising, tax on, 227n.11. *See also* Sumptuary taxes

Advisors on taxation: methodology for, 19–22, 195; role of, 19, 21, 217n.7. *See also* Tax reform

Agricultural taxation: case for, 18, 203; effects, 52, 68, 74; income tax, 96; presumptive taxation, 203, 213. *See also* Land tax

Aid, foreign, 30–31, 218n.9. *See also* Structural adjustment lending.

Alcohol taxes, 50, 124. *See also* Sumptuary taxes

Amnesty, tax, 199–200, 236n.17

Appeals, 116, 190, 192

Argentina, 150, 227n.5, 230n.6

Asher, M. G., 124

Assessment, guidelines for, 110–13. *See also* Presumptive taxation

Assignment of functions, 146, 147, 155, 161. *See also* Local government finance

Audit, 116, 200–201, 226n.18

Automobile taxes. *See* Fuel taxes; Vehicle taxes

Autonomy, local, 150, 153, 161. *See also* Local government finance

Bangladesh, 154

Bargaining about taxes, 110, 111, 192, 198

Basic needs and local government finance, 156

Bauer, P. T., 204, 207, 208

Bearer securities, 92
Benefit taxation, 7, 23, 194, 210–12; case for, 5–6, 214; earmarking, 172, 176, 179; urban finance, 6, 161–64; valorization tax, 166–67. *See also* Earmarking; Urban finance
Bequests, taxation of, 89. *See also* Death taxes
Best, M. H., 35
Blue returns in Japan, 226n.11
Bogota, 165, 230n.23
Bolivia: death tax, 138, 230n.21; evasion, 236n.20; presumptive taxation, 108–10; tax administration, 234n.1; tax reform, 225n.9, 226n.7, 235n.3
Booth, A., 124
Borrowing, 4; local government, 156, 162, 164
Brazil, 149
Britain. *See* United Kingdom
Budgeting, 175, 176–78; earmarking, 174–75, 178; local government, 157; politics of, 208–9; reform, 210
Buoyancy, tax, 216n.24. *See also* Elasticity

Cali, 51
Capacity tax, 79. *See also* Presumptive taxation
Capital bias, 65–66, 82, 222n.6; in public sector, 72. *See also* Capital-labor ratio
Capital formation. *See* Investment
Capital gains tax, 10, 92–93, 132; and death tax, 228n.8; on land, 166–67
Capital goods, tax on, 14, 77, 80. *See also* Investment
Capital income tax, 91–93; and globalization, 90; in open economy, 70, 220n.5, 230n.20. *See also* Dividends; Interest; Schedular taxes
Capital-labor ratio, 63–64. *See also* Capital bias
Capital levy, 135, 229n.12
Capital markets, 71–72
Casanegra de Jantscher, M., 189
Centralization: and earmarking, 177–78; of government structure, 145, 161; of tax administration, 115. *See also* Decentralization; Local government finance
Centrally planned economies, 3, 4
Charging. *See* User charges
Chelliah, R. J., 34
Chile, 44
Collection, tax, 116, 230n.22. *See also* Administration
Colombia: earmarking, 172, 174–75, 179; education deduction, 224n.19; fuel tax, 175; local finance, 150, 154; presumptive taxation, 228n.7; savings, 44; tax reform, 24, 218n.13; user charges, 51, 55–56; valorization tax, 162, 164, 165–68
Commodity taxes. *See* Indirect taxes
Compliance: proof of as enforcement device, 102, 114–15; voluntary, 87, 88, 193–94, 205
Comprehensive income tax. *See* Global income tax
Computerization, 114–15, 188, 195–96; and information returns, 103, 199
Consumption taxes. *See* Expenditure taxes; Indirect taxes
Corporation taxes. *See* Profits tax
Corruption, 117, 191, 192, 198, 212, 236n.12
Current payment, 105–7. *See also* Withholding
Customs duties. *See* Import taxes

Data problems, 36. *See also* Information
Death taxes, 134–37, 140–41, 228n.8, 229n.19. *See also* Wealth taxes
Decentralization: administration, 115; earmarking, 177–78; local government, 151–52. *See also* Centralization
Deficit finance, 4, 31
Depreciation allowances, 94
De Soto, H., 220n.8, 223n.18
Development plans and taxes, 29, 202
Displacement effect, 206
Distribution: and growth, 9–10, 41, 42–45; and local government, 53–54, 148–49; as policy objective, 43, 62; and product mix, 66; and taxes, 6–8, 41, 49. *See also* Incidence

Dividends, taxation of, 95–96. *See also* Capital income tax; Profits tax

Due, J. F., 18, 124

Earmarking, 23, 166, 171–80, 194, 233n.12. *See also* Benefit taxation; Valorization tax

Earned income tax, 89, 90–91, 133. *See also* Payroll tax; Schedular taxes; Wage income tax

Education: deductions for, 75, 223n.19; of taxpayers, 194

Effective tax rates, 220n.8, 236n.21. *See also* Rates

Elastiticty of substitution, 64–65. *See also* Capital-labor ratio

Elasticity, tax, 12–13, 86, 190, 216n.24

Elite administrators, 195, 235n.10

Employment: expense deduction, 91; incentives for, 73, 79, 224n.23; as policy objective, 62, 222n.1; and taxation, 15, 61–82; and trade, 67–68, 78

Equality of opportunity, 134

Equity. *See* Fairness

Equalization, 146, 155. *See also* Transfers

Estimated income tax. *See* Presumptive taxation

Ethical approach to tax reform, 20–22, 28

Evasion, tax, 25, 42, 190, 192, 200, 205; and progressivity, 107, 191, 224n.3

Excises, 14, 50, 58, 69, 98, 119–20, 122–24, 126, 213. *See also* Fuel taxes; Luxury taxes; Sumptuary taxes; Vehicle taxes

Exemptions: income tax, 73, 74, 90, 116, 186–87; indirect taxes, 59, 69, 127, 222n.14; property tax, 54, 140, 231n.8; valorization tax, 165

Expenditure, government: beneficiaries of, 6, 172, 211; earmarking, 173–74; importance of, 49, 205–6, 207; reform of, 208–9, 214; relation to taxes, 13, 36, 194, 205–10; in urban areas, 159–60. *See also* Benefit taxation; Budgeting; Please effect; Social security; Subsidies

Expenditure taxes, 89, 131, 216n.20, 224nn.4–5, 225n.6, 228n.6

Export taxes, 67, 70

Factor markets, unification of, 70–72

Factor substitution. *See* Capital-labor ratio

Fairness, in taxation, 6, 85, 194, 224n.1; and income tax, 85–86, 187; and wealth tax, 141. *See also* Ability to pay principle; Distribution; Equality of opportunity; Horizontal equity

Federalism, 147–48, 149–50. *See also* Local government finance; Intergovernmental fiscal relations; Transfers

Fees, business license, 109

Feldstein, M.S., 183, 184, 234n.2

Financial reform, need for, 71–72

Fine tuning, dangers of, 9, 14, 185, 224. *See also* Interventionist tax policy

Fiscal capacity. *See* Tax capacity

Fiscal effort. *See* Tax effort

Fiscal illusion, 233n.12

Fiscal mismatch. *See* Vertical imbalance

Flat-rate tax, 93–94, 101, 107, 225n.13. *See also* Rates

Food: exemption of, 59, 69–70, 127, 222n.14; taxes on, 51, 126

Foreign exchange gap, 10, 43, 44, 61

Foreign investment. *See* Multinational enterprises; Open economy

Foreign trade: and employment, 67–68; taxes on, 120, 122. *See also* Export taxes; Import taxes; Open economy

Forfait, 226n.13. *See also* Bargaining; Presumptive taxation

Fuel taxes, 57–58, 123, 172, 175. *See also* Vehicle taxes

Galbraith, J. K., 25

Gasoline tax. *See* Fuel taxes

Global income tax, 11, 18, 96–97, 131, 133; *vs.* schedular, 88–90, 225n.17; and withholding, 102

Grants. *See* Transfers

Goode, R., 18, 87

Growth: classical model, 42–43; and distribution, 9–10, 41, 42–45, 216n.14;

vs. equity, 132; and saving, 10, 29, 43, 216n.18; and tax rates, 45–46, 204; and taxation, 8–9, 41, 218n.13, 219n.22, 227n.19. *See also* Foreign exchange gap

Guatemala, 45–46, 50, 121, 190

Hard-to-tax groups, 26, 99, 105, 107–13. *See also* Agricultural taxation; Presumptive taxation; Professionals; Self-employed; Small business taxation

Hart, A. G., 199

Heller, W. W., 18

Hicks, U. K., 18

Hirschman, A. O., 204, 233n.9

Hood, C., 212

Horizontal equity, 13, 20, 50, 52, 129, 190, 194, 234; among poor, 58, 128. *See also* Distribution; Fairness

Horizontal imbalance. *See* Equalization

Hotel tax, 179

Human capital and taxation, 90–91, 133, 228n.3

Identification of taxpayers, 102, 104, 106, 113–14

Implicit taxes, 67, 220n.10

Import taxes, 14, 122, 126, 190, 227n.7

Incidence, 50–52; agricultural taxes, 74; indirect taxes, 50–51, 58–59, 124–27, 222n.13; payroll tax, 15–16, 76; profits tax, 95; property tax, 51, 54–55; uncertainty of, 10, 51, 60, 184, 222n.15; user charges, 51–52. *See also* Distribution; Progressivity; Regressivity

Incentives. *See* Tax incentives

Income distribution. *See* Distribution

Income tax, 85–97; ability to pay, 11, 85–86; administration, 98–118; conditions for, 87–88, 98–99; coverage, 86–87; exemptions, 73, 90, 91; international aspects, 89, 104; rates, 18, 45–46, 204, 211. *See also* Global income tax; Inflation adjustment; Personal income tax; Profits tax

Incrementalist approach: to local government finance, 158, 230n.9; to tax reform, 12, 17, 22, 27, 117

Indexation. *See* Inflation adjustment

India: administration, 196; federalism, 149, 150; income taxes, 204, 211; indirect taxes, 68–69, 126–27; local taxes, 154; tax reform, 202, 203, 206

Indirect substitution, 64, 222nn.3,7

Indirect taxes, 18, 47, 119–29; and employment, 68–70; exemptions, 59, 69, 127, 222n.14; and growth, 227n.19; and poor, 7, 50–51, 58–59, 124–27; rates, 59, 125–26. *See also* Excises; Sales taxes; Value-added tax

Indonesia, 69, 216n.12, 223n.13, 236n.13

Inflation, 4, 13, 124, 222n.6. *See also* Inflation adjustment

Inflation adjustment: current payments, 106; excises, 123, 227n.9; income tax, 93–94, 186–88

Informal economy, 70, 71, 220n.8, 223n.18. *See also* Modern sector

Information: in intergovernmental relations, 151, 157; in tax administration, 115, 192, 199, 228n.4

Information returns, 103, 199. *See also* Computerization

Institutionalization: of local government supervision, 151–52; of tax reform, 27, 185

Integration of income taxes, 95

Interest, taxes on, 92, 96, 225n.12. *See also* Capital income tax

Intergovernmental fiscal relations, 145–58. *See also* Federalism; Local government finance; Transfers

International comparisons, 16, 18–19, 29–37

International Monetary Fund, 32–36, 219n.13

Interventionist tax policy, 14–15, 82, 185. *See also* Fine tuning; Neutrality

Investment: from earmarked taxes, 166, 168–69; and growth, 9–10; tax incentives for, 8–9, 63, 91–93, 188, 222n.2. *See also* Capital goods

Israel, 108

Jamaica: exemption of food, 59, 127; growth and taxes, 46, 207; indirect taxes, 58–59, 124, 126–27, 221n.4,

235n.5; presumptive taxation, 226n.9; property tax, 54; tax administration, 226n.16, 235n.10, 236n.20; urban transit, 56–58
Japan, 226n.11

Kaldor, N., 18, 202–3, 207, 213, 234n.1
Kenya, 51
Keynes, J. M., 43, 45
Korea, 110, 199, 226n.11

Land adjustment, 231n.6
Land reform, 81
Land tax, 79, 80, 130, 136; administration, 139–40, 192; effects, 9, 52, 54; on potential, 203, 213; rates, 221n.8; and valorization tax, 167. See also Agricultural taxation; Property tax; Site value tax; Wealth taxes
Land value increment tax, 232n.10
Legal framework of taxes, 200
Life-line tariff, 55. See also User charges
Level of taxation, 202, 206. See also Development plans and taxes
Lewis, W. A., 29, 202, 207
Local government finance, 145–58; autonomy, 150, 153, 161; budgeting, 157; case for, 147–49, 151, 161; competition in, 147; and distribution, 148–49; importance of, 53, 136; monitoring, 151–52, 155; rural, 231n.3; stabilization, 147–48, 230n.6; and tax reform, 194. See also Federalism; Local revenues; Urban finance
Local revenues, 153–54, 160, 162–70
Lotteries, in tax administration, 199
Luxury taxes, 47, 59, 67, 221n.12. See also Excises

McLurer, C. E., Jr., 50
Malawi, 221n.1
Malaysia, 55, 149
Marsden, K. 29, 218n.3
Matching. See Information returns
Medellin, 165
Migration, 52, 74, 159
Minimum tax, 109, 225n.16, 235n.4
Mining and taxation, 33–34, 219n.19

Modern sector, taxation of, 15, 70–71. See also Informal economy
Monetization, 47, 74–75
Monitoring: of local governments, 151–52; of tax officials, 112, 116–17, 192, 198
Multinational enterprises, 82, 86, 89, 104
Musgrave, R. A., 108, 203, 234n.1

Nairobi, 51
Negotiation. See Bargaining about taxes
Net wealth tax, 133, 230n.23. See also Wealth taxes
Net worth method, 108
Netzer, D., 232n.10
Neutrality, 11, 20, 65, 216n.21, 217n.5, 234n.4. See also Interventionist tax policy
Nicaragua, 35, 206, 207
Nigeria, 149, 150, 192
Nonresident taxation, 104, 154, 225n.3. See also Multinational enterprises; Open economy

Octroi, 154
Open economy: constraint on taxation, 12, 70, 137–38, 220n.5, 230n.20; and employment, 67–68, 78; property tax, 54; tax incentives, 92, 216n.18. See also Foreign exchange gap; Nonresident taxation.
Optimal tariff, 227. See also Import taxes
Optimal taxation, 16, 19, 122, 123, 183, 215n.10, 216n.21, 217n.2
Output composition. See Product mix and taxation

Pakistan, 42–44, 79, 150, 216; indirect taxes, 126–27, 222n.13
Papanek, G. F., 42
Papua New Guinea, 150, 192, 225n.13, 227n.13
Pay-as-you-earn (P.A.Y.E.), 101. See also Withholding
Payroll tax, 15–16, 76–77. See also Social Security; Wage income tax
Peacock, A. T., 205–6
Penalties, 25, 116, 192, 200
Pepys, S., 236n.12

Personal income tax, 15–16, 46, 74, 75, 85–95, 186–88. *See also* Income tax

Peru, 220n.8

Philippines, 69, 70, 221n.12, 223n.19, 224n.23, 226n.16

Piecemeal reform. *See* Incrementalist approach

Please, S., 207, 208

Please effect, 30, 207, 218n.5

Political aspects, of tax reform, 12, 22–26, 46, 87–88, 98–99, 176, 187, 212

Poor: and government expenditure, 49, 50; and horizontal equity, 128; and indirect taxes, 7, 50–51, 58–59, 124–27; and taxation, 47, 49–60; and user charges, 55–58; and valorization tax, 166. *See also* Distribution

Population, 73, 224n.20

Poverty. *See* Poor

Positivistic approach to tax reform, 20–21, 195

Presumptive taxation, 98, 107–13, 200; in agriculture, 203, 213

Pricing of public services, 5, 172. *See also* Benefit taxation; User charges

Privatization of tax administration, 196–98

Product mix and taxation, 66–70

Production process, taxation and, 63. *See also* Capital-labor ratio

Professionals, taxation of, 110–13, 201. *See also* Presumptive taxation

Profits tax, 10, 18, 47, 93, 94–96, 106; effects, 42, 79; incidence, 95, 191; retained *vs.* distributed, 8, 72, 147

Progressivity, 10, 42, 50–52, 210; and evasion, 107, 191, 224n.3; personal income tax, 11, 86, 93; valorization tax, 166. *See also* Rates

Property tax, 54, 98, 113, 164; administration, 191, 237n.1; exemptions, 54, 140, 231n.8; incidence, 51, 54–55; as wealth tax, 141, 230n.23. *See also* Land tax; Real property; Wealth taxes

Public choice approach, 13. *See also* Political aspects

Public employees, taxation of, 100

Public enterprises. *See* State-owned enterprises

Public utilities. *See* Urban services; User charges

Rates: and administration, 115–16; ear-marked taxes, 166, 175, 180; income tax, 18, 45–46, 93–94, 204, 211; indirect taxes, 59, 122–23, 125–26, 227n.18; land tax, 221n.8. *See also* Effective tax rates; Flat-rate tax; Inflation adjustment; Progressivity; Regressivity

Real property, as base of wealth tax, 139–40. *See also* Property tax; Wealth taxes

Refunds, tax, 101–2

Regressivity, 49, 50–52, 55, 119, 125. *See also* Incidence; Progressivity

Redistributive taxation. *See* Distribution; Progressivity

Revenue sharing, 173. *See also* Transfers

Revenue targets, 116–17, 192, 197

Rezende, F., 225n.17

Risk-taking, 9

Road finance, 179. *See also* Fuel taxes; Vehicle taxes

Sales taxes, 121, 191. *See also* Indirect taxes

Sanctions. *See* Penalties

Savings: and foreign aid, 30; and growth, 10, 29, 43, 216n.18; and profits, 42; and taxes, 10, 30, 43, 91, 136, 208, 229nn.16, 19. *See also* Please effect

Schedular taxes, 11, 88–90, 96, 200, 201, 225n.17. *See also* Capital income tax; Global income tax; Wage income tax

Self-employed, taxation of, 91, 105. *See also* Presumptive taxation

Self-enforcing taxes, 203, 213, 237n.1

Self-finance, for large cities, 155, 161–64. *See also* Benefit taxation; Urban finance

Seligman, E.R.A., 223n.12

Services, taxes on, 70

Shoup, C. S., 32, 47, 123, 185–86, 203, 234n.1

Simons, H. C., 41

Simplicity, as guide to tax reform, 117, 139

Singapore, 162

Site value tax, 166–67, 169. *See also* Land tax

Small business taxation, 69–70, 71, 100, 108–10, 136–37, 191. *See also* Presumptive taxation

Smith, A., 20, 235n.8

Social security, 73, 77, 100, 224n.20. *See also* Payroll tax

Special assessments. *See* Valorization tax

Specific *vs.* ad valorem rates, 122–23, 227n.18. *See also* Excises

Spillovers, in local government finance, 148

Sri Lanka, 203

Stabilization, 12–13, 147–48, 230n.6

Stamp tax, 23

State-owned enterprises, 57, 72, 100, 173, 232n.5

Structural adjustment lending, 31, 237n.6. *See also* Aid

Subdivision finance, 164, 168. *See also* Local government finance; Urban finance

Subsidies, 77, 126, 227n.17

Sumptuary taxes, 50, 123–24, 221n.3, 227n.11. *See also* Alcohol taxes; Excises; Tobacco taxes

Sunset provision, for earmarking, 178, 180

Supply-side taxation, 7, 10, 42, 204, 207. *See also* Tax incentives

Surrey, S. S., 189, 196

Targets. *See* Revenue targets

Tariffs. *See* Import taxes

Takshiv, 108

Tax administration. *See* Administration

Tax capacity, 31, 33–34, 36

Tax design, 13–14, 16–17, 19, 23, 188

Tax effort, 29, 30, 31, 34–37, 157, 220n.26

Tax expenditures, 225n.14

Tax farming, 196–97, 235n.11

Tax handles, 122

Tax incentives, 44, 112, 190, 216n.12; capital utilization, 78–79; design of, 79–80; for employment, 73, 75, 79, 224n.23; for investment, 8–9, 78, 91–93, 188, 222n.2; for savings, 91–93

Tax protesting, 109

Tax reform: administrative constraint, 185, 189–201, 207, 212; benefit taxes, 210–12; and crisis, 22–23, 27; and expenditure, 205–10; institutionalization, 27, 185; instrumental approach, 131–32, 184; and local government finance, 194; package, 22–23, 216n.22; political conditions, 12, 22–25, 98–99; requirements for, 17, 19; rules for, 183–86, 226n.20; and simplicity, 117, 198–201; strategy of, 22–25; and tax design, 16–17, 188; and tax increases, 206; welfare methodology of, 19–22. *See also* Incrementalist approach; Open economy

Tax roll, 114, 226n.16. *See also* Identification of taxpayers

Technical assistance, 21. *See also* Advisors on taxation

Technology, 81

Third-party taxation, 197. *See also* Withholding

Tobacco taxes, 50, 58, 69, 179. *See also* Excises; Sumptuary taxes

Transfers, intergovernmental, 153, 154–56, 157, 160, 173, 210

Transformation of taxes, 223n.12

Two-gap model. *See* Foreign exchange gap

United Kingdom, 101, 205, 212

United States, 101, 200

Urban bias, 6, 215n.6

Urban finance, 6, 160–70

Urban services, 55–58, 155, 159–70, 211–12

Urban transit, 56–58, 163

Urbanization, 52–53, 159–50, 163, 167–68, 212

User charges, 4–5, 51–52, 55–57, 172, 179, 211

Utilization of capital, 14, 78–79

Valorization tax, 164–70, 176, 232nn.10,11

Valuation, 139–40

Value-added tax, 18, 98, 121, 129, 188, 199, 213; incidence, 58–59, 127. *See also* Indirect taxes

Veblen effect, 232

Vehicle taxes, 54, 123, 162, 172. *See also* Fuel taxes

Venezuela, 234n.1

Vertical equity. *See* Distribution; Progressivity

Vertical imbalance, 146, 155. *See also* Transfers

Vickrey, W. S., 228n.5

Wage income tax, 11, 15, 76–77, 89–91, 100–103. *See also* Earned income tax; Payroll tax

Water charges, 51, 55

Wealth taxes, 7, 12, 130–41, 213, 237n.7; administration, 139–40; effects, 136–38, 229nn.14,19; and income tax, 90, 132–33, 136, 141, 229n.14. *See also* Death taxes; Property tax

Wiseman, J., 205–6

Withholding, 92, 99–105, 116, 205, 213, 225n.3

Witt, P. C., 193

Work effort, 9